IN PURSUIT OF DEAD GEORGIANS

IN PURSUIT OF DEAD GEORGIANS

One Historian's Excursions into the History of His Adopted State

GEORGE R. LAMPLUGH

IN PURSUIT OF DEAD GEORGIANS
ONE HISTORIAN'S EXCURSIONS INTO THE HISTORY OF HIS ADOPTED STATE

iUniverse books may be ordered through booksellers or by contacting:

iUniverse
1663 Liberty Drive
Bloomington, IN 47403
www.iuniverse.com
1-800-Authors (1-800-288-4677)

ISBN: 978-1-4917-6791-7 (sc)
ISBN: 978-1-4917-6808-2 (e)

Library of Congress Control Number: 2015908198

Print information available on the last page.

iUniverse rev. date: 06/18/2015

Contents

Contents

Introduction

A Contingent Career: "You can't always get what you want"

Since I was first introduced to it, I've loved the term *contingent* to describe events in history that suggest there is no big, unstoppable ideological wave out there moving humanity in a preordained direction (e.g., democracy, Christianity, Marxism, progress, the Enlightenment). Rather, there are times when events are determined by human action, coincidence, or luck. Now that I have retired, when I'm in a retrospective mood—which is much of the time—I find myself focusing on the contingent events, coincidences, and (mostly good) luck that have brought me to this point. So, before you begin reading the essays in this volume—and their autobiographical introductions—you might want to peruse this modest effort to put my career as a historian in a broader context.

* * * * *

I grew up in Baltimore, Maryland, and Newark, Delaware, the oldest of three children in a struggling lower-middle- (or perhaps upper-lower-) class family. Only two members of my extended family had attended college—one, an uncle, studied engineering at the University of Delaware after World War II, thanks to the GI Bill; the other, an aunt, also attended Delaware a decade or so later. Whether my two siblings and I would be able to follow them to college was an open question when we were growing up.

I loved going to school and, early on, began to dream of attending college—the University of Delaware, of course, to study engineering, as my uncle George had. Yet my family really didn't have the financial wherewithal to make that possible. Meanwhile, even before I graduated from Newark High School, I had decided that engineering was not for me, despite my uncle's sterling example. I struggled with math and science, but, more importantly to me, I did not *enjoy* either subject; I was more interested in history and English.

In the fall of 1962, I entered the University of Delaware as a history education major, hoping to teach history in high school. Then, however, luck—or contingency?—intervened. The dean of the education school summoned entering freshmen to a meeting, where he outlined the curriculum for our next four years as education majors. When I learned that I would only study history at the survey level because of the department's requirement that I take various education courses, it did not set well with me. Within a few days, I exited the school of education for the school of arts and sciences (or, as we liked to call it, "air and sunshine") as a generic history major.

Then there was the larger world in which my college career unfolded, the era of the Vietnam War. It soon became clear that, if I were to have any hope of graduating from Delaware, I would have to join the advanced Army ROTC program. Basic ROTC was required of all able-bodied male students at Delaware for their first two years. The final two years, advanced ROTC, led to an officer's commission in the US Army and were elective, but any male who wished to graduate was "strongly advised" to sign up for the advanced course.

Although there were still a few ways to receive a draft deferment in mid-1964, they were rapidly disappearing, and none of those remaining applied to me. I enrolled in advanced ROTC, and, thanks to the program's stipend, along with money I earned as a dormitory floor advisor during my last two years and funds borrowed from my girlfriend's parents after my father declared bankruptcy, I was able to finish college.

My military obligation was two years of active duty in the US Army during what we now know was the height of American involvement in Vietnam (1966–1968). I started as a second lieutenant in the Quartermaster Corps, a combat support (as opposed to a combat) branch. I approached the QMC's basic officer course just as I would have an academic course at Delaware and did well in it. Likewise, I jumped into my advanced course (Open Mess Management, or how to run an officer's club) enthusiastically and was one of only two members of my class who did *not* go to Vietnam upon completion of the course. Instead, I wound up at Aberdeen Proving

Ground, Maryland, barely a half hour from the University of Delaware, where my girlfriend (and future wife) was finishing college.

My time in the US Army was undistinguished. As my tour of active duty was winding down, I began to consider what I would do next. I had married in June 1967, and, since I had eliminated three possible future careers (army officer, restaurant manager, and government bureaucrat) while on active duty, I decided that I would try history graduate school, with help from my new spouse.

Here's where contingency, coincidence, and luck enter the picture again. I hoped to attend the University of Wisconsin, Madison, but, alas, Wisconsin wasn't interested in me. Knowing that I needed backup schools, I also applied to my alma mater, the University of Delaware, which accepted me but offered little in the way of financial aid, so that seemed to be a nonstarter.

While an undergraduate at Delaware, I had taken a course in eighteenth-century English history from Professor Robert Smith. I had enjoyed the course material more than Professor Smith's presentation of it. Dr. Smith told us at the end of the year that he was leaving Delaware for Emory University in Atlanta, a school I'd never heard of. So, as I was plotting my history graduate school future on the eve of leaving the army, I sent an application to Emory (using Dr. Smith as a reference). Perhaps because of the combination of my academic record at Delaware, the Smith connection, and the fact that I had already completed my military obligation, I found a graduate school that seemed eager to have me; Emory offered a fellowship amounting to a "full ride."

* * * * *

History grad school was one of the most exciting times of my life. Emory supported me financially for five years; the GI Bill of the Vietnam era supplemented the university's contribution for my first two years; and my wife also was working. So I was being paid—and handsomely, based upon our Spartan lifestyle—to study a subject I truly loved while more or less ignoring what was going on in the wider world (i.e., the decline and fall of our effort in Vietnam).

Shortly after I arrived at Emory in 1968, I began to search for a dissertation topic. I thought that, since I was attending a school in Georgia, a Georgia history topic made sense because most of the primary sources should be readily available. It turned out that, although there were certainly several promising topics for a dissertation in the post-Revolutionary history of Georgia, many primary sources related to those topics either were not housed in the state or had been destroyed by the Civil War or by natural disasters. This shocked me at first, but eventually I was able to face the future with something approaching equanimity. I decided to pursue that elusive Georgia history, regardless of where I had to travel to do so.

In grad school, I practiced being a professor (teaching several classes of American history survey at Emory and a night course at nearby Georgia Tech); researched and wrote my dissertation; and became a father. It was, all in all, a weird, wonderful period. I had so much fun that, every now and then, I had to pinch myself to make sure I wasn't dreaming.

Yet the closer I got to the end of my dissertation, the more I realized there were few college-teaching jobs out there. In my last year at Emory, I sent out more than a hundred queries to universities, colleges, and junior colleges but got no nibbles. Because I still wanted to teach history, in a mood of calculated desperation I decided to investigate plying my trade at the secondary level in private, or independent, schools. (I thought at the time that my lack of education courses would not matter, but it turned out I was wrong.)

Operating under plan B, then, I received two offers: a girls' school in Alexandria, Virginia, was interested in me, as was a co-ed day school across town from Emory. The headmistress of the Alexandria school was so eager to hire me, not least because I was a male, that she dipped into her contingency fund to offer me what she obviously felt was a munificent salary of $7,500 (remember, this was 1973). It turned out, though, that the Westminster Schools, the coed day school across town, was willing to pay me the princely sum of $9,500. Since we now had a child and realized $7,500 would not go very far in the Washington, DC, metropolitan area, I agreed to join Westminster.

*****

When I started teaching at Westminster in the autumn of 1973, I did not anticipate staying for the long term. Surely something better (i.e., a college teaching post) would come along. But no; I found myself making the transition from "professor" to teacher. I came to like the school—and my students and colleagues—very much and spent the next thirty-seven years at Westminster, retiring in the spring of 2010.

During that period, I never forgot the lessons my Emory professors had taught me: "keeping up in my field"; sending a steady stream of book reviews and articles to professional journals; giving the occasional paper or public lecture; and publishing my dissertation so that search committees would be able to separate me from my rivals and, of course, offer me that endowed chair at Ivy U. I did all those things, culminating in the publication of my dissertation by the University of Delaware Press. (To this day, I don't know why a press at my alma mater published a book about politics in Georgia after the American Revolution. Put it down to contingency or luck.) When the book appeared in 1986, I had been on the Westminster faculty for thirteen years.

* * * * *

My first few years at Westminster were incredibly busy. I had to adjust to teaching in a high school, which involved creating several courses, not to mention learning how to deal with students in grades nine through twelve, much younger than any I had encountered before as a teacher. I also was required to take two education courses each year for the first five years so that I could be certified by Georgia. Moreover, mindful of the advice from my Emory teachers, I tried to carve out time to publish.

I took every opportunity to burnish my professorial credentials on the off chance that some desperate college or university sought me out. For example, one of my Emory professors, Dr. Bell Wiley, had established a pipeline with the book review editor of the newspaper in his Tennessee hometown. When he decided that he no longer wished to review history books for the *Jackson Sun*, Dr. Wiley graciously passed the job to me, and several of my early book reviews appeared in that paper.

The early 1970s led up to the American Revolution bicentennial celebration. Because my dissertation began with the Revolution in Georgia and carried the story into the early nineteenth century, I found myself in demand as a local expert on the Revolutionary era. I made my way onto the public stage as a writer of articles, book reviewer, public speaker, and even, on one occasion, a panelist on a cable television show in Augusta, Georgia. These engagements offered scholarly exposure, though they did not bring that coveted college or university teaching position.

I generally met my initial goal of publishing at least one article or book review annually, at least through the end of the 1990s. During the first decade of the twenty-first century, though, I abandoned book reviewing and contented myself with publishing an occasional article, because by then, I had decided to remain at Westminster, abandoning any hope of moving on to the college or university level. I had, in other words, decided I was destined to be a teacher rather than a professor.

*****

During the early years at Westminster, my dissertation director at Emory, Dr. James Rabun, annually forwarded notices of job vacancies in the college ranks, taken from the *American Historical Review*, and I dutifully applied for them, to no avail. Meanwhile, I drew on my liberal arts background to develop a number of courses at Westminster that were outside of my field. In addition to Advanced placement and regular American history (both in my field), I helped to create a course in ancient and medieval history that quickly became the department's introductory offering (evolving over the years into Origins of Western Society and then History of the Ancient World) and shortly supplemented it with courses in Modern European—and Advanced Placement Modern European—History; the South and the Sectional Image; and the History of the Modern American Civil Rights Movement.

In 1989, I became chairman of the history department, the only administrative position I ever actually coveted. For a variety of reasons, I decided that, as chairman, I would do what I could to move our curriculum away from the western civilization model and in the direction of world history, which would better reflect the world into which our students would move as adults. Of course, I had come up through high school, college, and grad school learning about the glories of *western* civilization—and my field was *American* history. Fortunately, I was able to take advantage of two summer programs designed to help broaden the secondary school history curriculum by incorporating world history—one at the National Humanities Center in North Carolina (1989), the other through the Woodrow Wilson National Fellowship Foundation at Princeton University (1993). These programs enabled me to nudge my school in the direction of world history, though I was unable to push quite as far as I'd hoped to by the time I stepped down as chairman.

*****

Perhaps a decade or so into my Westminster tenure, I realized that I was happy there and no longer desired to pursue a post on the college level. One of the hardest things I've ever had to do was inform Dr. Rabun, my Emory dissertation director, that, while I appreciated his efforts to try to line up a college job for me, I had decided to bloom where I was planted and stay at Westminster. Professor Rabun, while not happy (he continued to believe that I deserved "something better," for which I've always been grateful), accepted my decision.

The courses at Westminster were solid—for secondary school history offerings—and I really enjoyed my students, even freshmen in the introductory course I had created (which made me an oddity in my department, most of whose members preferred to teach older students). Moreover, my wife had secured a job in the school's elementary school library that enabled her to carve out a rewarding career for herself over the next four decades, and our sons were able to attend the school tuition-free. After a time, in other words, it would have taken quite an offer from a college to budge me from Atlanta, and that offer never came.

Once I decided to remain at Westminster, I began to consider the question of what I would pursue next in the area of scholarship (yes, I still remembered the advice of my Emory professors, despite my decision not to seek a college teaching job). I had originally proposed to study the evolution of political factions and parties in Georgia between 1776 and 1815 or so, but I had ended my dissertation in 1806, which turned out to be a logical—but not a fulfilling—conclusion.

Westminster developed a sabbatical program that would have been the envy of junior colleges and some small four-year colleges. In the mid-1990s, I put together a proposal that I hoped would allow me to continue the research I had outlined in my original dissertation prospectus. My idea was approved, and, beginning in 1996, the year of the Atlanta Olympics, I launched the new project. I aimed to follow the story in that earlier work to the point that personal and issue-oriented political factions in Georgia evolved into parties similar to those on the national level. Little did I know that this evolution would continue until the mid-1840s. Still, the goal, however remote, of fulfilling the promise I had made in my dissertation prospectus a quarter of a century earlier carried me through the rest of my Westminster career and into retirement.

*****

The transition from "professor" to teacher was long and bumpy, but, in the end, I was glad I had gone along for the ride. I enjoyed my students, who were bright, and their parents, who generally supported the school and its mission. The powers that be at Westminster usually kept out of the faculty's way and let us do our jobs. If I had not harbored hopes of becoming a college professor, I suspect that the transition to being "just a teacher" in a prep school would have been much smoother. It was not simply a matter of learning how to be a teacher; there also was the nagging feeling that I must keep up in my field and take whatever opportunities arose to publish and otherwise keep my name before the academic public, not to mention meeting my responsibilities as a husband and father.

As head of the history department, I was an "easy rider," keeping meetings to a minimum and supervising my charges in a low-key manner. I really enjoyed the opportunity to sit in on classes; go to bat for my colleagues at annual meetings with the administration; take part in the hiring process; and even deal with the occasional crises that arose with no warning. One thing I soon learned was that, when a crisis flared up, the day really flew by, because I had to teach my classes and try to put out the fire(s) at the same time; it was an exhilarating, rewarding experience. I never really came to enjoy the regular department heads meetings, however, when we usually sat around congratulating each other on how hard we worked but seldom made any substantive decisions. In fact, what we did more often than not was to raise a question and talk it to death—what I called the "black hole" approach to administration.

*****

Fortunately, by the time I retired, many Georgia newspapers for the years I was interested in were readily available online through the wonderful University of Georgia GALILEO website, as were a number of other collections of significant primary sources. What a contrast to my earlier travails at the Georgia Historical Society, Georgia Archives, Library of Congress, Duke University, University of North Carolina, and other sites, where, in order to work with hard copies or microfilm editions of antebellum newspapers and other documents, I had to travel hundreds of miles and stay in cheap motels, far from my family.

It was at this point that I retired, and, for the next few years, spent much of my time trolling through online antebellum Georgia newspapers and other document collections. Eventually, I was able to produce a lengthy manuscript, the sequel to my 1986 book. But, in addition, I have been assembling a collection of essays on Georgia history, some previously published in a number of historical journals, others that have not yet seen the light of day.

The present volume is an overview of how my career as a historian of Georgia and the South unfolded while I taught history in a prep school, armed with a PhD. Who knows? If my career had gone in another direction, I might have ended up at one or more colleges, plying my trade as a history professor. Instead, I made the best of what contingency, coincidence, and luck handed me for nearly forty years, and I don't regret a minute of it!

I dedicate this book to my family, and to my colleagues and students at The Westminster Schools, who taught me how to be a husband, father, teacher, and, believe it or not, historian.

Chapter 1

Georgia's Whigs Divided, 1775–1783

[**NOTE:** In the process of trying to find a publisher for my doctoral dissertation, I lucked onto the University of Delaware Press. The reviewers of the manuscript agreed that the first chapter, on the impact of the American Revolution in Georgia on factional alignments, was not needed, because "everyone already knew about that." Funny thing: the reason "everybody" already knew about the factional strife in Georgia was that I and several of my scholarly acquaintances (Ed Cashin, Hardy Jackson, and Ed Bridges, to name a few) had been beating that particular drum steadily over the past couple of years through journal articles and oral presentations. However, there really wasn't a whole lot I could do to counter my publisher's demand, so I gave in. What appears below is a slimmed-down version of that missing chapter. Unlike the reviewers and editors at the University of Delaware Press, I believe that what follows is essential information if one is to understand the forces that shaped Georgia politics *after* 1783.]

* * * * *

On the day that British Regulars clashed with colonial militia at Lexington and Concord in Massachusetts, a troubled resident of Savannah, Georgia, unburdened himself in a letter to a correspondent in England. As a Georgian, James Habersham recognized that the colonists had very real grievances against the mother country, but as president of Governor Sir James Wright's Council, he had an obligation to enforce the ministry's decrees. Torn by these conflicting loyalties, Habersham hoped for a compromise, but, by April 19, 1775, the last glimmer of his optimism had flickered and died:

> [A]s I find Government are determined to push matters to the utmost Extremity to bring the Americans to a Sense of their Duty, I cannot think of the Consequence, but with Horror and Grief and Indeed if conciliating Measures do not soon take Place, I expect no less than an open Breach amongst us, Father against Son, and Son against Father, and the dearest Connections broke through by the Violent Hands of Faction and Party.[1]

Though Habersham did not live to see it, events in Georgia between 1775 and 1783 bore out his somber prediction. More significantly, the Treaty of Paris did not resolve all the questions over which Georgia Whigs had divided during the war. These issues, transmuted by the alchemy of time and circumstance and stamped by the personalities of a series of skillful factional chieftains, defined the parameters of politics in the state for the next generation.

Political factionalism was not a new phenomenon in Georgia in 1775. Prior to 1763, disputes had flared up periodically aligning the governor of the colony against the Commons House of Assembly or the assembly against the council. Nevertheless, in 1763, Georgia hardly seemed ripe for revolution. The colony depended upon British troops to control the Creek Indians on her western frontier. The youngest of Britain's mainland colonies, Georgia had no long tradition of self-government. Since her Crown officials were paid by Parliament, the assembly lacked the leverage that control of the purse strings provided lower houses in her sister colonies. Moreover, the royal governor, Sir James Wright, was a conscientious public servant who owned over twenty-four thousand acres of land in the colony. Governor Wright had an understanding of Georgia's problems, an interest in her welfare, and a sizeable stake in her future.

Though seemingly insulated, the colony of Georgia could not remain oblivious to the repercussions of British imperial policy after 1763. The Commons House of Assembly joined with representative bodies in other colonies to protest both the Sugar and Stamp Acts, although the demurrers from Georgia were directed not at the power of Parliament to levy taxes but at the financial burden the exactions would place upon the colony's meager resources. Friends of colonial liberty did reside in Georgia, and, in conjunction with outside agitators from Charles Town, this Whig faction gradually increased its influence until, by September 1775, it had usurped most of the functions of the provincial government.[2]

Working outside established political channels, Georgia Whigs gradually had erected an effective counterregime, attested to in March 1776 when the frustrated Governor Wright departed the province.[3] The initial success of the revolutionary movement in Georgia came from the efforts of a number of individuals working in uneasy harness. Even before Sir James Wright sailed for England, events had been set in motion that would put the colony's new "governors" at each other's throats. The bones of contention varied, from profound philosophical differences to petty personality clashes. Ambition, rhetoric, and emotions widened the fissures in the edifice of cooperation and rendered ineffectual all attempts at unified direction of the war effort. It would be but slight exaggeration to say that, in Georgia during the American Revolution, adherents to the cause of independence devoted more time to squabbling among themselves than to combating the forces of George III.

The great imponderable in any study of political factionalism is the role of personality. When an ambitious leader justifies his conduct in terms of adherence to principle or assails another for deviating from that tenet, is his overriding motive to advance his own career or to maintain inviolate the creed he espouses? James Habersham warned of the folly of attempting to answer this question, when he wrote that "Liberty as well as religion, has many pretenders among its votaries, and both are too often made a block of Licentiousness, for Hypocrites can as easily cant the phrases of patriotism, as of Sanctity"[4]

Since royal officials in Georgia continued to adhere to the Crown as America moved toward a break with England, the new government would of necessity be entrusted to inexperienced men.[5] Moreover, few Georgians had military experience more extensive than militia duty. Given this vacuum in leadership inherited by the Whigs, it was natural that those who had led the colony thus far along the road to revolution should expect to guide her destinies on the battlefield and in council until the goal of independence had been attained. Problems arose, however, when the scope for advancement proved too narrow to encompass the pretensions of ambitious Georgians.

Two men stood at the center of the partisan strife that rocked Georgia: Button Gwinnett, leader of the more radical faction, a planter from Saint

John's Parish with a talent for shady financial practices and political maneuvering; and Lachlan McIntosh, a Scot from Saint Andrew's Parish, who attracted more conservative Georgians to his cause.[6] The rivalry between Gwinnett and McIntosh became so bitter that they fought a duel, in which Gwinnett perished, but his allies eventually succeeded in having McIntosh removed from command of Georgia's Continental Line. McIntosh's single-minded efforts to have his former rank restored and to discredit the leaders of the reconstituted radical faction kept the state in turmoil until 1783. The seeds of this contention apparently were sown at the very beginning of the Revolution.

Given the magnitude of the issues at stake, as late as 1775, many Georgians either had no desire to choose between loyalty to the Crown and allegiance to the patriots or were unwilling to act precipitately. For example, numerous residents of Savannah hesitated to cast their lots, as did the bulk of the colony's frontier settlers.[7] To force those laggards across the Rubicon, Button Gwinnett, whom his good friend Lyman Hall once described as a "Whig to Excess," organized a radical caucus called the Liberty Society.[8]

According to an unfriendly account published in 1777, Button Gwinnett formed the Liberty Society sometime in 1775 to arouse residents in outlying districts against obstructionists in Christ Church Parish (Savannah). To accomplish this end, Gwinnett "industriously insinuated that the views and interests of the town of Savannah were different from those of the State, and by his address and management persuaded many of the members, both to the southward and to the westward, that it was really so."[9] While it is true that men of a conservative bent were not confined to Savannah, the status of that town as the seat of royal government and as an active port with extensive commercial ties to the mother country enabled both the followers of Governor Sir James Wright and cautious Whigs to exert a restraining influence on more radical Georgians and their Carolina allies.

Writing some years after the Revolution, Lachlan McIntosh defended the caution of many Georgians during this period. Pointing to the colony's relative youth, the sparseness of her population, and her geographical proximity to both the Creek Indians and British troops in the Floridas, McIntosh argued that his fellow Georgians had been justified in

> not entering rashly into Measures of Such Magnitude, altho' there were some Men who without considering these circumstances were

> for rushing violently into them from Motives of Ambition Avarice & their own Circumstances [T]he Number of public Officers in that weak Colony were [*sic*] equal to those in the most populous, they were also of so long Standing and had so many advantages of which they did not fail to make the best use for themselves that they with their dependants [*sic*] possessed perhaps half the property in the Country which with the Straighten's [*sic*] circumstances of the rest gave them greater Influence by far than in any other Colonys [*sic*] and retarded their first Exertions greatly, ... when they [the cautious revolutionaries] once determined they entered into Measures with a Spirit Equal at least to any of these Colonys [*sic*] which had much less to fear.[10]

Gwinnett certainly could not have been ignorant of these factors or of the fact that Georgia was moving, if haltingly, along the road to independence. Therefore, it seems reasonable to assume that he established the Liberty Society as a radical pressure group that would keep the colony on its faltering course by prodding members of the Provincial Congress and by whipping up public opinion on behalf of the patriot cause.

Personal financial difficulties had kept Gwinnett out of public life between 1770 and 1775, but he threw himself wholeheartedly into the work of the Liberty Society. In January 1776, the Provincial Congress elected officers to command Georgia's First Continental Battalion. Reportedly as a result of "his influence and weight at the nightly meetings," Button Gwinnett secured appointment as colonel, or commanding officer, of the battalion over Samuel Elbert, a Savannah merchant.[11] No sooner had he been elected, however, than Gwinnett resigned the position. The Provincial Congress then arranged a compromise by appointing Gwinnett a member of the state's delegation to the Continental Congress, entrusting Lachlan McIntosh with command of the battalion and selecting Samuel Elbert, Gwinnett's former rival for the colonelcy, as lieutenant colonel.

The motives behind Gwinnett's lightning resignation remain obscure. A hostile writer asserts that several of the newly elected Continental officers and some Georgia militia officers objected to serving under him. On the other hand, he might have set his sights on bigger things and so preferred the Philadelphia post. A third possibility, which would be consonant with the claim by his critics that he was overly ambitious, is that Gwinnett had hoped to hold *both* of the military and civilian commissions but had been overruled by the Provincial Congress.[12] Gwinnett's biographer mentions the compromise but maintains that "the election of a delegate who had played no open or active part in carrying the province into the Continental Association has been given as one of the causes arousing against him a feeling of jealousy and resentment on the part of a powerful faction in the province."[13] While Gwinnett's appointment to Congress undoubtedly stirred up "a feeling of jealousy and resentment on the part of a powerful faction," the cause of this animosity might well have been that Gwinnett's role in the events of 1775 had been too "open" and "active" to suit a number of his contemporaries.

Button Gwinnett soon departed for Philadelphia, where he was to achieve something approaching immortality by signing his name to the Declaration of Independence. When he returned to Georgia the following summer, he carried with him a letter from John Hancock, president of the Continental Congress, informing Georgia president Archibald Bulloch that Congress had decided to expand the Georgia contingent of the Continental Line to brigade size, a move that would necessitate the appointment of a brigadier general from the state.[14] While leading Georgia political figures probably were unaware that Gwinnett already had attempted to advance his pretensions to the generalship in Philadelphia, President Bulloch, Lieutenant Colonel Samuel Elbert, and the state's continental agent, John Wereat, all suspected that Gwinnett's return presaged a new effort to secure political or military advancement.[15] It soon became clear that Gwinnett had his heart set on command of the new brigade. Nevertheless, since Lachlan McIntosh had performed creditably in the nine months he had commanded the state's Continental Line, the Continental Congress promoted him to brigadier general, though not without considerable agitation, both in Georgia and in Philadelphia.[16] Relations between the disappointed Gwinnett and the victorious McIntosh deteriorated rapidly. It would be easy to suggest a cause-and-effect relationship, but that is probably an oversimplification in view of the role the conduct of two of the general's brothers might have played in determining Gwinnett's actions.

In January 1777, following a series of complaints by settlers on Georgia's frontier that the state's Light Horse troops were ineffectual in protecting lives and property against bands of marauding Native Americans and Tories, the unit's commander, Lieutenant-Colonel William McIntosh, applied for a leave of absence "for his health" and eventually relinquished his command altogether. The House of Assembly scrutinized the colonel's conduct as leader of the Light Horse, acquitting him of negligence on two different occasions.[17] It is possible that the complaints against William McIntosh were valid to some degree and that the legislative investigations were undertaken in the public interest, but his brother the general did not think so. On December 15, 1776, Lachlan McIntosh complained to one of the state's delegates to the Continental Congress, George Walton, of the "Scandalous attempt[ts] on the character of my Bro[the]r William, Tho' I was the grand object." While the general went on to say that he did not need to inform Walton "of the *person* or his *Motives*" behind these allegations, his allusions to that man's "nocturnal Meetings" point clearly to Button Gwinnett, who was then serving as Speaker of the House of Assembly.[18]

Meanwhile, the imprudent conduct of another of the general's brothers, George McIntosh, led to charges of treasonable activity against him and to a campaign of character assassination directed at the general.[19] In June 1776, George McIntosh joined his brother-in-law, Sir Patrick Houstoun, and Robert Baillie, to purchase a brigantine to ship a cargo of rice to Surinam, Dutch Guiana. For McIntosh, a member of the Georgia Council of Safety, to unite in a commercial venture with Houstoun, whose conduct toward the American cause had thus far been equivocal, and Baillie, who made no secret of his continuing attachment to the mother country, was bad enough; but he then compounded the error by agreeing with his partners to sell a fourth interest in the vessel to the notorious William Panton, keeper of an Indian store on the St. John's River in British East Florida.[20]

The partners received clearance from the Georgia authorities for Surinam after posting bond to ensure that the ship would steer clear of British ports. No sooner had the brigantine sailed than Panton, who had shipped aboard her, ordered the captain to change course. Following a stop at St. Augustine, headquarters of British forces in East Florida, the vessel sailed to the British islands of Antigua and Jamaica, where William Panton's brother Thomas finally succeeded in selling the rice. Loaded with rum, sugar, and coffee purchased from proceeds of the sale, the ship returned to St. Augustine.

Reports of Panton's actions reached Savannah in August. At that time, George McIntosh denied complicity in the brigantine's change of course, convincing President Bulloch and the Council of Safety that "any person of common sense, for the profit that could be made upon sixty barrels of rice, which was his share of the cargo, would not forfeit a bond of £1,000 sterling."[21] Nothing more was heard of the affair for six months. During that lull, Lachlan McIntosh received promotion to brigadier general over Gwinnett, and the harried William McIntosh took his leave of absence from the Light Horse. Late in February 1777, President Bulloch died, and the Council of Safety elected Button Gwinnett to succeed him. On March 4, 1777, the council reassembled to sign the new president's commission, but George McIntosh, who had been absent on the occasion of Gwinnett's election, refused to affix his signature. This reportedly led to a heated exchange between the adamant councilor and the angry president.[22]

On March 16, President Gwinnett received a letter from John Hancock, president of the Continental Congress, covering an intercepted letter from Governor Patrick Tonyn of East Florida to Lord George Germain containing "the most convincing proof of the treasonable conduct of Mr. George M'Intosh of your state." On July 16, Tonyn had informed Germain of William Panton's success in procuring provisions for the garrison at St. Augustine and added that Panton had been

> greatly assisted by Mr. George M'Intosh, who is compelled to a tacit acquiescence with the distempered times, and is one of the Rebel Congress of Georgia, intentionally to mollify and temporize, and to be of all the service in his power. I am informed his principles are a loyal attachment to the King and Constitution. He would, my Lord, be in a dangerous situation were this known.

Even Lachlan McIntosh's good friend South Carolinian Henry Laurens, writing from Congress, informed him that nearly everyone believed George McIntosh's conduct censurable. According to Laurens, the general's brother was "in the class of those who wished the American Cause very well, but not *so well*, as to make any Sacrifice of his Interest in order to promote its welfare." Moreover, Laurens claimed that the general himself had "declare[d] your Sentiments to this effect about a Month before the unlucky transaction which has occasioned him & his family so much trouble."[23]

On the strength of this evidence, President Gwinnett ordered George McIntosh placed in irons and confined in the common jail. A short time later, the president departed for Sunbury to supervise preparations for an expedition against East Florida. In his absence, a number of McIntosh's friends, including four members of the Council of Safety, posted £20,000 bond, thereby securing the prisoner's temporary release.

Since the commander of Continental troops in the South, General Robert Howe, refused to have anything to do with the projected invasion of East Florida, the Continental officer with whom President Gwinnett was obliged to work was none other than General Lachlan McIntosh. Gwinnett probably distrusted the general in the wake of the incidents involving his brothers, and he might still have harbored some resentment over the earlier occasions on which McIntosh had bested him in the scramble for military rank. The two men soon became engaged in a controversy over the right of the president to call councils of war, and both eventually were asked by the other officers present to return to Savannah, leaving the command to Colonel Samuel Elbert.

Under the newly promulgated Georgia Constitution of 1777, the House of Assembly convened in May to elect the state's first governor. Gwinnett entered the lists, but once again his pretensions were denied, with the prize going to John Adam Treutlen. On the other hand, this same session of the assembly supported the former president in his contention that he had had the power to summon councils of war. During the investigation of this issue, General McIntosh reportedly called Gwinnett "A Scoundrel & Lying Rascal." A challenge from Gwinnett resulted. The two men met outside Savannah on May 16, and though both fell wounded, only Gwinnett's injuries proved fatal.

When the House of Assembly decided, soon after Gwinnett's death, to send George McIntosh under guard to Philadelphia for trial by the Continental Congress, Lachlan McIntosh could only have viewed the step as another instance of striking at him through one of his brothers. When the efforts of the general and other supporters of his brother failed to forestall the measure adopted by the assembly, George McIntosh went into hiding. He attempted to reach Philadelphia on his own in July, believing that only in this way could he be sure of receiving a fair trial, but he was overtaken in North Carolina by a party of soldiers from Georgia, who escorted him the rest of the way. After the Continental Congress had agreed with Governor Treutlen that they had the power to try the prisoner, a committee decided that there was insufficient evidence to warrant a trial. McIntosh was released and returned to Georgia.[24]

The civil authorities had taken no immediate action against General McIntosh following his fatal encounter with Gwinnett, but the slain man's friends did not remain idle. Pressing for McIntosh's arrest, they also launched a coordinated campaign to secure his removal from command of the Georgia Line. Spearheading these efforts were members of the Liberty Society.

On July 1, approximately seventy-five citizens of Savannah signed a petition urging the Continental Congress to suspend McIntosh from command. Copies of this petition were distributed to other parts of the state, along with a circular letter over the signature of the president of the Liberty Society, William Belcher, urging that McIntosh's attempts "to weaken or oppose the civil power" be rebuked by the popular will. According to a hostile source, leading members of the Liberty Society left the seat of government and traveled throughout their respective counties to urge that the petition be signed: Joseph Wood toured Chatham County, Lyman Hall and Benjamin Andrew kept up the ferment in Liberty, while George Wells spoke against McIntosh in Richmond County and the Ceded Lands. If we can believe this same jaundiced observer, Governor Treutlen himself returned to Effingham County, "where he demeaned himself so much, as to go to an Election the other day for a vacancy, & would not suffer a Man to vote 'till he first signed a petition against the General."[25]

At the same time, the House of Assembly agreed to ask Congress to remove General McIntosh from command. Moreover, the legislature elected two of the leading members of the Liberty Society, Joseph Wood and Edward Langworthy, to represent the state in Philadelphia.[26] These measures were not enacted without resistance from McIntosh and his allies. One of the McIntosh clan's most zealous defenders was John Wereat, the state's continental agent. Wereat aided General McIntosh in the pamphlet warfare raging over the conduct of George McIntosh and also dispatched letters to Henry Laurens and George Walton in Congress, excoriating the activities of the Liberty Society and painting a bleak picture of affairs in Georgia.[27]

Both Walton and Laurens found it necessary to defend General McIntosh in Congress against aspersions emanating from Georgia. As early as July 14, McIntosh had intimated to Walton that he would not be averse to a transfer, and, on August 5, in response to a request from Walton, General George Washington proved amenable to bringing McIntosh northward, so the beleaguered Scot had his honorable exit and the Liberty Society rid Georgia, at least temporarily, of a man they considered untrustworthy.[28] Even prominent conservative Whig Joseph Clay, a Savannah merchant, was relieved at McIntosh's transfer because "'twas impossible for him to have, or give any satisfaction here, prejudice was so strong against him."[29]

With the departure of Lachlan McIntosh, factional strife subsided in Georgia, while the fortunes of war began to run strongly against the state. As 1778 drew to a close, British forces captured Savannah in the face of ineffectual opposition from General Robert Howe. With the Whig government on the run, even the most contentious Georgians were preoccupied with survival. The Liberty Society presumably was a casualty of war. Some of its members undoubtedly sought shelter within British lines, while others fled to the Carolinas or joined partisan bands in the backcountry. In mid-1779, with the American cause in Georgia at its lowest ebb, General Lachlan McIntosh was ordered back to the state. Upon his arrival in Augusta, he discovered that his enemies were still determined to humiliate him. This time, the remnants of the old Gwinnett-Liberty Society clique succeeded in having McIntosh suspended from command, primarily because of the unscrupulous conduct of their new leader, McIntosh's former defender, George Walton.[30]

Following the fall of Savannah, a few members of the House of Assembly gathered at Augusta. Lacking a quorum, those present styled themselves a "convention" and chose an executive council presided over by William Glascock. Since the sudden arrival of the British at the gates of the capital had prevented election of a governor, the executive council tried to keep government in existence until a chief executive could legally be chosen. Even the council soon found its continued existence in peril, for the British sent a force to Augusta, which arrived in February 1779. After the British withdrew, remnants of the assembly returned and, late in July, chose a so-called Supreme Executive Council. On August 6, this body elected as its president the conscience of the state's conservative Whigs, John Wereat.

Under Wereat's leadership, the Supreme Executive Council demonstrated that it was "willing and able to act as Georgia's executive over the part of the state subject to its authority, but it was weak and at times had to content itself with requests rather than with orders."[31] The council also was a constitutional anomaly, but, given the distempered state of the times, it was better than no government at all. Realizing its tenuous position, the Supreme Executive Council issued a proclamation on November 4, 1779, urging those who had resided in the low country prior to the reduction of Savannah to return to the state by December

1, when they would elect a new House of Assembly. The proclamation further ordered the assembly thus elected to convene at Augusta on the first Tuesday in January 1780.[32]

At this point, George Walton reappeared on the political scene. He had been captured at the fall of Savannah and remained a prisoner on parole until exchanged almost a year later. Upon his release, Walton went to Augusta and consummated a political marriage of convenience with Richard Howley, a Sunbury attorney, and George Wells, reputedly one of the most important members of the Liberty Society and Button Gwinnett's second during his duel with McIntosh. Late in November 1779, these three men and some of their supporters adopted the title of "House of Assembly" and elected Walton governor of Georgia and delegate to Congress. When the executive council chosen by this rump assembly met for the first time, its members selected Howley as council president. Two extralegal bodies now competed for the dubious distinction of "governing" the small portion of Georgia still under Whig control.

The Walton regime did its best to undermine public confidence in Wereat's council, charging that it was an illegal body composed of Tories. Not content to stop there, Governor Walton sent to Congress documents calling for removal of General Lachlan McIntosh from command, on the grounds that both the state militia and the Continental troops stationed in Georgia were dissatisfied with McIntosh and refused to serve under him. One of these items, an address from the House of Assembly, bore the signature of William Glascock, Speaker of the House. Another purported to be a resolve of the executive council, while Governor Walton himself added a cover letter enlarging upon the sentiments of both bodies. On the strength of these petitions, the Continental Congress relieved McIntosh from command on February 14, 1780.

For the next three years, McIntosh strove to clear his name. When he confronted William Glascock with a copy of the assembly's address, the Speaker denied having any knowledge of the document and wrote a letter to Congress labeling his signature on the petition a "flagrant forgery." McIntosh also amassed affidavits from prominent Georgia politicians and officers in the Georgia militia and the Continental army imprisoned with him in Charles Town after the capture of that city by the British in 1780, denying allegations contained in the packet sent under Walton's seal. Upon being exchanged in the summer of 1781, McIntosh repaired to Philadelphia, where, despite the presence of both Walton and

Howley in Congress, that body rescinded its resolves of February 1780 and reinstated McIntosh as a brigadier on active duty. The general next shifted his efforts for vindication to Georgia, and, on February 1, 1783, the House of Assembly, acting upon evidence compiled by an investigating committee, declared that Glascock's signature appeared to be a forgery and that the charges leveled against McIntosh in the communications of 1779 were without foundation. Although the assembly also instructed Georgia's attorney general to institute legal action against the perpetrators of these nefarious proceedings, no prosecution was ever undertaken: one day prior to the issuance of these instructions, the assembly had elected as chief justice of Georgia, and the man who would preside over any legal action, none other than George Walton.[33]

The motives behind Walton's complete reversal of position between 1775 and 1779 remain a mystery. Since McIntosh and John Wereat were close friends, the key to the "forged letter incident" may lie in Walton's opposition to the Supreme Executive Council rather than in any late-blooming hatred on his part toward the general.[34] To be sure, the Supreme Executive Council was an extralegal body, but it is difficult to see how a "House of Assembly" convened without popular mandate by a small number of returning refugees had any better claim to legitimacy, especially because, only a few weeks before, the council had ordered elections to be held in December. Conservative Whigs were to claim that Walton and his supporters had organized their "assembly" solely to influence the outcome of these elections, and the results appear to bear them out. In January 1780, the newly elected House of Assembly chose Richard Howley both governor and delegate to Congress, where eventually he joined George Walton. Furthermore, the executive council, elected from among members of the House of Assembly, named George Wells as its president.

But was political advantage the sole reason Walton turned on Wereat and McIntosh? As commander of the militia at the fall of Savannah, Walton observed the effects of still another dispute between Governor John Houstoun and General Robert Howe, and the experience left a bitter taste in his mouth. Then, in September and October 1779, a joint French and American force had laid siege to Savannah but failed to recapture it. Lachlan McIntosh played a conspicuous military role in that unsuccessful attack, while John Wereat had been present in his capacity as de facto governor of Georgia.[35] The magnitude of this failure left the state in a more exposed position than ever.

Walton had been grievously wounded in the unsuccessful defense of Savannah in December 1778, and, when the Franco-American expedition besieged the capital the following year, he had been in Sunbury, a paroled prisoner. It is possible that he attributed his own recent misfortunes and the futile assault on Savannah in 1779 to the failure of the state's military and political leadership. If so, he might well have decided that what Georgia needed at this critical juncture was the inspired guidance of George Walton. If these assumptions are correct, then—in Walton's eyes, at least—the end sought certainly would justify the means necessary to attain it. Upon his release from captivity, two obstacles barred Walton's road to power: the Supreme Executive Council and General McIntosh, who Walton believed, with some justice, tacitly supported the body presided over by his friend Wereat.[36]

Whatever his reasons, George Walton's apparent apostasy was merely the most striking manifestation of factional politics among Georgia Whigs during the American Revolution. Amid the shifting alliances and personal bickering that characterized the years between 1775 and 1783, few Whigs lost sight of the objective all claimed to be seeking, American independence, a goal that until 1781 appeared increasingly unattainable. Not surprisingly, in their attempts to explain the inability of Georgians to unite in the war effort, factional leaders arrived at different conclusions, conclusions based upon sometimes irreconcilable perceptions of the nature of the government and the society they sought to create and the instruments at their disposal.

* * * * *

When the last British transport sailed away from Savannah in July 1782, the future of Georgia appeared bright. Although the war had exacted a high price in lives and property, all good Whigs could now work together to overcome common problems. Yet there was another side to this coin of victory. Internecine strife among the state's leaders had been bitter, and their ability to cooperate in the postwar period depended upon the speed with which they resolved those divisive issues.

The end of hostilities settled the troublous question of control of the military, but other sources of wartime friction remained. Loyalists who entertained hopes of returning to Georgia had to be dealt with, as did Whigs who had been forced by circumstances temporarily to accept protection from the British. The process of disposing of confiscated Loyalist property had not yet run its course. The supposedly radical Georgia Constitution of

1777 survived the war, but even its strongest advocates could not say with certainty how it would stand up under the strains imposed by political, economic, and social adjustments attendant upon the peace.

The Revolution had taken its toll among those who had occupied central positions in the factional strife of the period. Gwinnett had fallen in the duel with McIntosh; George Wells had been slain in a duel with the truculent young protégé of John Wereat, James Jackson; John Adam Treutlen had been murdered by Tories in South Carolina; George McIntosh had died shortly after his return from Philadelphia; age and pecuniary distress combined to restrict Lachlan McIntosh's postwar political activities; McIntosh's wartime ally, John Wereat, served throughout the 1780s as state auditor, but the position he occupied, while crucial for postwar recovery, was perhaps the least political office in the gift of the state.

There would be no shortage of ambitious men willing and able to replace those who had fallen by the wayside. Returning veterans like the three talented Habersham brothers and James Jackson played prominent roles in Georgia politics after the war, including George Mathews, who led a party of Virginia settlers into the Broad River Valley of up-country Georgia and experienced a meteoric rise to eminence in his new home, as did Nathaniel Pendleton, nephew of Edmund Pendleton of Virginia and former aide to General Nathanael Greene; General "Mad Anthony" Wayne; Abraham Baldwin, a transplanted Connecticut Yankee; and James Gunn, a former captain in the Virginia Line.

Returning soldiers or "principal people," Old Georgians or newcomers, leaders of the postwar generation had to tackle the manifold problems of a frontier state, exacerbated by almost a decade of bitter warfare. To do so, incumbents and their would-be successors worked to politicize the militia, brand opponents with opprobrious epithets, and manipulate county grand juries. Representatives from the rapidly growing up-country appealed to newly awakened sectional pride, while their coastal counterparts frequently sneered at the pretensions of anyone living west of Savannah. If all else failed, inveterate political foes could adjust their differences, sometimes with finality, on the field of honor. In short, just as sources of division persisted in Georgia after the Revolution, the tactics adopted by the new order of political warlords had in many cases had been developed and tested by the factious Whigs of the Revolutionary era.

Chapter 2

William Few's Brownsborough Plan

[**NOTE:** This brief article was extracted from a chapter in my dissertation. I also was trying to complete the dissertation, and publishing this article helped me later, when I had to reduce the length of my manuscript for the folks at the University of Delaware Press. I leaped at the chance to sum up the article in a few sentences in the book, citing the fuller, published version in my notes. The finished essay appeared in *Richmond County History* 5 (Winter 1973), 40–46.]

* * * * *

The structure of Georgia politics after the American Revolution was a multistoried edifice. Historians traditionally have examined only the upper floors, neglecting the all-important foundation, the position occupied by a politician in his county of residence. Most state legislators held additional posts in the counties they represented, usually serving as local magistrates and militia officers. For most such "versatile Georgians," who normally spent less than two months each year in the legislature, the cultivation of support on the local level was a continuous process, a duty that no one with political ambitions could afford to shirk.[1]

The relative importance of local influence to Georgia politicians is nowhere better illustrated than by an episode in the postwar career of William Few, who was perhaps the most influential up-country man at the end of the American Revolution. Between 1783 and 1785, Few bent every effort to a single end: to have the Richmond County courthouse and jail, and hence the county polling place, constructed in the settlement of Brownsborough rather than in Augusta. Although this meant leaving the

Continental Congress before the expiration of his term in January 1783—and probably contributed to the fact that Few disregarded his reelection to that body in 1784—he obviously felt that solidifying his position in his home county was worth the sacrifice.[2]

At its creation in 1777, Richmond County stretched for more than thirty miles along the southwest bank of the Savannah River and extended almost forty miles into the back country. The population at the beginning of the Revolution must have been spread fairly evenly across the settled portions of Richmond, despite the fact that the major town, Augusta, hugged the Savannah River, for two militia battalions were organized to defend it, one for the upper part of the county and one for the lower.[3] There were at least two other settlements in Richmond in 1777: Wrightsborough, near the center, in what is now McDuffie County; and Brownsborough, situated between Wrightsborough and Augusta in an area that later became part of Columbia County.[4] The Fews had migrated to Georgia from North Carolina in 1771 and settled at Wrightsborough, but sometime before 1776 they had removed to the Kiokee District, presumably at or near Brownsborough.[5]

Early in the Revolution, the House of Assembly appointed three men, Few's father, William Few Sr., William Jackson, and John Pratt, as commissioners to arrange for the construction of a county courthouse and jail in Richmond County. The commissioners entered into a contract with William Candler and Benjamin Few, who agreed to erect the buildings at Brownsborough, presumably because that village was more centrally located than Augusta. In January 1780, however, the assembly, claiming that "the remote situation of Brownsborough renders it a very unsafe place for a Jail and Court House," ordered the facilities to be built at Augusta. Nearly two years later, in November 1781, the executive council indicated that this solution also had proved impracticable. Noting that "some doubts may arise respecting the place for holding the annual election in the County of Richmond," the council recommended that magistrates and electors meet at Brownsborough for that purpose.[6]

The question of the location of the county seat had not been resolved by January 1783, when the House of Assembly appointed two Richmond representatives, William Few Jr. and Robert Middleton, "to bring in a Bill for Establishing a Town and Building a Court house and Jail" in that county.[7] These instructions made it clear that Augusta, which had only six months before lost the state capital to Savannah following the evacuation of that port by the British, was to be bypassed in selecting the site for the county seat. Furthermore, William Few Jr.'s presence on the committee suggested that the bill would resurrect the abortive assignment given his father during the Revolution.

Few and Middleton brought in their bill, but after two readings and an uneventful trip to the executive council, the measure apparently became bottled up, perhaps as the result of parliamentary maneuvering by the Augusta representatives.[8] Few implied as much on February 16, when he moved that the commissioners appointed during the Revolution to oversee the building of the courthouse and jail be empowered to require the original contractors to keep their end of the bargain, or, if that were not feasible, that they be authorized to find other individuals who were willing "to build or finish the Court House and Jail in the County of Richmond agreeable to the vote and determination of a Majority of the freemen of that County." Apparently, neither Few nor other Richmond residents beyond the immediate environs of Augusta would countenance further delay. Nevertheless, the House voted to postpone consideration of the issue until the next session, with five of the six Richmond delegates in attendance opposing further delay.[9]

James Jackson of Chatham, who had cast his vote in favor of postponing action until the ensuing meeting of the legislature, later reported that Few was angry at the defeat of his motion. If Jackson was correct, Few attributed the failure of his initial effort to pressure exerted by Augusta lawyers, who would have been inconvenienced were the courthouse located in another part of the county:

> I have been amazed at the attempt of the execution on the threats of the Honorable Mr. Few since the falling of his Brownsborough plan—An Association has been actually begun in [Richmond] County and is now pushing forward for the total exclusion of Lawyers and with them why not Law [?]—Many Plebeians have joined his standard but the sensible see the disguise[.] It has been rejected by many with disdain and it is by some conjectured the High mettled hobby horse [Few] rides will some day give him a tricky fall[.][10]

The Augusta politicians must have been confident that, having frustrated Few's stratagem, their town would be made the county seat at the next meeting of the assembly, for they held elections there in December 1783 to choose the Richmond legislative delegation. Not to be outdone,

Few and his Brownsborough faction held their own canvass. When the assembly convened in January 1784, the double return from Richmond County was referred to the committee on privileges and elections.

On January 8, the committee submitted a report based on information furnished them by Few, spokesman for the Brownsborough slate, and William Glascock of Augusta. Both men agreed that every county election since the adoption of the constitution of 1777 had been held at Brownsborough except one; which had been conducted at "little Kiokee," evidently at a site near the creek of that name. Although the constitution was silent on the question, the committee recommended that, because Brownsborough customarily had been the location of the country polling place, the return from that settlement be accepted as valid. The full House rejected the report, however, choosing instead to seat as representatives from Richmond County the ten candidates with the greatest number of votes from among the twenty returned by the electors at Augusta and Brownsborough.[11]

A comparison of the names of those finally seated with the published list of those chosen at Augusta reveals that Few emerged from the electoral skirmish victorious. Only three of the ten men picked by voters in Augusta actually received a place on the compromise delegation from Richmond. The other seven, including William and Benjamin Few and their brother-in-law, Greenbury Lee, might have had some support in Augusta on election day, but the bulk of their votes must have come from outside the town. Few and his allies from the hinterland of Richmond County had furnished convincing proof that Brownsborough had at least as much claim to be the county seat as did Augusta.[12]

Despite William Few's successful execution of this revised "Brownsborough plan," the legislature refused to revive a separate measure dealing with Richmond's public buildings, choosing instead to incorporate the requirements of that county in an omnibus measure designed to facilitate construction or repair of jails and courthouses throughout the state.[13] The architects of this bill attempted to avoid bruising the sensibilities of either Richmond faction by providing that the necessary structures be erected "at the place where the road crosses the little Kiokee Creek leading to the meeting house, and that the superior Courts be held at Augusta till a Jail and Court house are built, and that elections be held at the place fixed on [as the site for the facilities]."

Following the third reading of the proposed bill on February 26, William Few indicated that he found the wording of the measure unsatisfactory. Few proposed that, in order to determine the location most convenient to a majority of the county's residents, a plebiscite should be held at the "Kiokees [*sic*] Meeting House," at which time voters would select from among three alternative sites for the county's public buildings: Augusta; "where the [militia] Battalion line crosses the little Kiokee"; and Brownsborough. This amendment was defeated, 15–22, with half of the Richmond delegation, including William Few, Benjamin Few, and Greenbury Lee, voting for it, and the other half against it. Few and his allies tried again, moving that the facilities be constructed "At the Little Kiokee on the new road which leads from Augusta to the Kiokee meeting house where the said road Crosses the Little Kiokee Creek." This motion also failed, 14–18, with the Richmond delegation split as before. Finally, the House approved the wording of the committee report by a vote of 22–8, with Few and his adherents in opposition to the last.

The controversy had not yet run its course. One month later, the Richmond County grand jury presented as a grievance "the repeated contention for the fixing the court-house of this county" and recommended that "such attempts be suppressed until a revisal [*sic*] of the Constitution."[14] The state constitution was not overhauled for another five years, and even then, the frame of government said nothing about the location of Richmond's public buildings. On the other hand, the new constitution, unlike the earlier one, did not specify county boundaries, an omission intended to make easier the creation of new counties. Between 1784 and 1789, new settlers continued to swell Richmond County's population, and hence the incidences of crime and litigation, so a single courthouse and jail to serve residents in an area of more than 1,200 square miles became increasingly unrealistic.

By the autumn of 1789, an Augusta resident was moved to urge his fellow citizens to vote at the ensuing election "for men who are in favor of a division of the county, that court-buildings and trials may be erected and established.—a large, growing and commercial town, without these establishments, is unprecedented in America, or the world." The assembly responded by designating Brownsborough, Kiokee Creek, and Augusta as locations for the Richmond court sessions, but this effort at compromise ran afoul of Superior Court Judge George Walton, who objected that the new arrangement forced his court "to move about in the woods." In

December 1790, the legislature acted to alleviate these inconveniences, creating a new county, Columbia, from the northeast corner of Richmond, "virtually giving William Few his own county," where he remained the leading political figure until he left Georgia a decade later.[15]

Available sources offer little information on Few's motives—or those of his opponents—in all of this. For many of Richmond's widely dispersed residents, Brownsborough was a more convenient location for the courthouse than Augusta, and this seems to have been Few's major concern. The outcome of the disputed election of December 1783 indicates that, had the county seat been awarded to Brownsborough, Few's position among Richmond voters would probably have been enhanced, but this consideration might be irrelevant in view of the impressive string of public positions Few occupied during the 1780s, including service in the Continental Congress and the Philadelphia Convention, culminating in his election as one of Georgia's first US senators under the new federal constitution. Although those opposed to making Brownsborough the county seat might have acted at least partly from a desire to avoid the personal inconvenience of having to travel there for court sessions and voting, they also obviously seemed to feel that Augusta's importance to the social, political, and economic life of Georgia's piedmont region ought to outweigh the fact that Brownsborough traditionally had been the county polling place.

Finally, it must be noted that the controversy over William Few's "Brownsborough plan" agitated a major up-country county for at least two years and perhaps longer. Although there is no way of knowing with any degree of certainty, it is interesting to speculate about the effects of this dissension upon both the successive legislative delegations from the county and upon the state as a whole. At the very least, the dispute should warn the historian to proceed with caution when attempting to explain the course of Georgia history during this period in terms of the rivalry between a monolithic "up-country" and an equally unified "low country."

Chapter 3

George Walton, Chief Justice of Georgia, 1783–1785

[**NOTE:** One of the things our Emory professors inculcated in us was the importance of publishing—articles, book reviews, even books if we were lucky, in order to show ourselves worthy of college or university teaching posts—and I tried to do as I'd been taught, despite the fact that I fetched up at a prep school. My initial publications appeared well before I finished grad school: a book review in 1970 in the *Atlanta Journal-Constitution* and an article in the spring 1972 issue of the *Journal of Negro History*. Once I signed on at The Westminster Schools, I continued to try to crank out at least one piece annually, but I had begun to rethink my career plan; perhaps, I reasoned, prep school teaching was not that bad a way to practice as an historian. Still, I continued to give papers and publish articles and reviews on the off chance that some institution of higher learning unexpectedly targeted me for its faculty. But no …

In 1981, I published two articles drawn from an early chapter in my dissertation; one, about the controversial tenure as Chief Justice of Georgia of George Walton, who had aided the radical Whigs in ousting John Wereat and the Supreme Executive Council during the Revolution, appeared in the *Georgia Historical Quarterly* 65 (Summer 1981): 82–91.]

* * * * *

Although the manifold problems vexing Georgia after the American Revolution formed a kind of Gordian knot, they impinged upon the careers of political leaders of the state at different points and in different ways.[1] As chief justice of Georgia between 1783 and 1785, George Walton played an important role in shaping public opinion in a frontier state struggling with the burdens of its newly won independence. Moreover, Walton's conduct during the Revolution had made him a controversial figure, and the vicissitudes he faced while chief justice indicated the extent to which animosities bred during the War for Independence persisted into the postwar period.

By 1783, Walton had behind him an impressive record of achievement. He had been a prime mover in the agitation that culminated in Georgia's break with England, member of the Provincial Congress and House of Assembly, governor, delegate to the Continental Congress, and signer of the Declaration of Independence.

On the other hand, Walton's shift from inveterate assailant of Button Gwinnett's "radical" Whig faction to midwife of a reconstituted radical group after Gwinnett's death in 1777 had alienated supporters of General Lachlan McIntosh. Moreover, his part in securing McIntosh's suspension from Continental command in February 1780 had discredited him in the eyes of many. Speaker of the House William Glascock, who allegedly had signed the crucial anti-McIntosh Assembly address forwarded by Walton to Philadelphia, subsequently denied any knowledge of the document and labeled his signature on it "a flagrant forgery." For three years following his suspension, McIntosh sought vindication. In the summer of 1781, he finally convinced Congress to rescind the resolves of February 1780 and to reinstate him as a brigadier general on active duty.[2]

The general then shifted his efforts for vindication to Georgia, and, on February 1, 1783, the House of Assembly, acting upon evidence compiled by an investigating committee, declared that Speaker Glascock's signature appeared to be a forgery and that the charges leveled against McIntosh in the communications of 1779 had been without foundation. Although the Assembly also instructed the attorney general to institute legal action against the perpetrators of those nefarious proceedings, no prosecution was undertaken. One day prior to the issuance of those instructions, the legislature had elected as chief justice of Georgia, and the man who would preside over any legal action, none other than George Walton.[3]

In sum, George Walton had as good a claim as anyone in post-Revolutionary Georgia, and a better claim than most to political preferment, but his road was of necessity a rocky one until the passions stirred by wartime divisions had cooled.

Adherents of Lachlan McIntosh pursued Walton as tenaciously as Walton and his friends had hounded the general during the war. No sooner had the House of Assembly elected him chief justice than a notice appeared over the signature of General McIntosh's son William declaring Walton "a *Coward and a Villain*" and promising that, if he attempted to perform the duties of his new office, young McIntosh and his friends would "assist in pulling him of[f] of a Bench which ought to be filled with an Unblemished Character." This was no idle threat, for shortly thereafter, William McIntosh accosted Walton in the streets of Savannah and chastised him with a horse whip that, McIntosh gloated, had been "well laid on."[4]

The anti-Walton group also took its case to the public in a series of letters to the *Georgia Gazette*. The first journalistic assailant, who signed himself "A Citizen," termed Walton's judicial appointment, by the same body that also was considering charges of forgery against him, "an inexplicable paradox, a solecism in politics, which the world will never be able to comprehend, unless publick infamy shall be considered as the only recommendation to publick trust." This indictment called forth a bitter defense of Walton from "Scourge." "Hercules Wormwood" and "A Whip," the latter probably William McIntosh, joined the fray on March 6, hinting that "Scourge" was George Walton himself, an allegation "Scourge" took pains to deny.[5]

Still smarting from the humiliation of his public flogging, the chief justice found himself, on March 4, 1783, confronting the regular session of the Chatham County grand jury. As his glance swept over the eighteen men seated opposite, Walton must have realized that this would be no ordinary session, for among those staring back at him were three members of the clan McIntosh, including General Lachlan McIntosh, and McIntosh's unswerving ally, John Wereat. His suspicions were confirmed when, instead of the usual presentments dealing with the prevalence of immorality and the disgraceful condition of roads and ferries, the foreman, William Gibbons, Sr., attempted to lay before the court a searing indictment of its presiding officer's conduct while governor late in 1779 and of the assembly's "flagrant imposition" in electing Walton chief justice while he was still "liable to a criminal prosecution."[6]

Not surprisingly, Walton declined to accept the presentments, and the grand jury adamantly refused to proceed to other business unless he did so. Finally, the panel members retired from the courtroom to seek the opinion of Georgia's attorney general, Samuel Stirk, on the legality of their action. Stirk ruled that a grand jury could submit their presentments in any order it desired. The jurymen returned triumphantly to court, only to discover that the wily chief justice had adjourned the session in their absence. Unwilling to allow Walton to escape so easily, Gibbons and his associates went before the governor and council the next day, demanding that Walton be suspended for the present term, "thereby enabling them to pursue the functions of their body, and to preserve the current of Justice, which must otherwise become stagnant." The executive promptly complied with their request. Thus, after three years of feverish but frustrated activity, Lachlan McIntosh secured a modicum of revenge against his erstwhile ally.[7]

Walton's treatment at the hands of the irate Chatham grand jury evidently had no adverse effect on the prevailing opinion of his legal ability. Not only was he reinstated as chief justice by the governor and council in time to ride the autumn judicial circuit, but he also was reelected by the ensuing legislature. Anyone reading his charges to various grand juries during 1784 might have concluded that the events of the preceding year had chastened the volatile magistrate. This conclusion would have been erroneous: George Walton took the high road only to secure a better vantage point from which to assail his adversaries.

On March 2, 1784, the chief justice delivered a charge to the Chatham grand jury that suggested that readers of the *Georgia Gazette* had taken recent calls for constitutional revision to heart. He instructed the members of the panel that, if they felt it necessary to point out the "infirmity" of the Constitution of 1777, they should do so "with great good temper." They responded by presenting, at the head of their list of grievances, "the too large representation of this county, and the state in general, in the House of Assembly, the expence [*sic*] of which becomes too burthensome for the circumstances of the inhabitants thereof," and by recommending constitutional reform. Walton offered a similar charge at each of the remaining stops on his circuit, and with the exception of Effingham, each grand jury supported alteration of the frame of government.[8]

By the time he set out on his second circuit ride in 1784, the chief justice had had a change of heart. For example, when he met the Wilkes County grand jury, he asserted that the time for amending the constitution had not yet arrived. Although he had informed the Liberty County grand jury in April that residents of "the counties lying on Savannah River are promoting petitions" calling for constitutional revision, it might have become evident by November that there was insufficient popular support for such a move.[9] Yet, in the fall of 1784, Walton had an even more compelling reason to reorder his priorities: by that time he had embarked upon a determined campaign to rid Georgia of "Tories" and their sympathizers.

Between July and September 1784, George Walton contributed to the *Georgia Gazette* a series of essays over the signature of "Brutus" that constituted an all-out attack upon the administration of Governor John Houstoun. The "Brutus" letters were attributed to Walton by three different sources, although by indirection, as was customary in the eighteenth century. That no one publicly denied the accuracy of these attributions, as for instance "Scourge" had done in March 1783 when he was accused of being Walton, further strengthens the claims by contemporaries that the chief justice was "Brutus."[10]

"Brutus" pointed out that, in his February message to the legislature, Governor Houstoun had asked for guidance on only a single article in the definitive treaty of peace, that regarding restitution of confiscated property. Although Walton avoided a direct assertion that Houstoun had acted out of a desire to aid Loyalists in recovering their confiscated estates, he charged that "the new administration gave birth to hopes which encouraged [Tories] into high expectations." He declared further that the amercement policy being pursued by the assembly was both pusillanimous and wrong-headed, because Whigs and Tories were "like fire and water which essay to each other's destruction whenever brought into contact." While he refused to speculate about whether the "airs of abominable audacity" recently assumed by Georgia Tories arose from a belief that the state government was in the hands of their friends or from a contemplated "bold attempt" on that government, "Brutus" warned his fellow citizens to be on their guard, arguing that "a longer acquiescence in measures which produce such effects is unpardonable."[11]

Walton next shifted his attention to attempts by British merchants to collect debts from virtuous but impecunious Whigs. The merchants had been rebuffed by Chief Justice Walton, "Brutus" wrote, but, "meeting with encouragement" ("They said the Governor wished the matter tried," he added in a footnote), they renewed their efforts. However, the chief justice had demonstrated that he "could not be driven from the grounds of his former decisions." Convinced they would not receive satisfaction from the judiciary, British creditors turned to their allies in the executive branch.

There they secured what no former administration had been willing to grant—the sale of public property at auction in order to raise sufficient funds to pay them for supplies furnished General Wayne's army in the waning days of the Revolution. In view of the pitiful plaints of distressed Whigs that had thus far gone unheeded by the Houstoun administration, "Brutus" asserted that "without being accountable for the charge, I confess the management of the business has something very like collusion in it."[12]

Why Walton harbored such animosity toward John Houstoun is not clear; it is also not clear the extent to which the chief justice himself believed what he wrote. What is beyond cavil is that Walton had portrayed contemporary events as a continuing struggle between Whigs and Tories of the Revolutionary era. When someone eventually replied to Walton's charges, he, too, admitted the existence of two contending factions, but he eschewed fastening upon them the labels chosen by the chief justice.

The pamphlet *Cursory Remarks on Men and Measures in Georgia*, by "A Citizen," was "scattered about the streets" of Savannah late in 1784. According to the anonymous author, confiscated property lay at the heart of factional strife in the state. He categorized one group, which had as its "two principle [*sic*] heroes" Walton and an unidentified ally, presumably Richard Howley, as "a most powerful combination of individuals zealously embarked in the scheme of advancing their private fortunes on the ruins of every thing [*sic*] that is dear and valuable to the community." Opposing this rapacious clique was "a more virtuous, though a less active set of citizens … counteracting knavery and vociferation with reason and argument." Walton and his supporters had "plunged themselves into an abyss of debt" in their pursuit of confiscated property, and, facing financial ruin, they were attempting to extricate themselves by "an internal revolution." To this end, they were using every means in their power to "create distrust and jealousy against those whose fortunes offer a security for confidence, and whose private characters command respect and esteem."[13]

"A Citizen" charged that Walton, Howley, and others of their ilk had no intention of paying for the confiscated property they had purchased. Hence, they were not satisfied when the legislature tried to relieve the distress of those who were unable to meet their obligations by allowing them a period of one year during which audited certificates would be accepted for one half of the sum due the state. When state officials remained adamant in insisting that the modified payment terms be complied with, the writer asserted, the "redoubtable duumvirate" at the head of the unscrupulous purchasers turned their fire upon the Houstoun administration in the "Brutus" letters. To conceal their own rapacity, the authors of the essays had summoned the hobgoblin of toryism in an attempt to discredit a group of conscientious public servants. If the people of Georgia permitted these tactics to succeed, warned the pamphleteer, "we may lay our accounts to be the dupes of every factious demagogue who wants a step ladder to climb into consequence, or feels lust of being richer than his neighbor."[14]

Between the conclusion of the "Brutus" letters and the appearance of *Cursory Remarks*, George Walton continued to castigate men and measures. In Savannah, he criticized the legislature for inactivity and coupled this charge with a critique of the measures that body *had* enacted. In Wilkes County, Walton made a thinly veiled attack on those who had sprung to the defense of the Houstoun administration. In Liberty County, he criticized the governor for summoning the legislature to meet in Savannah rather than in Augusta. Urging that legislators be required to gather in Augusta, the chief justice delivered a summary of the argument he had advanced in "Brutus, No.8." In the peroration, he raised the specter of sectional animosity, arguing that "as free governments are instituted for the ease and convenience of the greatest number, and as the western people have generally and cheerfully met below [in Savannah], it is but reasonable that they should expect the eastern Members to meet above [in Augusta] in their turn, were it not for the necessity [to meet in Augusta] created by law."[15]

Despite George Walton's refusal to abandon his vendetta against the Houstoun administration and the blatant attempt by the author of *Cursory Remarks* to injure his chances for reelection, the House of Assembly appointed him to a third consecutive one-year term as chief justice. During 1785, Walton turned his seemingly boundless energy to the task of securing grand jury presentments favorable to investing the Continental Congress with the power to levy an impost, or customs duty, on imports, thereby strengthening the national government under the Articles of Confederation. His efforts in this direction probably earned him the grudging respect of some of his Chatham County adversaries, and they were received enthusiastically by several members of Congress. Walton's yeoman service on behalf of bolstering Congress marked the turning point in his postwar career: he called off his hunt for "Tories," and in turn, his critics relented in their pursuit of him.[16]

After his retirement from his judicial post in 1786, George Walton practiced law in Savannah and continued to cultivate the good opinion of low countrymen. In May of that year, he was chosen a member of the Chatham County delegation to the House of Assembly, the first of a series of offices to which he would be elected during the remainder of the decade, culminating in his elevation to the governorship in 1789.[17]

Throughout the 1780s, George Walton was one of the most outspoken men in Georgia. This was partly the result of his volatile temperament and partly in consequence of his three years as chief justice, a post that provided a perfect forum for publicizing his opinions. In a state with a constitution that limited the powers of the governor, and with a legislature that struggled with only mixed success to bring order out of the near chaos of the Revolution, Walton used his position as head of the state judiciary to cajole, persuade, and educate Georgians on the issues of the day. Consistency was not his strong suit, but this probably says as much about the ephemeral nature of some of the disputes in which he became involved as it does about Walton himself.

Chapter 4

Waiting for the Steamboat: The Political Career of Thomas Gibbons, 1783–1789

[**NOTE:** The research trip I took in the autumn of 1971 in pursuit of Thomas Gibbons might have been the most enjoyable one I've ever experienced. Not only did I have the opportunity to reconnect with my family in Delaware but I also drove to northern New Jersey, following in Gibbons's wake after his departure from Georgia early in the nineteenth century. First, I spent time with a private collector of Gibbons's manuscripts in Chatham, where we drank bourbon in front of a wood fire, looked at documents, and discussed "Ole Tom's" role in Georgia politics, with which my host was only tangentially familiar, since his collection mostly focused on his hero's life in New Jersey.

The next day, I went to Drew University in Madison, located on property formerly owned by Gibbons, where I met the director of the school's Rose Memorial Library. He showed me a "baleful" portrait of Gibbons (which I included in the published version of my dissertation), as well as a prized item in the university's collection of Gibbons Family Papers, an "anatomically correct" anti-Jefferson political cartoon (drawn by Gibbons, I think). This article appeared, under a different title, in the *Atlanta Historical Journal* 25 (Fall 1981): 37–44.]

* * * * *

Most students of American history know the name of Thomas Gibbons, if at all, through his involvement in the famous Supreme Court case of *Gibbons v. Ogden* (1824), which was decided over a decade after he had abandoned Georgia for the financially more salubrious climes of New

Jersey. Yet his political career between 1783 and 1789 reveals much about the nature of Georgia politics in general and of low-country political culture in particular. At the end of the American Revolution, the ambitious young lawyer found himself handicapped by his "Tory" sympathies during the conflict. Gibbons overcame the stigma of "toryism" in a surprisingly short time, displaying a remarkable degree of political astuteness that nearly enabled him to revolutionize Georgia politics.

Thomas Gibbons, a native Georgian, had adhered to the Crown during the Revolution, while his brothers had thrown in their lot with the Whigs. Like other families throughout the colonies, the Gibbonses were determined to save their property, regardless of which side prevailed on the battlefield.[1] During the British occupation, Gibbons practiced law in Savannah, where his willingness to defend Whigs accused of treason against the king seems to have earned him the enmity of royal officials and his fellow Loyalists.[2] Although included in the confiscation and banishment legislation of May 4, 1782, and arrested by Georgia Whigs following the departure of the British from Savannah, Gibbons evidently harbored no doubt that, once state authorities were informed of his reasons for accepting British protection and of his conduct between 1776 and 1782, he would be restored to citizenship. On January 13, 1783, he petitioned the House of Assembly to be placed on the Amercement Act, which readmitted a number of Georgians tainted by "toryism" to citizenship under certain restrictions.[3]

On July 24, 1783, the assembly placed Thomas Gibbons's name on the Amercement Act by legislative resolution, but this resolution, as well as several others lessening the penalties for "toryism," ran afoul of the state's fervent Whig governor, Lyman Hall, and his council, who refused to comply with its terms. The legislature finally embodied the resolutions respecting penitent Tories in a new amercement bill on February 21, 1785.[4] The debate on this measure indicated that neither the Chatham County delegation in general nor representative James Jackson in particular was willing to forgive or forget the apostasy of Thomas Gibbons.

During the third reading of the amercement bill, one legislator moved that the name of Thomas Gibbons be removed from the measure, thereby permitting him to be restored to citizenship without penalty.[5] This was not an unusual request; similar motions were made on behalf of several former Tories. The response of the House, which defeated the suggestion, 17–27, was also not surprising, for this fate awaited most such proposals.

All eight of the representatives from Chatham County opposed any further alleviation of the punishment for Gibbons's transgressions.

Later that same day, however, James Jackson, a Revolutionary hero and rising tidewater politician, reopened consideration of Gibbons's case. He proposed that Gibbons "be not allowed to plead and practice in the Courts of Law in this state for 14 years." As written, the amercement bill provided that, in addition to being fined 12 percent of the value of their property, Loyalists in the same category as Gibbons were to be prohibited from voting and holding office for fourteen years. If Jackson's amendment were passed, Thomas Gibbons would also be singled out for the additional penalty of being barred from practicing his chosen profession for fourteen years. This proposal obviously appeared too stringent to most of the members from Chatham, for six of them voted against it, and only two—Jackson and James Gunn—voted for it. Nevertheless, the House approved the amendment, 25–18.

There are several possible explanations for the depth of the hostility displayed toward Thomas Gibbons by James Jackson and a majority of the House of Assembly. It is conceivable that Jackson and Gibbons had clashed, either verbally or physically, or both, during the tense period immediately prior to the outbreak of the Revolution or subsequent to the recapture of Savannah by the Whigs. Neither Gibbons nor Jackson was particularly reticent or self-effacing; convinced of the rectitude of his own conduct, each might have moved aggressively on a course leading toward a collision with the other. Even if Gibbons had defended Whigs trapped behind British lines, it is doubtful that patriots as vocal as Jackson would have agreed that this conduct outweighed the apparent tenacity with which Gibbons had clung to the British standard and the persistent rumor that he had somehow betrayed the confidence of General Benjamin Lincoln during the war. Although the House of Assembly had displayed lenity toward Loyalists engaged in certain critical occupations,[6] there was certainly no shortage of lawyers in the state in 1785. Finally, the propensity demonstrated by Gibbons during the British occupation for offering his counsel to those who espoused the unpopular American cause might have disturbed a number of Georgians. A man who defended Whigs under a Tory regime almost certainly would be willing to serve as attorney for Tories or their creditors seeking satisfaction from a Whig regime that had already begun to divide confiscated property among its adherents.

Gibbons must have had a glib tongue or powerful connections, or both, for scarcely eighteen months after the legislature had forbidden him to follow his chosen profession, its members reversed that decision and readmitted him to the bar.[7] Within a month, he took steps to demonstrate that Whig suspicions regarding his probable conduct if permitted to practice law were well founded. The ensuing controversy eventually aligned a number of influential Savannah residents, including his nemesis James Jackson, against Thomas Gibbons.

On September 14, 1786, Benjamin Fishbourn, former aide-de-camp to General Anthony Wayne and son-in-law of James Jackson's "foster father," John Wereat, publicly denounced Thomas Gibbons for pressing a suit against him seeking to recover some confiscated property in his possession. The outraged Fishbourn explained that he felt it necessary to warn his fellow citizens against such "vile and malicious proceedings," asserting that Gibbons had declared that "let him *once be admitted* [to the bar], he would overturn the whole Confiscation Law, … and that he would make the purchasers of such property sweat for their hardiness." Gibbons promptly challenged Fishbourn, and only the combined efforts of their seconds resolved the dispute short of a duel.[8]

No sooner had he settled his differences with Benjamin Fishbourn than Thomas Gibbons was accosted "in an ungentlemanly style" by a Mr. Davies, who, speaking for himself and for General James Jackson, told Gibbons that he could choose between the two of them for his next opponent.[9] Gibbons immediately selected Jackson, and the two agreed upon a meeting place, but, when word of their plans became common knowledge, they decided to postpone the encounter. When Jackson made no effort to renew his challenge during the next nine days, Gibbons accused the general of having "trespassed on my indulgence." Jackson responded by dispatching an agent who was to "tell when and where Mr. Gibbons may satiate his Tory appetite, by shooting as much as he pleased" at him. After the two had exchanged shots on the field of honor without injury, Gibbons's second suggested that the antagonists shake hands. According to Jackson's second, "the General was backward in doing it, and when he did do it, he said, 'I shake hands only on this affair, as it is a private one; in a publick [*sic*] cause, I shall always be your enemy, Mr. Gibbons.'" Events were to show that this feeling was mutual.

Although Benjamin Fishbourn later implied that Davies and Jackson "were induced to pursue the line of conduct they did toward Mr. Gibbons out of respect to me," the explanation for the rash of challenges confronting Gibbons in the fall of 1786 is more complex than that. Jackson, of course, might have been angered by the assembly's action in permitting Gibbons to resume his law practice. Davies had clearly indicated the source of his dissatisfaction when he asked Gibbons whether he would "sue for old debts as far back as 1778." Jackson's personal animus and Davies's fear that Gibbons would be a zealous advocate for Tories and their creditors were fed in turn by still another factor, the sense of frustration then pervading Chatham County over a series of setbacks administered to low-country pride during 1786. Gibbons's willingness to prosecute purchasers of confiscated property was the proverbial last straw.

In his report of a "Whig Meeting" on September 18, *Georgia Gazette* editor James Johnston commented that "we do not find any thing [*sic*] of consequence was done at it." Indeed, there was little that residents of Savannah could do about the removal of the state capital to Augusta, the suspension of their magistrates by the governor and council, or the emission of £50,000 of paper money by the legislature, but they could and did turn upon Thomas Gibbons.[10] Those in attendance apparently sent words to Gibbons that he must refrain from offering his services to persons desiring to press judgments against good Whigs or be prepared to face the consequences, for Gibbons delayed answering their resolves until after he had dealt with Jackson, explaining that "it was my wish to adjust this matter first, and then turn my face toward these inhabitants, or some of them." As a lawyer, he declared, he was bound to seek equal justice for rich and poor, not simply to enlist in popular causes, adding that "I shall on these principles do my duty, and set the consequences at defiance."

By his actions in September and October 1786, Thomas Gibbons demonstrated convincingly that he had the courage of his convictions. This evidently stood him in good stead both with the legislature and with the voters of Chatham County. In February 1787, the House of Assembly passed a law restoring to Gibbons and eight other former Loyalists all rights of citizenship. Thereafter, Gibbons represented Chatham in the assembly (1787–1789); in the convention to ratify the federal Constitution; and in the state constitutional convention of 1789.[11] Nevertheless, this popularity did nothing to dispel the aura of controversy that had enveloped Gibbons since the end of the American Revolution.

Gibbons continued to refurbish his reputation at every opportunity. For example, he refused a challenge growing out of a Fourth of July dispute in 1788, but, when one of the principals publicly accused him of treasonous conduct during the Revolution, he published a series of affidavits in support of his contention that he had been guilty of no untoward activities during that period.[12] In September 1789, General Benjamin Lincoln passed through Savannah, and Gibbons secured a statement from Lincoln that he hoped would finally lay to rest the charge raised by "the rioter, the leader of mobs, and the disappointed candidate" that he had betrayed Lincoln's confidence during the Revolution.[13]

General Lincoln's reply was crucial to Thomas Gibbons in the autumn of 1789, for he was in the midst of a bitter election campaign.[14] The Georgia Constitution of 1789 had reduced representation of Chatham County in the legislature from fourteen to six (one senator and five representatives). Under the Constitution of 1777, it had been possible for both established local figures and relative newcomers like Thomas Gibbons to secure a seat on the delegation, but the reduction provided in the new frame of government forced even proper gentlemen to sully their hands in the dirty business of electioneering. In October 1789, residents of Savannah were treated to a public display of how far politics had moved since the end of the Revolution.

On October 1, "A Planter" urged "Planters, Tradesmen, Shopkeepers, and other Voters, of Chatham County" not to elect Thomas Gibbons to represent them in the new state senate. Not only had Gibbons made himself obnoxious to other members of the House of Assembly during his tenure in that body, "A Planter" charged, but on a number of occasions, he had attempted "to sacrifice the interests of his constituents, in favor of that of other counties, most probably to gain an influence with them." "A Planter" asserted that, before the last election, Gibbons had held nightly meetings at which he used "every artifice" to ensure that only those persons were elected who would be subservient to his leadership. As a result of Gibbons's "party designs," "two thirds of our Members last year were men so entirely ignorant of all legislative proceedings that they must necessarily have been dependent on the opinions of others [i.e., Thomas Gibbons]." To make matters worse, Gibbons and his adherents had actively campaigned for their posts:

> How have the magnificent promises of that party been fulfilled? Last session the tender of paper money was to be repealed, and other statuatory [*sic*] laws passed to secure the honest tradesman the fruits of his labour. What was done? 5000*L* of the money was burnt, and

> the tender of the rest extended five years ... I understand they are repeating the same promises to obtain your suffrage at the ensuing election, which I suppose they will fulfil [*sic*], by burning 5000*L* more, and making the rest a tender for 14 years, after the example of the honest people of Rhode Island.

The pseudonymous writer concluded on a note that, though implicit in similar election-eve exhortations since 1783, had seldom been expressed publicly: "Be cautious in trusting those who fawn on you and court your suffrage; it is a strong indication they have some personal views of their own. It appears to me the extreme of impudence for one man to ask another for a vote."[15]

The timing of this scathing attack was masterly, for, under the new state constitution, the general election was to be held on the first Monday in October, three days *before* the next issue of the *Georgia Gazette* went to press. Gibbons and a candidate for the state House of Representatives, Robert Montfort, who also had felt the sting of "A Planter's" invective, replied by the only method available to them, a broadside. Gibbons answered a number of the specific charges raised by "A Planter," but his response to the most potent of them seemed to concede the point to his opponent: "I will add, that, if I am a party man, or ever was, I was drove [*sic*] to the measure."

Not to be outdone, "A Planter" issued a handbill of his own, in which he revealed, perhaps inadvertently, the extent to which the style of campaigning adopted by Gibbons and his supporters had challenged the ingenuity of men accustomed to the deferential politics of years gone by:

> Mr. G. and his party wish to insinuate that a number of gentlemen have formed a party against the mechanics:--I do not believe it. I have never been at any night meeting of any side, which in a free government, I think improper. But, as far as I am able to judge from appearances, and what I have heard, it is a story whispered into the ears of the mechanics (a respectable and judicious body of men) merely to create a prejudice against certain persons who had formerly served you for many years with honor. These are the arts of designing men, who have no other political pursuits but their own success, and that of their friends.[16]

At the ensuing election, Thomas Gibbons and the other candidates mentioned with varying degrees of venom by "A Planter" went down to defeat. William Stephens, elected over Gibbons to the state senate, and three of those chosen representatives—Joseph Habersham, James Cochran, and Samuel Stirk—certainly fit "A Planter's" description of "persons who had formerly served you for many years with honor," against whom the "Gibbons Party" supposedly had been conducting their whispering campaign.[17]

Election-eve commentary was nothing new in Georgia, but the admonition that voters should select the "right" candidates to govern them finally was made explicit in "A Planter's" attack. The major change revealed by the 1789 campaign in Chatham County was a shift in tactics employed by prospective candidates. The plaints of "A Planter" notwithstanding, candidates in previous elections had engaged in electioneering, but of a subtle, perhaps unconscious variety: the Revolutionary hero, the local magistrate, the militia battalion or regimental commander, the incumbent officeholder, all had "campaigned" for office by virtue of their positions of authority, their bearing, their social standing, or their ability to command the respect of potential voters. Status, not programs; personalities, not issues—these had been the touchstones of Georgia politics.[18]

This began to change with the entry of Thomas Gibbons into public life. In the eyes of many of his contemporaries, Gibbons was culpable not because he had somehow discarded his reputation as a "Tory" and managed to secure election to stations of trust but because he had begun, toward the end of the 1780s, actively, even blatantly, to seek office. More damning still, not only had he exploited discontent by offering specific proposals for the consideration of the electorate but he also had gathered about him a coterie of like-minded individuals who were willing and able to echo his views.

To be sure, voters in 1789 rejected this appeal, aided by the indignant cries of the "proper gentlemen" whom Gibbons's tactics suddenly had aroused from their torpor. Admittedly, the opposition to Gibbons might have been fostered as much by the reduction in the size of the legislative delegation under the new constitution as by an instinctive distaste for his style of electioneering. If "A Planter" is any indication, then the anti-Gibbons forces proved adept at modifying the rather pristine campaign methods of yore.

Thomas Gibbons went on to serve several terms as mayor of Savannah in the 1790s; otherwise, he contented himself with his lucrative law practice, his plantations, and his role as leader of Savannah's small but vocal Federalist clique. His efforts to build a solid base for Federalism in Georgia were unavailing. For this failure, Gibbons's contentious and sometimes unscrupulous conduct deserves at least part of the blame. James Jackson, Georgia's leading Jeffersonian Republican, was more successful than Gibbons in electioneering and party management in the 1790s. Bearing the cross of "Toryism" in the 1780s, Gibbons had nothing to lose and everything to gain by challenging the conventional style of politics in Georgia. A decade later, however, he was a member of Savannah's economic elite and the port's most prominent Federalist. The Federalists, the party of George Washington and Alexander Hamilton, were not much given to "revolution"; after 1789, Thomas Gibbons was not, either.

Chapter 5

Farewell to the Revolution: Georgia in 1785

[**NOTE:** This was the first article on Georgia history I published, in the *Georgia Historical Quarterly* 56 (Fall 1972): 387–402. The format for yearlong courses in Emory's history graduate school was conventional class work during the fall and winter quarters (e.g., lectures, tests, book reviews), followed by a spring quarter during which the student researched and wrote a seminar paper in each of his major courses. This piece was the product of Dr. James Rabun's Era of the American Revolution course. Obviously, I was already taking to heart my mentor's advice that I needed to publish in order to get my name out there and, thus, gain an advantage over rivals for college-teaching positions when the time came.

I undertook a study of Georgia in 1785 because, at the time, I was considering doing my doctoral dissertation on the state's history during the so-called "Confederation Period," the years between adoption of the Articles of Confederation as the nation's first constitution in 1777, and the decision to jettison the Articles for the federal Constitution a decade later. A decade seems like a mighty short time span for a dissertation, I know, and that's probably why, in the end, I decided to go in a different direction, even if I still stuck to Georgia history.

One other note on this article: the editor who accepted it for the *Georgia Historical Quarterly*, the legendary E. Merton Coulter, evidently misplaced the manuscript for a time, and, when he did lay hands on it again, decided that it was too long for that journal. Still, he evidently regretted losing the manuscript and offered to publish it if I was willing to cut it judiciously. Well, as we PhDs were wont to ask in those days, "Is the pope Catholic?" "Cut it, Dr. Coulter? Why certainly, sir—by how many pages? Oh, is that enough? Fine, yes, sir, here ya go ..."

This essay helps furnish the context within which the factional infighting of the Revolutionary era evolved after the war; it also highlights several issues that continued to dominate Georgia politics for a long time after the adoption of the new government created by the Philadelphia Convention.]

*****

With the British evacuation of Savannah in July 1782, the government of the state of Georgia, created by the Constitution of 1777, finally had an opportunity to govern. The House of Assembly began at once to repair physical destruction; reestablish law and order; woo settlers to the state as a buffer against Native American and Spanish neighbors; dispose of a vast quantity of land; deal with those Georgians who had been on the losing side in the Revolution; and raise enough money to meet the state's financial obligations. So overwhelming were these tasks that, of the twenty-eight bills passed between 1781 and 1784, all but three were aimed either at alleviating conditions brought on by the war or lubricating the creaky wheels of state government.[1]

Less than one-third of the laws enacted by the legislature in 1785 were directly related to recovery, including an amercement act, readmitting certain Georgia Loyalists to citizenship upon payment of a fine and other civil penalties; a law repealing portions of earlier land legislation; a measure to ascertain the specie value of Georgia treasury certificates and bills of credit issued during the Revolution; and a law validating deeds issued since the outbreak of hostilities with Britain, even though they might have been deficient in point of form.

The House of Assembly looked toward the future instead of the past in other areas, like religion, marriage, and education. In both their complexity and their philosophical overtones, many of these bills stood in marked contrast to earlier legislation. The smooth-running committee system that the assembly had developed by 1785 seemingly afforded more time for rumination on the part of members charged with drawing up legislation. In addition to its more reasoned approach toward writing laws, the assembly also demonstrated that feelings toward Loyalists had mellowed a bit. Of the twenty-one individuals who had petitioned either to be removed from the confiscation and banishment acts or permitted to return to the state from exile, six received favorable action.

An examination of several issues reveals just how far along the road to recovery Georgia had come since the last British ship sailed away from Savannah. For instance, the Revolution had left in its wake a staggering legacy of destruction. Grand juries constantly berated local citizens for failing to maintain roads. Where they existed at all, ferries were haphazard affairs, often lacking even a rudimentary shelter at the landing. While the 1785 assembly session did consider a bill for establishing ferries throughout the state, the measure dropped from sight after February 16.[2]

Various obstructions, both natural and man-made, had accumulated in the state's rivers and creeks since the outbreak of the Revolution, and these, too, posed problems for the unwary traveler. Grand juries in the coastal counties called attention to the sad state of repair of that area's public buildings and places of worship, while up-country grand juries complained of the almost complete lack of those structures.[3]

If one traveled any distance from a settlement in 1785, there was the constant threat of predatory creatures of both the two-legged and four-legged variety. Three years of punitive expeditions by the Georgia militia had not eliminated the bands of robbers preying upon frontier settlements. Although Georgia's relations with Native American neighbors were marked more by tension and mutual distrust than violence, at least one sizeable raid by the Creeks during 1785 was recorded. Of course, if one managed to avoid both the banditti and the Indians, one still had to cope with beasts of the Georgia forests. A bill to encourage the killing of "Bears, Wolves, Panthers, and Wild Cats" made the rounds of the assembly at the 1785 session, but it was tabled on February 17.[4]

A bane of eighteenth-century existence was smallpox. Savannah was rife with reports of the dread disease during the summer of 1785, but prompt action by the governor and council and Chatham County justices of the peace apparently nipped the threat of an epidemic in the bud.[5] Savannah also confronted other problems of health, sanitation, and fire safety. On February 21, the assembly passed an act "for better regulating the Town of Savannah and the Hamlets thereof" intended to consolidate existing ordinances. This omnibus measure dealt with a bewildering variety of town concerns, including rubbish disposal, privies, water supply, fire prevention, and public auctions.[6]

Rice cultivation in Georgia had been badly crippled during the Revolution by damage to plantations and by the removal of slaves at the behest of the British. The low-country planters clung tenaciously to their old money crop, however, and by 1785, Governor Samuel Elbert could reassure the state's congressional delegation that the rice crop would be a good one. Although rapidly increasing up-country farmers raised corn and wheat, their staple crop was tobacco. Recognizing that "the cultivation of tobacco is very considerable and if properly attended to will become a most valuable article of exportation from the State," the House of Assembly enacted a law on February 21, 1785, establishing a system of tobacco inspection.[7]

Although Georgia's tariff policies were relatively simple in 1785, pressure was building that culminated in passage of a detailed act in 1786. The ports of Savannah and Sunbury had reopened by 1785, but they were not operating at peak efficiency. Rotting hulks and other objects sunk during the Revolution still obstructed the Savannah River. If less bothered by channel obstructions, the smaller port of Sunbury, Liberty County, lost revenue for another reason, the lack of a "proper lighthouse." In a state as financially straitened as Georgia, no source of revenue could be overlooked, and, on April 26, 1785, the executive council moved to close a loophole in the collection of imposts, appointing a customs official for smaller ports beyond the jurisdiction of the collector at Sunbury.[8]

Many Georgians regarded the extensive trade between the up-country and the state of South Carolina, upon which no duties were levied, as a primary cause of the flight of specie from the state, because the Carolinians would not accept in payment the up-country's staple commodity, tobacco. Although the assembly took no action in this matter during 1785, a provision of the Tariff Act of 1786 imposed on goods of foreign manufacture imported overland the same duties levied on similar items brought in by ship. The collector for these overland duties was to reside in Augusta.[9]

The Land Office Act of 1777 had included several provisions to encourage industry in Georgia, one offering a hundred acres of land to anyone establishing a grist mill. Grist mills must have been flourishing by 1785, for the assembly appointed a committee to bring in a bill to regulate them, although the measure was not finally enacted until January 1786. Other Georgians toyed with the notion of encouraging shipbuilding. The 1785 legislative session considered a motion "to lay a duty on every Ton

Measure of live-Oak exported from ... this State, and for the encouragement of Ship building within the same," but the measure was tabled.[10]

Although life in Georgia in 1785 could be grim, there were opportunities to improve the mind and refresh the spirit. On January 27, the assembly passed a law "for the more full and complete Establishment of a public School of Learning in this State."[11] The philosophic preamble to this measure envisioned a day when the young Georgians no longer would be sent elsewhere for school, but instead would receive careful instruction in American principles in the state itself. To further this end, the education statute chartered the University of Georgia and created the Senatus Academicus, composed of a board of trustees and a board of visitors, to oversee its operation. All publicly supported schools in the state were to be considered part of the university and governed by its regulations. Even though the University of Georgia did not open its doors until 1801 and many local academies existed only on paper, this measure is still regarded as a landmark in the history of education in the state.

The members of the assembly also waxed philosophic in the preamble to the act "for the regular establishment and support of the public duties of Religion," signed into law on February 21. Arguing that "the Knowledge and practice of the principles of the Christian Religion" was "no less necessary to present, than to future happiness," the lawmakers attempted to tax each Georgian to support the religion of his choice, a procedure they believed implicit in the provisions of the Constitution of 1777 establishing the principle of religious toleration.[12] In February, the House of Assembly ruled on the side of both religious toleration and personal convenience when it declared that marriages performed by justices of the peace, like those performed by ministers of the gospel, would be valid, so long as marriage banns had been announced for eight days or a license obtained from the governor.[13]

Georgians also required outlets for the exuberance that was a natural product of life on the American frontier. For families in isolated settlements, amusements were closely akin to everyday activities. On the other hand, as a substantial town and an active port, Savannah naturally imparted a more cosmopolitan flavor to her citizens' amusements. Residents with any pretensions to culture could patronize plays that were occasionally offered, trip the light fantastic in Mr. Godwin's dancing school, or study music under the tutelage of John Hiwill.[14]

Savannah residents who preferred good fellowship to intellectual stimulation could find that, as well. There were at least ten taverns in town by 1785, all of them featuring a variety of spirituous liquors and some offering facilities for games such as "skittle alley," shuffleboard, and billiards. More genteel companionship could be found at Burt and Stebbins's newly opened Savannah Coffee House, which boasted victuals of the "first qualities from the cellar and stall," as well as accommodations for lodging, dining, and private entertaining. In addition, the proprietors kept a book of marine intelligence, and, as a final inducement, Burt and Stebbins promised that "all the principal newspapers will be procured from the different states in the Union."[15]

During 1785, the government of Georgia was lax in responding to popular pressure over the condition of public buildings, although positive steps were taken, or at least contemplated, to restore commerce to its prewar level. Lowland agriculture still bore the scars of war, but up-country farmers were enjoying success with a new money crop, tobacco. The House of Assembly showed surprising foresight in legislation dealing with education and religion.

No doubt more ought to have been done, but Georgia did not exist in a vacuum. Like it or not, her affairs were bound to those of her sister states. Georgia also became involved in controversies with her neighbors—Spaniards, Native Americans, and South Carolinians. Whether involvement in these imbroglios was of its own volition or inadvertent, required exertions on the part of the state government sometimes limited the government's ability to deal with internal affairs.

At the core of Georgia's "foreign" entanglements in the postwar years was her hunger for land, which seemed insatiable. State officials fretted over securing land from the Indians and supported ambitious schemes of speculators and others to extend the state's boundaries. The year 1785 also saw the revival of the dispute over the boundary between Georgia and South Carolina, a source of friction with roots in the colonial era.

Following Britain's evacuation of Savannah, the state government moved quickly to reassert authority over Indian tribes along the frontiers. In October 1782, a band of Cherokees signed the Treaty of Long Swamp, ceding to the state a large tract of land between the Oconee and Tugaloo Rivers. Cherokee representatives and commissioners from Georgia met at Augusta in May 1783 to ratify this treaty, and, in November of that year, representatives from only two of one hundred Creek towns also assented to the settlement.[16]

By 1785, the Creeks were dominated by Alexander McGillivray, the son of a Scottish trader, Lachlan McGillivray, and a Creek woman.[17] McGillivray's ability as a diplomat was exceeded only by his hatred for Georgia, since that state had both confiscated his father's property during the Revolution and, so he believed, used the threat of force to secure Creek ratification of the Long Swamp treaty. Fortified by what he considered a pledge from Spain to aid him if need be, McGillivray was determined not to submit to the terms of that pact without a fight. However, as far as Georgia was concerned, the question had been settled at Augusta. One of the provisions of the Land Act of February 22, 1785, called for appointment of commissioners by both Georgia and the Creeks, who were to meet as soon as possible to determine the new boundary line, "agreeable to treaty, and according to Law, endeavouring [*sic*] to obtain for the white people as large a compass of ground as they can."[18] Clearly, the assembly, which sought the land in order to create a "Bounty Reserve" sufficient to meet Georgia's Revolutionary War obligations, would brook neither interference nor delay.

The talks sent by Governor Elbert to the headmen of the Cherokees and Creeks did not indicate that he harbored misgivings about the justice of the state's demands. Furthermore, in a letter to Indian trader William Clark, Elbert implied that he did not anticipate a large turnout at the meeting and that the Georgia commissioners were prepared to conclude an agreement no matter how few Indians attended.[19] The day after Governor Elbert sent the letter to Clark, he received intelligence from William Houstoun, Georgia's lone congressional delegate, that threatened to upset the state's plans. Houstoun informed him that Congress had appointed its own commissioners to arrange treaties with the southern Indians and that no Georgian had been selected to conduct those negotiations. Although Elbert urged Houstoun to protest the exclusion of a Georgian from the congressional commission, he made no plans to cancel the state's proposed meeting with the Creeks and Cherokees. In fact, on June 9, he instructed Elijah Clarke, one of those elected to represent Georgia at the Board's Bluff parley, to hurry to the meeting place, since "it is a business of the first consequence to the State, and should not be delayed, especially as the Commissioners from Congress will shortly be on the same errand, and if we get thro' [*sic*] with this before they commence, it may be a capital point gained."[20]

Less than two weeks later, Georgia's game was up. On June 21, a discouraged Governor Elbert reported to the state's congressional delegation that he had learned from the Creeks' interpreter, Timothy Bernard, that a "talk" sent by the congressional commissioners had "been the means of preventing the Indians meeting us agreeable to their appointment, nor I suppose we shall be able to do anything with them until the general treaty." Elbert and the council thereupon adopted new tactics. The governor informed the three congressional appointees, Benjamin Hawkins, Andrew Pickens, and Joseph Martin, that he planned to have several persons attend the Galphinton meeting, "as Congress has been so very kind as to indulge the State with that privilege." The instructions from the executive council to the Georgia commissioners ordered them to aid the congressional representatives "in forwarding their business as far as they by the Articles of Confederation and perpetual Union are authorized to go," but strictly charged them "to protest against any measures that may appear to them to exceed the powers given by the Confederation aforesaid, and which may be contrary to the constitution and Laws of this State."[21]

After the frenzied preparations, the meeting at Galphinton was anticlimactic. The commissioners from Congress, who expected to meet representatives from one hundred towns, arrived near the end of October to find only two Creek chiefs and sixty warriors awaiting them. By November 8, it had become clear that no more Native Americans would arrive, so the commissioners distributed a few trinkets and departed without a treaty. The next day, Georgia representatives Elijah Clarke and John Twiggs induced those Creeks present both to confirm the Treaty of Augusta and to cede to the state a tract of land between the Altamaha and St. Marys Rivers.[22]

The congressional commissioners did negotiate a treaty with the Cherokees at Hopewell in South Carolina. This agreement pleased Georgia not a bit. In fact, on February 11, 1786, a committee of the Georgia Assembly attacked the actions of the congressional negotiators at Galphinton and Hopewell, declaring that they had violated the Articles of Confederation. The committee also recommended a protest to Congress and declared null and void every action taken by the emissaries from New York that violated Georgia's "rights & privileges."[23] Alexander McGillivray and his followers disavowed the Treaty of Galphinton, just as they had the earlier agreements of Long Swamp and Augusta. Another "unjust" treaty in the pockets of Georgia negotiators and the constant incursions made into Creek territory by land-hungry Georgians served only to increase tension between the two sides. Within a very short time, Georgia-Creek relations moved from the council fire to the battleground.

Land hunger also bulked large in the fantastic series of events that unfolded during 1785 as a result of the creation by the House of Assembly of Bourbon County, in territory claimed by both Georgia and Spain in West Florida. In January, the legislature began to consider a petition from Thomas Green and others, residents of the area around Natchez. On February 7, the Speaker of the House signed into law a bill "laying out a District of land situate on the river Mississippi and within the limits of this State into a County to be called Bourbon." The assembly appointed Thomas Green one of the justices of the peace for the new county and empowered the magistrates to administer an oath of allegiance to other residents and to enroll them in the Georgia militia. In its instructions to the Bourbon County justices, the legislature emphasized clearly that its support for Green's venture was to be of the moral variety, rather than military in nature. For example, the sixth article admonished the magistrates that they were "not without further orders and authority to engage in any dispute with either the Spaniards or the Indians about Territorial claims ... or any other matter whatsoever which may eventually involve this State in a contest. Should you or the people under you by any misconduct or breach of these instructions draw on such, it will not be considered that you have any claim to the protection or support of your fellow Citizens in this quarter of the State."[24]

So, armed with best wishes from the Georgia legislature but little else, Thomas Green set out for Natchez to beard the Spaniard in his den. While the authorities in Natchez were, to say the least, a bit confused when Green called on them, the Spanish viceroy, Bernardo de Galvez, was driven into a veritable paroxysm of fury at the news of Green's mission. Spanish officials gave the justices of the peace of Bourbon County two weeks to leave West Florida, and, aware that they could expect no help from Georgia, the Green party beat a hasty retreat.

In contrast to the storm clouds that hovered over Georgia's relations with West Florida, an aura of calm marked her dealings with East Florida. Even this tranquility was deceptive, for suspicion and tension lurked just beneath the surface. Throughout 1785, the presence of British Loyalists in

East Florida and the problem of maintaining law and order on both sides of the St. Marys River between the two neighbors exacerbated an already unstable situation.

When, in May 1785, William Pengree, "a gentleman of character and property who has long been a resident ... in East Florida," inquired of Governor Elbert about settling in Georgia, Elbert not only encouraged Pengree but also asked him to sound out gentlemen of similar standing in that province about removing to Georgia. However, this was a sensitive issue, and hostility toward strangers thought to be from south of the St. Marys proved sufficient to sidetrack Pengree's recruiting effort. In September, he informed Elbert that his party of thirty prospective settlers had abandoned their scheme because of "Various Reports of Individuals that they shd [*sic*] be cut off by private Parties sent out for this purpose, without Publick [*sic*] Authority Law or Tryal."[25]

Suspicions harbored toward Georgia by Governor Zespedes of East Florida were reflected in his ambiguous reactions to overtures from the state suggesting they cooperate in apprehending raiders who made existence perilous for settlers on both sides of the St. Marys. In February 1785, Governor Elbert was informed that Zespedes had indicated a willingness to adopt such measures, and, in May, the justice of the peace on the Spanish side of the river, Henry O'Neill, and his Georgia counterpart, Alexander Semple, had broached the subject again to their superiors. Nevertheless, on May 24, Governor Zespedes's secretary told O'Neill that the governor felt he lacked authority to approve joint operations against the bandits, since "every nation considers it to be one of the prerogatives of its sovereignty to protect within its territory every foreigner who comes to it seeking asylum."[26] While a lingering animus in the minds of Georgians against Loyalist refugees probably necessitated a distinction such as that drawn by Governor Zespedes, it certainly complicated the already unenviable task of hard-pressed Spanish and American local officials responsible for maintaining law and order on the Georgia-Florida frontier.

The cessation of hostilities between the new United States and her former mother country brought to the fore two unresolved territorial questions between Georgia and South Carolina: the location of Georgia's northern boundary, which had been imperfectly defined in her colonial charter; and South Carolina's claim to land south of the Altamaha River in Georgia. Efforts to settle these disputes had been made in 1783 and 1784 but had died before reaching maturity. In 1785, both states seemed willing to negotiate, appointing commissioners, but the Georgia Assembly bound her emissaries to claim the full extent of territory granted by both her colonial charter and a royal proclamation issued in 1763. Because these instructions amounted to a restatement of Georgia's previous position, South Carolina broke off negotiations, choosing instead to petition Congress to decide the issue under Article IX of the Articles of Confederation. Here the matter rested for the remainder of the year.[27]

During 1785, Georgia's relations with the Continental Congress centered around three questions, in addition to the issue of Indian affairs: representation; the request by Congress for the power to levy an impost; and financial obligations. Georgia's congressional delegates were elected from, and could continue to sit and vote in, the assembly. This, combined with the distance from Savannah to New York and the sporadic salary payments to congressmen, made a prospective delegate reluctant to leave home and hearth. Of the five men chosen by the assembly to represent Georgia in Congress, for example, only one, William Houstoun, actually was present in New York City before May 30. Since the Articles of Confederation stipulated that no state could be represented in Congress by fewer than two members, Georgia was, for all intents and purposes, unrepresented in the national legislature for the first five months of the year.[28]

Easily the most controversial question confronting Georgia during 1785 was the congressional request of April 18, 1783, for the power to levy an impost. Because the measure was designed to furnish Congress with an assured income independent of the notoriously ineffectual requisition system, a much broader issue was at stake: the nature of the central government. In spite of pleas from Congress in December 1784 and January 1785 urging a decision, the House of Assembly delayed acting upon the request.

Even a legislative body as nimble as the Georgia Assembly in evading a decision on the impost question could not withstand public pressure indefinitely. At each stop on his circuit during 1785, Chief Justice George Walton used his charge to inveigh against the dilatory tactics of the legislature, and grand juries invariable presented as a grievance the assembly's delay in approving the congressional impost request.[29] The state's only newspaper, the *Georgia Gazette*, contained numerous items underlining weaknesses in the central government, and it also chronicled activities of northern merchants attempting to combat restrictions imposed on American trade by Great Britain. From time to time, local correspondents offered advice on steps to be taken to strengthen Congress; most of these writers envisioned bolstering the Articles of Confederation through the addition of the impost power.[30] In mid-September, Governor Elbert informed Georgia's congressional delegates that the next session of the assembly would act upon the impost, and, on February 13, 1786, the legislature approved the measure.[31]

Georgia was also derelict in her duty to Congress under the requisition system. For example, reports from the Board of the Treasury indicated that the state had paid not a jot on a $24,905 assessment stemming from the requisition of October 1781, and, as late as July 1785, also had not contributed anything toward her share of the 1784 tax burden. Unfortunately for Congress, Georgia had its hands full trying to meet obligations within its own borders. Even after the state's auditor, John Wereat, reduced to specie value paper claims against the state that had accumulated during the Revolution, Georgia still faced the problem of laying its hands on sufficient hard money to make good its obligations, reduced though they now were.[32]

The state had hoped to obtain specie from three main sources: the sale of confiscated estates; tax collections; and import duties. But this optimism proved groundless. In 1785, legislators turned to another option, enticing paper claims out of circulation by providing that audited certificates would be accepted in payment for up to one-half of an individual's tax assessment and as payment in full for confiscated property purchased from the state.[33] Yet the Revolution had so deranged Georgia's economy that these measures, too, failed to accomplish the desired end. Faced with a chronic lack of specie, then, both the state government and the private sector were reduced to something approaching the barter system. The best that can be said of Georgia's fiscal relations with Congress is that the spirit was willing, but the flesh was weak.[34]

Burdened with the opprobrium of representing a state that had insufficient delegates on the floor of Congress, delayed approval of the desperately needed impost power, and lagged far behind in her financial obligations, a despondent William Houstoun wrote Governor Elbert in April that "it is very seriously talked of, either to make a tryal [*sic*] of voting Georgia out of the Union or to fall upon some means of taking coercive measures against her. In truth I do not think at any one time since the existence of Georgia she has been in a worse situation than at present." In spite of Houstoun's pessimism, Congress took no punitive action against the state. By June, John Habersham—who, along with Abraham Baldwin, had been at Houstoun's side since the end of May—could inform Savannah merchant Joseph Clay that "from our being so long unrepresented, and the indifference shewn [*sic*] to our Foederal [*sic*] requisitions, I was led to suppose we should frequently be reminded of the delinquency of Georgia; but whether it is because the States have all been in some degree culpable, or that our distresses and consequent inability are considered, the subject has seldom been touched upon."[35]

Without examining the years still to come before Georgia ratified the federal Constitution, it would be presumptuous to characterize the events of 1785 as *the* turning point in Georgia's history during the Confederation Period, yet several things are clear. Laws passed by the assembly marked a definite break with the emphasis on postwar recovery that had dominated the years between 1781 and 1784. The mania of her citizens for land and their continuing animosity toward Loyalists living on her borders embroiled Georgia in controversies with her neighbors. These disputes in turn distracted the attention of the state government from the important task of recovery set in motion by earlier legislation. Conscious both of its weakness in the face of the combined forces of the Spaniards and Native Americans and of the need to strengthen ties with the central government, Georgia was either unwilling, in the case of Indian affairs, or unable, with regard to her financial obligations to Congress, to signify, however symbolically, her commitment to the principle of union.

On the other hand, one cannot read the laws passed in 1785 or peruse the pages of the state's newspaper without detecting a note of optimism and—more importantly, perhaps—a measure of pride, both in the achievements of the American Revolution and in the future prospects of both Georgia and the United States. Lacking such elements, no venture in state-making could hope to succeed. Much remained to be done when the newly elected House of Assembly convened in January 1786, but prospects for success had increased immeasurably as a result of what had happened in Georgia in 1785.

And yet, despite all that had taken place by the end of 1785 and that would be accomplished subsequently, conflicts in several of these areas—most notably, the state's land claims, the presence of Native American tribes within her boundaries, and her relations with the central government—would continue to shape, and warp, the state's history for the next half century and foster a system of factional politics that would be unfathomable to most outside observers, as well as to some poor, befuddled souls who lived in Georgia.

Chapter 6

Georgia and the Federal Constitution

[**NOTE**: This essay originated as a talk delivered during the celebration of the bicentennial of the federal Constitution at the quarterly meeting of Historic Jonesboro / Clayton County (Georgia). I did not think that, as a high school teacher, I would ever be asked to address a local historical group, but I was wrong, thanks to the efforts of scholarly acquaintances Hardy Jackson and Brad Rice, faculty members at what was then Clayton Junior College and is now Clayton State University. A home, "Stately Oaks" (supposedly built in the 1840s), and a 1901 one-room schoolhouse, where the talk actually was given, were the venue. While my written talk lasted only twenty-five to thirty minutes, the actual presentation, including questions and answers afterward, stretched the event out. My journal records that "I had a *great* time! Funny, once I lapse into my 'performance' role, I cease to care about what I must look like to my audience. And I was every bit the performer tonight."]

* * * * *

On December 31, 1787, a convention meeting in Augusta ratified the proposed federal Constitution. Georgia was the fourth state to ratify and one of only three to do so unanimously. Thus, at first glance there does not appear to be much of a story here: politically astute Georgians, recognizing the peril in which their nation stood under the notoriously ineffectual Articles of Confederation, enthusiastically supported the new Constitution created by an assembly of demigods in Philadelphia. The reality was a good deal more complex.

To begin with, it is possible to see Georgia's prompt approval of the Constitution less as a fervent embrace of the new than as a decisive rejection of the old. One scholar who takes this line goes so far as to label the action of the Augusta ratifying convention as nothing less than "Georgia's first act of secession from the United States."[1] In truth, Georgia's relations with the Confederation Congress could hardly have been worse in 1787. Throughout the 1780s, the state was consistently in arrears in its financial obligations to Congress under the requisition system and, for a variety of reasons, was seldom fully represented in that body. Another sore point was Georgia's vast land claims, which extended south to Spanish Florida and westward to the Mississippi River. Native American tribes, Spaniards, and the American Congress all coveted this territory, while Georgia desired to open the lands to settlement under its own authority but was unable to do so.[2]

At the heart of the ill will between Georgia and Congress was the question of Indian relations. In order to open its western territory to white settlement, Georgia had to normalize relations with its Indian neighbors, who had supported the British during the American Revolution. To do this, state officials negotiated a series of treaties with the Creeks in 1783 (at Augusta), 1785 (Galphinton), and 1786 (Shoulderbone). Unfortunately for the prospects of peace along the southern frontier, only a few Creek chiefs were willing to sign away tribal lands at these treaty sessions; others, including the most influential Creek leader, Alexander McGillivray, denounced each treaty in turn and refused to recognize its validity. Moreover, Congress moved to assert control over the southern Indians, a step that gave hope to the Creeks but angered Georgians. The result of all this frontier intrigue was a steady deterioration in relations between Georgia and the Creeks, on the one hand, and between the state and Congress on the other. Violence flared in the backcountry between white settlers and the Creeks, and a full-scale Indian war loomed on the horizon.

It was in this context of frontier tensions and political alienation that Georgia reacted to the possibility of a reinvigorated central government. The Assembly considered the report of the Annapolis Convention, which paved the way for the more famous gathering in Philadelphia, in January and February 1787. On February 10, the assembly elected William Few, Abraham Baldwin, William Pierce, George Walton, William Houstoun, and Nathaniel Pendleton as delegates to represent Georgia in Philadelphia, where a convention would assemble in May to consider revision of the

Articles of Confederation. Four of those chosen by the assembly actually attended the Philadelphia Convention; except for a period of about ten days in late July and early August, the state had at least two delegates present. Abraham Baldwin attended throughout and was the state's outstanding delegate; William Few was in Philadelphia except for a month when he had to attend a congressional session in New York City; William Pierce remained from May 31 to about July 1, and he spent much of that time taking notes on personalities and proceedings of the convention that have proven useful to scholars ever since; William Houstoun arrived at the convention on June 11 and remained until about July 26.[3]

Georgia's convention delegates did not speak very often: Abraham Baldwin took the floor eight times; William Houstoun, seven; William Pierce, four; and William Few, not at all. In the course of debate, Baldwin and Pierce favored a stronger central government, but they also hoped to protect the rights of the states. Baldwin believed that the first branch of the proposed bicameral national legislature should represent the people and the second the states. He also insisted that the new government should have some contact with the people and that the states needed to surrender some of their sovereignty; otherwise, he felt, the new government would be no improvement over the old one. In short, the Georgia delegation in Philadelphia usually voted with the "large states" or "stronger central government" group in the convention.

Abraham Baldwin and William Houstoun, the only Georgians present in early July, played key roles in helping to resolve a knotty problem and, according to some scholars, helped to save the Philadelphia Convention. At the time, delegates were badly split over the question of the basis for representation in the upper house of the proposed national legislature and seemed about to break up in disarray. On July 2, the convention voted on a crucial motion by Oliver Ellsworth of Connecticut that the states have equal representation in the Senate. The vote was by states, which meant that members of each state delegation had to settle the issue among themselves before their state's one vote could be cast and counted. With eleven states represented at Philadelphia, the vote on Ellsworth's proposal stood at five to five when Georgia's turn came. Abraham Baldwin, who had previously announced that he would oppose the motion, instead voted for it, and William Houstoun voted against it; this split the Georgia delegation, so the state's vote could not be cast. The tie stood, and the convention had time to devise and adopt the famous "Connecticut Compromise," which provided for proportional representation in the House of Representatives and equal representation in the Senate.

Ordinarily, Georgia's delegation would have voted with the large states, which opposed Ellsworth's motion. If both Georgians present had done so, the large states would have defeated the proposal by one vote, and the small states probably would have gone home. This time, though, Baldwin reversed his earlier stand and voted for Ellsworth's motion. Why? The only direct evidence on this question is a statement from a Maryland delegate, Luther Martin, who said that Baldwin voted as he did in order to preserve the tie, buy time for compromise, and thus prevent the immediate breakup of the convention. Moreover, Baldwin was a native of Connecticut, and he knew several of the delegates from that state personally. A final, tantalizing bit of circumstantial evidence supporting Martin's assertion is that, when the convention subsequently approved the "Connecticut Compromise" by one vote, Baldwin reverted to type and voted against the proposal.

The members of the Georgia delegation at Philadelphia also took an active interest in another potentially divisive question, the foreign slave trade. Abraham Baldwin joined delegates from South Carolina in arguing that slavery was a local matter that should be left to the states, and he asserted that Georgia would oppose any attempt to restrict one of its "favorite prerogatives." Baldwin also claimed that states still allowing the foreign slave trade would probably abolish it shortly if left alone. Only the Carolinas and Georgia favored further importation of slaves from abroad. The other states were able to carry another compromise measure, allowing the foreign slave trade to continue until 1808, at which time Congress could examine the question again.

William Few and Abraham Baldwin signed the finished Constitution, and William Pierce said he would have if he had been in Philadelphia at the time. Pierce did not believe the Constitution was perfect, but he felt that it was probably the best one possible under the circumstances. There is also no reason to believe that William Houstoun would not have signed the Constitution had he been present in Philadelphia when the convention ended. With the end of the convention, the fate of the proposed Constitution was in the hands of the states.

After the Philadelphia Convention adjourned, William Pierce and William Few returned to Congress and were present when that body voted to send the proposed Constitution to the states. In late September, Pierce wrote to Virginia's St. George Tucker, giving his general impressions of the convention and its handiwork. He explained that, while he had been in New York on important business when the convention delegates signed the finished document, he certainly would have signed had he been present. Yes, there were objections that could be made about the new Constitution, but, Pierce averred, "The dissonant interests of the different parts of the Union, made it impossible to give it any other shape or form." Certainly, he admitted, there was fear that the new frame of government would reduce the power of the individual states, but, "as individuals in society ... give up a part of their national rights to secure the rest, so the different states should render a portion of their interests to secure the good of the whole."[4]

A week later, Pierce sailed for Savannah carrying a copy of the new frame of government with him. He arrived on October 10, and three days later, the proposed Constitution was published in the state press. Within a week, a special session of the assembly, which was meeting to consider Indian troubles many Georgians blamed on the Confederation Congress, called for election of a ratifying convention in December.

Surviving evidence suggests that public debate in Georgia over the wisdom of ratifying the new Constitution was extremely one-sided. Only one opponent of the proposed frame of government evidently took his case to the people through the press. This writer, who called himself "A Georgian," asserted that the powers granted the central government in the proposed Constitution were too strong, and he protested the absence of a bill of rights. Supporters of the Constitution confined themselves to heaping abuse on "A Georgian." "Demosthenes Minor," for example, contended that, if the Constitution were not speedily adopted, "we shall be shamed in history, cursed by posterity, the scoff of nations, and the jest of fools."[5] One of these writers even argued that opposition to ratification amounted to "toryism," which he defined as a desire to destroy the institutions won on the battlefield at the cost of the "blood of all *real Georgians*, as well as all other Whig Americans."[6]

Likewise, only a single private letter has been found that advised against the complete adoption of the Constitution in Georgia. On December 17, 1787, General Lachlan McIntosh of Revolutionary War fame wrote to his good friend John Wereat, who had been elected to the state ratifying convention and would be chosen the convention's president. McIntosh suggested that the Constitution be ratified but with the proviso that another convention be called in twenty years to consider amending the document again. McIntosh realized that the southern states would be in a minority in the new government, and he hoped to protect southern interests, specifically the region's "peculiar institution" of slavery, from attack by the majority, which he believed to be antislavery.[7]

The Georgia ratifying convention opened on Friday, December 28, 1787, in Augusta, with twenty-four delegates in attendance from ten of the state's eleven counties.[8] Attendees reviewed the Constitution on Saturday. At the end of the session, Joseph Habersham, a member from Chatham County, told his wife that the document would "[probably be sp]eedily adopted by this state, as it seems to have a good many friends in the convention."[9] Indeed it did, for, when the delegates reconvened on Monday morning, December 31, they ratified the Constitution without a single dissenting vote. Two days later, the formal approval and signing of the ratification document took place. As the last delegate signed his name, two field pieces positioned opposite the state house fired thirteen shots in salute. On January 5, 1788, the convention met for the last time, agreed to send a letter to the Confederation Congress announcing Georgia's ratification of the proposed Constitution, and ordered its journal published. Convention president John Wereat carried the ratification document with him to New York City, where he personally presented it to the Congress on May 5, 1788.

Ever since 1913, when Charles A. Beard published his controversial book, *An Economic Interpretation of the Constitution of the United States*, arguing that the Founding Fathers were motivated less by patriotism in ratifying the Constitution than by their desire to protect their own economic interests, the task of explaining ratification has become a veritable cottage industry among American historians. Without entering into this debate, there were several reasons for the strongly pro-Constitution sentiment in Georgia. The most important was the general disgust felt toward the Confederation Congress over the question of Indian relations. As one historian put it, "The crux of the disagreement was that the state wanted to negotiate without interference from congressional agents, but once a treaty was signed, Georgia officials wanted federal assistance in enforcing its provisions. Not surprisingly, Congress rejected this role."[10] For nearly two years before the Philadelphia Convention, Georgia had faced the threat of war with the Creeks, and Georgia's leaders knew that the state could not protect itself unaided. So, many Georgians hoped for a stronger central government as a bulwark against the Indians.

If the frontier hoped for protection against the Indians, Savannah and the coast wanted better trade regulations and an end to state-issued paper money. As Savannah merchant Joseph Clay informed a European correspondent in June 1788, "it is to the operation of the [federal] constitution, we look up to as a means to enable us to discharge all our Contracts with faithfullness [*sic*] & honour, & not only so, but to enable us to extend our Commercial views in all its [*sic*] branches."[11] Moreover, despite Lachlan McIntosh's misgivings, Georgians who owned or hoped to own slaves apparently were reassured by the compromise that delayed congressional consideration of the foreign slave trade until 1808.

There are several other factors that could be cited with the aid of the historian's most effective weapon, twenty-twenty hindsight, to explain Georgia's overwhelming ratification of the new federal Constitution. Instead, let me close with an evocative contemporary opinion that I discovered in the course of my research but have seen published nowhere else. Georgia's prompt, unanimous ratification of the Constitution raised hackles across the Savannah River in South Carolina, where that action was criticized as hasty. When word of this criticism reached Savannah, a resident of the port, probably the influential William O'Bryen Sr., penned a reply to the Charleston *Daily Advertiser* over the signature of "A Georgia Backwoodsman." He conveyed in a brief passage the feelings of one comparing the hopes of 1776 to the realities of 1788:

> It ought to be considered, that the infantine situation of Georgia makes it more her interest to form a solid compact which will give health and vigour to the extremest parts of the political body than any other state. The imbecility of her situation requires the efficient hand of a powerful government, having grown more grey in political disquietude and calamity than her sister states, although she has only the constitutional strength of infancy to support her. They also feel that constant movement in the human mind of providing against future contingent misfortunes, and endeavouring to profit herself by the advantage of melancholy experience ... All men saw no alternative.[12]

Chapter 7

John Wereat and Georgia, 1776–1799

[**NOTE:** One of the unalloyed pleasures of my doctoral research was the opportunity to make the acquaintance of John Wereat. At first, his was simply a name on a list of Georgia's governors during the American Revolution, apparently a figure about whom little else was known. As I began to plow through primary sources on my dissertation topic, however, I discovered that, first of all, Mr. Wereat had perhaps the most distinctive, and the clearest, penmanship I had ever seen. More significantly, as I investigated factionalism among Georgia's Whigs, it soon became clear that Wereat was a central figure in a story that had not been told.

Before long, I realized that an article about Wereat's role in the Revolution in Georgia was a real possibility. In the course of my research, I visited the Georgia Historical Society in Savannah, and I still remember the astonishment I felt when the longtime director of the GHS, Lilla M. Hawes, took me down to the basement and showed me a portrait of John Wereat. Now I had a face to put with the handwriting and with his role in the roiling factionalism of the Revolutionary era. Eventually, I prepared a paper on Wereat and the Revolution for a symposium on Georgia and the American Revolution at the Department of Archives and History in Atlanta.

Having done that, I was eager, for my own satisfaction if for no other reason, to study Wereat's career after the Revolution. It turned out that he served as state auditor-general for a decade or so after the war, an unexciting but significant position, and then, in the mid- to late 1790s, Wereat became embroiled in the controversy over the Yazoo land fraud, an event that, I would discover, shaped—and warped—the history of Georgia for the next four decades. My "biography" of John Wereat ultimately took the form of three articles, published in two different journals, but here they are presented in a single essay.[1]]

*****

John Wereat, a twenty-nine-year-old native of the West Country of England, arrived in Savannah early in 1759 to take up a partnership with William Handley, a merchant who had resided in the Georgia port since 1754. Handley was related to Wereat's wife, the former Hannah Wilkinson, and it was with his encouragement that the young couple had decided to move to Georgia.[2] Wereat's first sixteen years in the colony were marred by financial problems that blighted his career as a merchant, but these reverses did not prevent him from carving out a place for himself in the plantation society of the low country. To satisfy creditors, he was forced to dispose of almost three thousand acres during the 1760s, but he managed nevertheless to save his "best lands."[3] These, along with his property in slaves, served as collateral for additional loans that he used to improve his remaining holdings along Georgia's rice coast.[4] Despite his setbacks, John Wereat was a man of property by 1775.

Though available evidence does not connect his name to anti-British activity in Georgia prior to 1775, Wereat apparently made no secret of his opposition to the mother country's American policy. Whatever the specific grounds for his stand, Wereat's views must have been acceptable to

> disaffected low-country residents, for he sat in each of the provincial congresses that assembled prior to the drafting of the Constitution of 1777, first as a representative from St. Andrew's Parish and then, in January 1776, as a member for the town and district of Savannah.[5]

Although elevated to the Council of Safety in February 1776, John Wereat had decided by July that he could be of more use to Georgia in another capacity. A trip to Philadelphia resulted in his appointment as the state's continental agent, responsible for provisioning American vessels that called in Georgia ports, disposing of captured enemy ships, and furnishing cargoes for the *Georgia Packet*, which sailed regularly between Savannah and Philadelphia.[6]

Wereat had hardly entered upon his new duties when he was drawn into the vortex of factionalism. Serious differences of opinion had first emerged in the summer of 1774, over the wisdom of acceding to the

Continental Association and of sending delegates to the Continental Congress. Dissidents in Christ Church Parish were willing to countenance protests against British policy, but they hesitated to align themselves irrevocably with the growing colonial resistance movement. Anti-British elements in St. John's Parish, led by Button Gwinnett, rejected the claims to leadership advanced by the Christ Church group and demanded an end to temporizing. Early in 1775, Gwinnett organized a radical pressure group, the Liberty Society, in order to speed the colony toward a break with the mother country.[7] Over the next year, the basis for factional alignments shifted, from disagreement over the proper tactics of resistance to the question of who would guide the colony's destiny on the battlefield and in council until the goal of independence had been attained. The rivalry between Button Gwinnett and John Wereat's good friend Lachlan McIntosh sprang from this clash of ambitions. The dispute between the two became more acrimonious thereafter until it produced the celebrated duel of May 1777, as the result of which Gwinnett perished.[8]

Following Gwinnett's demise, his friends in the Liberty Society circulated petitions throughout the state, demanding McIntosh's removal from command of Georgia's Continental Line. The timely intervention of George Walton in Philadelphia secured for McIntosh a transfer to Washington's army. Before his departure, the general engaged in a polemic campaign against the machinations of the Liberty Society. McIntosh's most zealous supporter in this effort was John Wereat, who aided him in the pamphlet warfare raging over the allegedly treasonous conduct of McIntosh's brother George.[9]

In letters to members of the Continental Congress, Wereat asserted that the minions of the Liberty Society controlled the executive and legislative departments of state government, obstructed the judiciary, and labeled with "the hateful name of Torey [*sic*] ... every Man who is not of their party." According to Wereat, the radicals had launched their campaign of character assassination "in order to raise themselves fortunes, & political fame upon the ruins of the real Friends of their Country and the American Cause." He blamed the Constitution of 1777, which reflected the views of Gwinnett and his allies, for the state's plight. Wereat implied that the increased county representation provided in the new frame of government had combined with reduced property requirements for voting to render helpless the "best part of the community," thereby producing a situation in which "neither Liberty, or [*sic*] property are secure."[10]

Confronted by the apparent stranglehold of the Liberty Society on the executive and legislative branches of Georgia's government, Wereat turned to the October session of the Chatham County grand jury. The grand jury's deliberations fully justified his optimism, for the jurymen presented as grievances the treatment accorded George McIntosh by the governor and council and the unconstitutional interference of the executive department in the affairs of the judiciary.[11]

By March 1778, the conduct of the House of Assembly had strengthened Wereat's belief that its members were motivated by avarice, not patriotism. He criticized a new law to proscribe over one hundred Georgians and authorize the sale of their property. Wereat argued that even the most culpable of those affected by the legislation, men who had refused to take an oath of allegiance to the United States, had had one-half of their property secured to them by the state. It seemed clear that in this instance the "plighted faith" of the state had been "set at nought" by "opportunity, convenience and the private views of particular individuals." To make matters worse, the legislators also had approved an increase in their salaries; Wereat predicted that this expense alone would exceed projected tax revenues.[12]

The fall of Savannah to the British at the end of 1778 put the Whig government on the run; even the most contentious Georgians were preoccupied with survival. John Wereat followed retreating American forces northward and eventually reached Charleston. Meanwhile, a few members of the House of Assembly gathered at Augusta, styled themselves a "convention," and chose an executive council to preside over the state until elections could be held. This council was forced to flee when British troops entered Augusta on January 31, 1779. After the British withdrew from the town in mid-February, scattered patriots, Wereat among them, began to return. Early in July, the executive council informed Congress of the deplorable conditions in Georgia and pleaded for military and financial aid. Two weeks later, the remnants of the House of Assembly in desperation chose a Supreme Executive Council to govern those sections of the state still in Whig hands. On August 6, 1779, the members of the Supreme Executive Council elected as their president the conscience of Georgia's conservative Whigs, John Wereat.[13]

The composition of the Supreme Executive Council mirrored the chaos of the times. Five of the council's nine members, including Wereat, had ties with Chatham County on the coast, which was under British control. The only area of the state where the council could hope to exercise more than nominal authority, the up-country, had but four representatives; two of them, William Few and John Dooly, commanded military units in the field, so their attendance at meetings of the council was infrequent.

At least three councilors were probably chosen to allay fears in Congress of a repetition of the disputes that had marred earlier efforts at cooperation between state and Continental officials. President Wereat was both Georgia's continental agent and a warm friend of General Lachlan McIntosh, who had returned to Georgia in mid-1779 as commander of the Continental Line. Joseph Clay, whose duties as paymaster general for the state obliged him to miss most of the council meetings, was the man through whom Congress would channel financial aid. Joseph Habersham had been McIntosh's second in the duel with Gwinnett.

Thus, the loss of the capital, the dispersal of the state's constitutionally elected officials, and the dire need for congressional assistance had transferred the reins of government from the radical to the conservative Whig faction. Wereat and his allies set out at once to demonstrate that they acted out of selfless patriotism rather than the selfish opportunism they ascribed to the radicals. They made this point explicitly upon taking office, when they agreed to serve without pay. On August 6, in a statement regarding the extent of their powers, the members of the council moved further to reassure Georgians of their fitness to govern. In a slap at Gwinnett's successor as chief executive of Georgia, John Adam Treutlen, whom both Wereat and the Chatham County grand jury had accused of abusing his authority, the councilors asserted that they did not intend "to contravene or destroy the Constitution" by exercising either legislative or judicial powers.[14] Aware that the Supreme Executive Council was not sanctioned by the Constitution of 1777, the councilors also circulated petitions in the up-country seeking popular approval of the temporary delegation to their hands of executive authority, until elections for a House of Assembly could be held.[15]

The petitions failed to sway Colonel George Wells of the Richmond County militia, who had assumed leadership of the Liberty Society following Gwinnett's death. Wells attacked the council as unconstitutional and dominated by Tories. Perhaps in response to Wells's strictures, a number of citizens in his militia district petitioned to have his election as colonel set aside. When Wells was permitted by the council to examine that petition, he refused to return it, which gave the councilors the excuse they needed to declare his militia post vacant. Wells responded by spreading rumors that the state's lower counties had elected representatives to a new House of Assembly. These reports prompted Wilkes County residents to call for their own elections, a move the council acted quickly to prevent.[16]

A chronic lack of funds enfeebled the Supreme Executive Council during its brief, tempestuous tenure. Even the presence on the council of the state's Continental paymaster, Joseph Clay, failed to secure $500,000 appropriated by Congress for Georgia. Though it was better than no government at all, the council had not been established in accordance with the state constitution, so Clay's hands were tied.[17] Events on the battlefield also dealt Wereat's government a telling blow. During the Franco-American siege of Savannah, an optimistic President Wereat negotiated with British authorities for an exchange of prisoners, even going so far as to claim the restored colonial governor, Sir James Wright, as a prisoner on parole. Neither Wereat's bravado nor the efforts of the allied military force carried the day; when the siege was lifted, the president and his councilors trudged wearily back to Augusta.[18]

Shortly after his return to the Whig capital, Wereat set December 1, 1779, for the election of a new House of Assembly, which was to convene in Augusta on the first Tuesday in January 1780. Presumably to avert a resurgence of the radical faction, he also published in a South Carolina newspaper a proclamation informing exiles from the Georgia low country of the scheduled poll.[19]

At this point, Lachlan McIntosh's former defender, George Walton, arrived in Augusta and, in a move that stunned conservative Whigs, formed an alliance with two prominent radicals, George Wells and Richard Howley. These three men and some of their supporters, calling themselves a "House of Assembly," elected Walton governor of Georgia and delegate to Congress. Two extralegal bodies now competed for the dubious distinction of "governing" the small area that remained under Whig control.

There is scant evidence to suggest that the House of Assembly convened by Walton, Howley, and Wells late in November 1779 had any better claim to legitimacy than the Supreme Executive Council, especially since Wereat already had ordered elections for the assembly to be held on December 1.[20] There is also nothing to indicate that conservatives attempted to resist what they could only have regarded as a usurpation of their authority. In fact, Wereat asserted that many prominent conservative Whigs had by mid-January 1780 abandoned Georgia and sought refuge in South Carolina.

Evidently, Walton's coup, if such it was, succeeded in large part because Georgia conservatives had convinced themselves that there was nothing left in the state worth conserving.[21]

Walton and his "government" promptly revived the smoldering animus against General Lachlan McIntosh. This time efforts to secure his removal from command included the apparent forgery of Speaker William Glascock's signature on a purported assembly resolution that led Congress in February 1780 to relieve McIntosh of all command responsibilities. Unaware of the radical maneuver, McIntosh departed for Charleston in mid-December 1779, but, when he learned of the documents sent by Walton to Congress, he wrote at once to Wereat, informing him of the plot and asking that the matter be brought before the House of Assembly. Wereat, elected to the legislature in December 1779, offered the general scant hope that the action of the Walton-dominated assembly could be reversed. Though Walton had left for Philadelphia, he had been succeeded as governor by another radical, Richard Howley. Wereat asserted that "the Triumvirate that rules this poor State" was not interested in justice; greed was its ruling passion. The exodus of conservative Whigs from Georgia had left a few men like himself virtually powerless "to check and discourage the wicked & designing whose principles & policy is to raise themselves to wealth & opulence on the ruins of honest & inoffensive individuals & of the whole state."[22]

Wereat was so discouraged that he, too, contemplated a "retreat" to South Carolina. He reported that the assembly had empowered the governor to suspend public officials who associated with known or suspected enemies of the American cause. Because his opposition to the radical faction was well known, Wereat fully expected Howley to invoke this resolution and expel him from the House. He confided to General McIntosh that, under the circumstances, expulsion would be "far from being in the least disgraceful."[23]

So long as his friend McIntosh's reputation was still under a cloud, however, a "retreat" to South Carolina was out of the question for John Wereat. As foreman of the Richmond County grand jury in March 1780, he used presentments to bring before the public his concern for economy in government and his animosity toward the "Mutilated Assembly" organized by Walton. Wereat also collected affidavits from Georgians who had served under McIntosh and added a lengthy encomium of his own on the general's conduct. He might also have helped persuade William Glascock to declare to Congress that the signature alleged to be his on the assembly resolution of 1779 was a "flagrant forgery."[24]

John Wereat and Lachlan McIntosh were reunited late in 1780 because of American military defeats. McIntosh became a prisoner of war in May, when Charleston fell to the British. Wereat was among those taken prisoner a few weeks later, when British troops under Thomas Brown entered Augusta. Following an unsuccessful attempt by Whig partisans to retake the town in September, Brown sent twenty-three of the "worst characters" among his Whig captives, including John Wereat, to Charleston.[25]

Though plagued by gout, Wereat did what he could to keep up the spirits of his fellow prisoner. McIntosh chafed at the knowledge that, despite affidavits submitted by Wereat and others, a congressional committee had decided not to recommend his reinstatement in the Continental Line. As they awaited a rumored prisoner exchange, Wereat and McIntosh continued to gather evidence they hoped might lead to a new investigation of the charges against the general.[26]

Following their release from captivity in the summer of 1781, the two friends set off together for Philadelphia, McIntosh to try to clear his name and Wereat to settle his accounts as Georgia's continental agent. The end of the war was in sight by the time Wereat returned to Georgia early in 1782, so he began to take stock of his present condition and future prospects. He estimated his financial losses during the Revolution at almost £2,400. In submitting his account to the state, Wereat commented bitterly, "I don't expect to be reimbursed a Shilling of it." He hoped for more success in recovering debts through the courts, and he urged his attorney "to push this business immediately."[27]

Wereat greeted the British evacuation of Savannah in July 1782 with mixed feelings. His own affairs in a shambles, he complained that "those who deserted their country and remained with the Enemy have made money"; yet he also agreed "to forgive anyone now the war is at an end."[28] In a poignant letter to an exiled Georgia Loyalist, Wereat recalled a discussion during the heady days before the outbreak of hostilities:

> I have in the course of this business found your prediction fully verified, and cannot pretend to say that every Man who has been professedly an American was actuated by a regard for justice or an inviolable attachment to the rights of this Country, and that many who had very little pretention [*sic*] to public trust and confidence, have wormed themselves into appointments of the first consequence,

> and into great fortunes, while others more deserving have been reduced very considerably.[29]

Based on his own experience, then, John Wereat believed that the American Revolution had drastically altered the world he had known before 1775. Once the colonial "establishment" had been ousted, well-to-do Whigs had assumed that direction of affairs would pass smoothly to men of property like themselves. They had reckoned without the assiduity and ability of the radical leadership. Firebrands like Button Gwinnett and George Wells did not survive the war, but their handiwork, the Georgia Constitution of 1777, lived on. The fabric of an ordered society dominated by the "best part of the community," which Wereat and other conservative Whigs had tried to preserve in the midst of revolution, lay in tatters. The ravages of wartime had wreaked havoc on the state's economy and blighted the hopes of many Georgians, perhaps beyond repair.

Some of Wereat's misgivings regarding the future direction of the state were assuaged as his financial position improved after 1783. In short, with time the gains of independence became evident enough to John Wereat; yet, given his conservative perception of the course of the American Revolution in Georgia, he could not help thinking wistfully in 1783 of what had been lost.

* * * * *

Conservative Whigs dominated assembly committees between 1782 and 1784. John Wereat described the state's new governor, John Martin, as a "principled Whig and an honest Man" and averred that "while the good of the State is his object, I think it the Duty of every good Citizen of it to be aiding and assisting and to make the Government as happy to him as possible."[30] Throughout the first decade of the state's existence in the young American republic, no one worked harder to smooth the transition to peacetime than John Wereat, who had a hand in solving some of the knottiest problems facing Georgia and proved himself a versatile and dedicated public servant.

It seems likely that, had he wished to do so, Wereat could have become a fixture in the House of Assembly. In fact, he had the distinction in 1782 of being elected to the legislature at least three separate times by two different constituencies. He was returned from Chatham County twice in April but was disqualified on each occasion by a technicality. After finally being permitted to take his seat on the Chatham delegation, Wereat also was returned from Richmond. He chose to represent the latter county and was replaced as representative for Chatham by his protégé, James Jackson.[31]

Wereat had been instrumental in bringing the fifteen-year-old Jackson to Savannah from England in 1772, and the young man had lived with Wereat's family while reading law. During the Revolution, Wereat and Jackson had corresponded regularly, and each had shown himself solicitous of the health and fortunes of the other. Indeed, Jackson might have been acting on Wereat's behalf when, in February 1780, he shot and killed George Wells, the leader of the radical faction that had recently displaced Wereat's conservative Whig government, in a duel.[32]

Thus, when Wereat sought an attorney to represent his friend General McIntosh in the prosecution of former radical George Walton, who allegedly had resorted to forgery in order to secure McIntosh's suspension from command in 1780, he turned to Jackson. Jackson declined to act in the matter, pointing out that he still had to answer for killing George Wells, Walton's former ally. Although Wereat was disappointed by Jackson's decision, he did not try to change it. McIntosh and Wereat gained a measure of revenge against Walton a few months later when, as members of the Chatham County grand jury, they had Walton suspended temporarily from his post as chief justice.[33]

Wereat's political career and his desire for vengeance against wartime opponents were insignificant compared to the problems facing Georgia, a fact Wereat himself soon recognized. The war had disrupted agriculture throughout the state. The situation around Augusta was particularly acute in 1782. In March, Wereat journeyed to South Carolina to procure "a small supply of Rice" that would "enable the people in the back part of the State to subsist 'til the Crops of Wheat comes [*sic*] in."[34] The following summer, Wereat was sent, along with William McIntosh and Samuel Stirk, by Governor Martin to British East Florida to negotiate with that province's royal governor, Patrick Tonyn, an end to raids by military forces across the St. Marys River. The Georgia emissaries met a cool reception in St. Augustine. While they awaited Governor Tonyn's reply, Wereat renewed his acquaintance with several exiled Georgia Loyalists who had taken up residence in the town.[35]

Shortly after his return from East Florida, John Wereat was elected the state's auditor general. He was the natural choice for the position: as Georgia's continental agent during the Revolution, he had demonstrated an impressive knowledge of finance, earned a reputation for probity, and, not least important considering the state's tangled obligations to Congress, made a number of influential friends in Philadelphia.

Georgia had financed the Revolution almost entirely on credit. In February 1783, the House of Assembly established tables of depreciation for Georgia and continental currency. Much of Wereat's work as auditor involved reducing claims against the state and Congress to their specie value and issuing "audited certificates" showing the amount of the depreciated obligation.[36] Another of his responsibilities was to provide Georgia Loyalists with affidavits attesting to the quantity and value of their property seized by the state under a confiscation and banishment law of May 1782. Loyalists used these affidavits to support claims for compensation from the British government. No doubt Wereat furnished most of the statements routinely, but his continued high regard for a few of the exiles occasionally must have made the chore less onerous.[37]

Wereat's work as auditor consumed both time and patience and led him to neglect his private affairs. Especially galling were the various changes made by Congress in the types of evidence required to support claims against the United States. Wartime conditions had made the preservation of necessary records haphazard at best; in other instances the state already had assumed certain congressional obligations, destroyed the original certificates of indebtedness, and issued new ones.[38]

Auditor Wereat also was required to make frequent—and expensive—journeys between Savannah and Augusta with his records and papers. Because his salary was usually in arrears, he was forced to finance some trips on official business out of his own pocket, but even this expedient did not always prove feasible. On November 8, 1784, for example, Wereat sought badly needed funds from Governor John Houstoun. He explained that "if I could make any shift I wou'd not apply, or if I could get any of my own; but ever since I came down [to Savannah, from Augusta] I have not seen a shilling either public or private but six dollars I borrowed. Mrs. Smith called on me for half a years [*sic*] rent which I cou'd not pay, and which is an expence [*sic*] *I* shou'd not be at but for the public business."[39]

That John Wereat was reelected annually as auditor for a decade testifies to the esteem in which the legislature held his efforts. Further evidence of the respect he commanded came in December 1787, when he was chosen to preside over the state convention that unanimously ratified the new Constitution of the United States. Convention delegates voted Wereat their thanks "for his able and impartial conduct in the chair."[40]

Late in 1790, Wereat took on a new responsibility that not only added to his burdens of office but also required long absences from Georgia. On December 1, the legislature unanimously elected him state agent in settling outstanding claims against the United States. To some extent, this was a continuation of his duties as auditor during the 1780s; now, however, he was authorized to present the demands before a three-member board of commissioners in Philadelphia.[41]

As Wereat struggled to put the state's accounts in order before leaving for Philadelphia in the spring of 1791, he met frustration on every hand. For example, a visit to Georgia's continental loan officer, Richard Wylly, revealed that Wylly expected Wereat to present to the federal board of commissioners certain certificates received after the expiration of the deadline set by Congress, others that had been issued by unauthorized persons, and still others with neither name nor date inserted. The exasperated state agent pointed out to Governor Edward Telfair that "these charges will certainly be met at Philadelphia and how I shall be able to face them I know not, I thought those already in my possession were more than enough."[42]

The situation did not improve once Wereat arrived in the national capital. Since one of the federal commissioners was absent, Wereat found that he would not be able officially to present Georgia's claims for at least a month. Moreover, the two commissioners who were present demanded that Wereat justify the state's claims for reimbursement of expenses incurred defending Georgia against Indian depredations in 1786 and 1788. Although he conceded that no act of Congress had sanctioned the mobilization of the Georgia militia during these alarms, Wereat argued that Congress "does not say, a State shall not arm for its defense when attacked, but admits it, was not this the case the Union would not be the protectors but the oppressors of the State by subjecting it to Savage Cruelty." To add to Wereat's difficulties, his unexpectedly long stay in Philadelphia meant that his funds would be exhausted before he could conclude his business, and he, his daughter, and his granddaughter had arrived in the city during an outbreak of smallpox.[43]

Wereat frequently received letters from friends in Georgia asking to be apprised of the status of their claims before the board of commissioners. Baffled by the seemingly senseless requirements, these correspondents invariably pleaded with Wereat to appeal personally on their behalf before the commissioners. Though he sympathized with their plight, Georgia's agent tactfully replied that the matter was beyond his control. He usually suggested that the claimant present his case in a petition to the state legislature, though in one instance "Old Mr. Wereat" did promise to speak with Secretary of the Treasury Alexander Hamilton in support of a Savannah acquaintance.[44]

After Wereat returned to Georgia in October 1791, the finance committee of the state House of Representatives approved his actions as agent, reporting that he had "done what was possible towards the settlement during his stay in Philadelphia and that the accounts are now in a favorable train for that purpose." Before leaving for the federal capital again in the spring of 1792, Wereat took steps to ensure that the duties of the auditor's office would be carried on in his absence. In a move that ultimately proved ill-advised, he deputized his nephew Thomas Collier to act as auditor. Wereat's departure also was marred by a family crisis: his widowed daughter, Ann, married Dr. Michael Burke against her father's wishes. Rumor had it that, as a consequence, Wereat had vowed never to speak to Ann again and that he had altered his will in order to settle his property on his granddaughter Eliza and his nephew Thomas Collier.[45]

In Philadelphia, Wereat busied himself once more with the task of presenting and defending Georgia's claims before the board of commissioners. He also was the logical choice to represent the state in another matter of importance in the federal capital. Almost a year before his appointment as state agent, he had written Governor Telfair that, in the face of several suits instituted against Georgia by individuals seeking to recover pre-Revolutionary debts sequestered by the state, "I think the time is now come to see whether the [May 1782] Act of Confiscation ... is in force or not." Telfair subsequently authorized Wereat to retain local counsel in Philadelphia to represent Georgia "in support of the Claims of the State arising under" the 1782 measure. When the suits reached the lower federal courts, the decisions went against Georgia, and her law officers recommended to Telfair that the state file for a writ of error with the United States Supreme Court and seek an injunction "to stay the proceedings until the same shall be determined or to seek such other relief as in their justice will seem proper." On July 17, 1792, the governor forwarded to Wereat power of attorney to employ counsel in one of the suits, *Georgia v. Brailsford.*[46]

On August 10, 1792, Wereat informed Governor Telfair that the lawyers he had hired, Alexander James Dallas and Jared Ingersoll, had filed the state's bill in equity in the *Brailsford* case and that the Supreme Court had issued a temporary injunction. Wereat evinced some concern over the attorneys' fees, for, he gently reminded Telfair, "they won't eat Tobacco, I must try to raise the Money for a Bill [of credit], and if no Cash is in the Treasury to discharge it I should think you cou'd order as much Tobacco to be sold as would make up the Sum." He also brought the governor up to date on the saga of the Georgia claims, reporting that, while the state's accounts with the federal government might soon be closed, the commissioners' term of office had recently expired and no reappointments had yet been made.[47]

Wereat returned to Georgia in the autumn of 1792 with the state claims still in limbo. Most of Georgia's accounts had been examined, but the deadline for the final settlement was July 1, 1793. Therefore, Wereat recommended that Governor Telfair appoint someone to represent the state before the federal board during the closing, in order to urge upon the commissioners "the necessity of the exercise of the equitable powers vested in them by Congress, without which the State must inevitably be a very great looser [*sic*]."[48] Telfair took the auditor's advice; not surprisingly, he convinced Wereat himself to return to Philadelphia to complete the work he had begun.

John Wereat remained at his post in the capital until early August 1793. At least partly as the result of his efforts during nearly three years as Georgia's agent, the federal government agreed to assume $246,030 of Georgia's debt contracted during the Revolution, out of the $300,000 maximum permitted by law. Moreover, the final report of the board of commissioners, issued in June 1793, ruled that in the matter of the state's claims, the federal government owed Georgia $20,000.[49]

Shortly after he returned from his final trip to Philadelphia, Wereat found himself in the middle of a dispute concerning the conduct of his deputy—and nephew—Thomas Collier, during his absence. "An Augustian" accused Collier of having extorted fees for services included in his duties as deputy auditor. Though the critic denied that Wereat himself had been guilty of misconduct during his long tenure as auditor, he did question his judgment in having appointed Collier. He also warned Wereat that "how far this [appointment of Collier] and your living in Savannah [rather than in the state capital of Augusta] may operate against your re-appointment, is a subject of legislative deliberation."[50]

The following week, a writer signing himself "A. B." defended Wereat against the allegations of "An Augustian." He asserted that Wereat had not lived in Savannah for eight years; in fact, he wrote, "Instead of saying the Auditor lives in Savannah, he might with equal propriety have said, at Philadelphia." Wereat's long absences from Georgia had dictated the appointment of a deputy, "A. B." continued. Wereat could not have foreseen the untoward practices complained of; if Collier were guilty as charged, then the governor ought to fire him. "A. B." further contended that "An Augustian's" letter was an indirect attack on Wereat's reputation, an attempt to disgrace him in the eyes of the public, "whose servant he has long been, ... without impeachment or reproach, and whose favorable opinion I have often heard him declare was his greatest ambition, whether in or out of office, to deserve."[51]

The charges and countercharges in the press occurred shortly before the legislature was to elect state officials for 1794. Available evidence does not reveal whether John Wereat intended to stand for reelection as auditor. Certainly his numerous trips between Georgia and Philadelphia had been fatiguing, and his private affairs had suffered neglect throughout the decade he had held that office. Perhaps the final settlement of Georgia's accounts, to which he had devoted so much time and energy between 1791 and 1793, had convinced Wereat that he could now retire. If he had planned to offer his services for another year, then perhaps he was stung by "An Augustian's" electioneering attack and changed his mind. Whatever the reason, the legislature chose Abraham Jones as auditor. John Wereat retired to his plantation near Hardwick, in Bryan County.[52]

* * * * *

For many Georgians, the state's vast land claims, extending westward to the Mississippi River and southward to Florida, promised to solve financial problems bequeathed by the struggle for independence. During and immediately after the Revolution, the Georgia legislature attempted to attract settlers with lands granted either by headright or as bounty to soldiers, but skillful speculators quickly turned these to private advantage. Land and other property confiscated from Georgia Tories also found a ready market among men of a speculative bent.

In the mid-1780s, legislators acquiesced in North Carolina speculator William Blount's abortive project to establish a new Georgia county in the bend of the Tennessee River at Muscle Shoals and supported another unsuccessful effort to create a county, to be called Bourbon, in the area around Natchez claimed by both Georgia and Spain. Finally, in 1788, increasingly aware of the encumbrances placed upon the state by her extensive western land claims, the legislature approved a measure ceding the southern portion of that territory to the government of the United States, but the ensuing negotiations foundered over the terms proposed by Georgia for surrender of the lands.[53]

Following the rejection by Congress of the proposed Georgia cession, the state legislature reverted to precedents established by the Muscle Shoals and Bourbon County speculations and decided to transfer the Yazoo lands to venturesome entrepreneurs. In December 1789, the General Assembly granted about twenty-five million acres of the western lands to the South Carolina, Virginia, and Tennessee Yazoo companies for just over $200,000; however, in June 1790, the legislature effectively nullified the sale by insisting that only gold and silver, not depreciated Georgia paper currency, be accepted in payment from the purchasing companies.[54]

Before retiring as state auditor, John Wereat's attitude toward speculation could best be described as ambivalent. On the one hand, Wereat purchased at sales of confiscated property "very valuable Tide Land" for a northern acquaintance, as well as four hundred acres on the Great Satilla River and three hundred acres in Columbia County for himself. On the other hand, no evidence links Wereat to any of the bizarre speculative ventures that caused turmoil in Georgia during the first decade after the Revolution. In fact, his lone surviving recorded comment, in a letter to his close friend Lachlan McIntosh in the summer of 1784, suggested that he viewed the spectacle with grim resignation.[55]

Despite this earlier ambivalence, Wereat's willingness to assist three Pennsylvanians in purchasing western lands from Georgia drew him into the vortex of speculation in 1794. Between 1790 and 1793, while Wereat sojourned periodically in Philadelphia as Georgia's agent for settling the state's Revolutionary accounts with the new federal government, Governor Edward Telfair authorized him to retain local counsel to represent the state before the United States Supreme Court. On each occasion, Wereat employed two leading members of the Philadelphia bar, Alexander James Dallas and Jared Ingersoll. When Dallas, Ingersoll, and their friend Albert

Gallatin decided, in the spring of 1794, to speculate in Georgia lands, it probably seemed natural for them to send Wereat their powers of attorney to serve as their spokesman before the General Assembly. Financial losses sustained during the Revolution and during his long career in public service had left Wereat's private affairs in disarray, so perhaps he had come to see land speculation as a means to recoup his fortune.[56]

Interest in Georgia's western territory, quiescent since the nullification of the Yazoo sale in 1790, revived in the summer of 1793, when federal district judge Nathaniel Pendleton, an opponent of the 1789 transaction, joined forty-nine others in an effort to purchase five million acres in the Natchez district. Although Pendleton failed to convince a legislative committee of the wisdom of his venture, he continued to advocate it over the next year, broaching the idea to a number of the state's leading political figures.[57]

Other interested observers, ranging from up-country Georgians to representatives of the various unsuccessful 1789 Yazoo companies, perceived that, despite Pendleton's failure in 1793, the time was ripe for a renewed effort to purchase Georgia's western lands. In November 1794, one of the partners in the old Virginia Yazoo Company warned his agent in Augusta that "the extent and variety of the applications which will be made to the present session of the [Georgia] Assembly, will not a little embarrass the members, and, I fear, increase your difficulties."[58] At about the same time, a Chatham County representative reportedly told Judge Pendleton, who had come to Augusta to further his land scheme, that a large majority of the legislators favored the sale of the western territory and that a bill to allow it would be passed by both houses.[59]

It is in the context of this rising speculative fever that John Wereat's activities in the summer of 1794 must be viewed. Between the receipt in May 1794 of Dallas and Ingersoll's powers of attorney and late August, John Wereat and William Gibbons Jr., who had been a member of the South Carolina Yazoo Company in 1789, apparently discussed making a joint bid before the legislature and decided to seek advice from Wereat's good friend, and Gibbons's brother-in-law, former Governor Edward Telfair.[60] Evidently, Telfair advised against a joint venture, for when Wereat submitted the first formal offer to purchase western lands from the Georgia legislature on November 12, 1794, he only did so in the names of Dallas and Ingersoll, seeking to buy the old South Carolina Yazoo Company grant at the original price of $66,964.[61]

On November 24, the state House of Representatives drew up a bill for disposing of certain parts of the western territory. The bill was reported on the following day and turned over to a joint House-Senate committee. Bids came thick and fast once the bill was reported: from the old Virginia Yazoo Company on November 25; from the Georgia Company, led by the state's Federalist senator, James Gunn, and from the Georgia Mississippi Company, both on November 26; from Edward Telfair on behalf of William Gibbons Jr. two days later; and from Zachariah Cox of the Tennessee Yazoo Company of 1789 on December 3.[62]

The territory sought by Gunn's Georgia Company included the area of the old South Carolina Company grant, which Wereat also hoped to buy, as well as extensive acreage lying between the Tombigbee and the Alabama and Coosa Rivers. Since the price offered by the Georgia Company exceeded what Wereat was authorized by his Philadelphia principals to make, his bid fell by the wayside. Telfair's offer on behalf of Gibbons was also rejected. On December 8, the joint committee reported out a bill embodying the proposals of the Georgia, Georgia Mississippi, Tennessee, and Virginia companies.[63]

Following the rejection of his initial proposal, John Wereat threw caution to the winds. By December 11, he had joined militia general John Twiggs, former senator William Few, and Edward Telfair, acting once again for William Gibbons Jr. to form the Georgia Union Company. On that date, while the House of Representatives was considering the Yazoo bill following its second reading, the organizers of the Georgia Union Company submitted a bid to purchase the lands desired by both the Georgia and Georgia Mississippi companies. Although the new company's offer was superior on paper to those of their competitors, Wereat and his associates had little cash on hand for a down payment. Wereat had even included as part of his company's down payment a $10,000 bank bill drawn on Dallas, Ingersoll, and Gallatin in Philadelphia, and he had done so without consulting the Pennsylvanians. According to Dallas's biographer, because of this, "the three partners promptly disowned any connection with the offer." The point was moot, anyway, for the House rejected the late-blooming organization's bid. Despite subsequent efforts to increase their down payment and a desperate attempt to purchase all of the western territory, the principals of the Georgia Union Company were out of the running.[64]

The house passed the Yazoo bill on December 13, the senate one week later. The measure next was sent to Governor George Mathews. Prospective purchasers urged the governor to sign; the organizers of the Georgia Union Company dispatched a letter to Mathews arguing that, despite the legislature's rejection, theirs had been the superior bid.[65] Governor Mathews vetoed the act on December 29, claiming, among other things, that the sum offered was inadequate and that the sale of land in the public domain to companies was monopolistic and would "prevent or retard settlements, population, and agriculture."[66]

The house reacted immediately to the veto message, sending a committee to confer with the governor. Within forty-eight hours, this committee brought in a new bill, the so-called "Supplementary Act," designed to answer the chief executive's objections.[67] Once more, Wereat tried to dissuade Mathews from signing. To his own copy of a letter to the governor written on January 3, 1795, Wereat added the following "Remark": "The within proposals offered a larger Sum to the State than all the other applicants to the amount of three hundred thousand dollars, which alone would have relieved the Citizens of the State of Georgia from taxes for near sixteen years to come."[68]

On January 5, 1795, while the Supplementary Act was still on Governor Mathews's desk, Wereat explained his actions in a letter to Alexander James Dallas. He emphasized the presumed superiority of the Georgia Union Company's bid and hinted at unsavory methods used by the four successful companies: "The majority of the Assembly are execrated by their constituents and even their lives threatened when they return. A party of armed Men are now near this town [Augusta], whose object is said to be to prevent the passing of the Bill, by an application to the Governor to withhold his Signature." In a postscript added after he learned that Mathews had signed the Supplementary Act, Wereat informed Dallas that he had sent a copy of the governor's veto message of the earlier Yazoo bill to Georgia senator James Jackson in Philadelphia. Then, Wereat asked Dallas, "As the [Supplementary] Act has doubtless been obtained by corruption and fraud, will not the [state constitutional] Convention who are to meet in May have it in their power to declare [the Supplementary Act] null and void?"[69]

The motives of Wereat and the other associates of the Georgia Union Company were the subject of dispute at the time and remain unclear to this day. According to a hostile source commenting in the aftermath of the

Yazoo sale, each of the principals in the company had applied individually to the other, better-financed organizations "and had actually engaged to be concerned, but not being gratified by the companies altogether as they wished, they concerted with others to defeat the sale totally."[70] Even if this assertion were true, it conveniently overlooks the widespread corruption rumored to have accompanied the sale. As the Yazoo bill and its successor, the Supplementary Act, made their way through the legislature, representatives of the four Yazoo companies distributed sub-shares in their purchases to pliant legislators, state officials, and influential up-country men. Those who accepted the proffered sub-shares "were not to pay any money therefore in advance, and were particularly indulged, until the whole of the purchase money was payable at the treasury." In the interim they could raise the purchase money either by disposing of their holdings on their own or by selling them back to members of the purchasing companies.[71]

Wereat and his partners were silent on the matter of corruption in their letters to Governor Mathews, attempting to persuade him to veto both the Yazoo and Supplementary acts. Instead, they emphasized the superiority of the Georgia Union Company's bid, ignoring the fact that their offer was long on promises to pay but short on hard cash. Perhaps Wereat believed that taking the high ground with the governor held out the greatest chance for success. On the other hand, Wereat referred specifically to "corruption and fraud" in the postscript of his letter to Dallas and revealed his plan to attack the sale in the upcoming constitutional convention. If Wereat's correspondence with Georgia US senator James Jackson were extant, it would almost certainly include a detailed indictment of the Yazoo business, for Wereat had no need to be vague or tactful with his protégé. Moreover, if an anonymous critic was correct, Wereat and his partners did not confine their opposition to the Yazoo sale to letters. Writing in the Augusta *Southern Centinel* on January 15, 1795, "Expono" charged that the "party of armed men" mentioned in Wereat's letter to Dallas, who put pressure on Governor Mathews to veto the Supplementary Act, had actually been raised and led by two of the organizers of the Georgia Union Company, probably John Twiggs and William Few. In short, it seems likely that even if, as their opponents charged, Wereat and his associates opposed Yazoo out of disappointment, they also were moved by a sense of outrage over the corruption that had accompanied the sale and had helped to frustrate their plans.

In the aftermath of the Yazoo sale, the state was plunged into turmoil, as champions and opponents of the transaction vied with one another in the press, in the streets, and at the polls. Wereat's partners, William Few, John Twiggs, and Edward Telfair, argued in the press with pro-Yazoo forces, but Wereat himself did not, despite ample provocation. On October 29, 1795, for example, the *Southern Centinel* printed a letter supposedly found along the roadside by "A Traveller." Laboriously composed in what was purported to be Edward Telfair's Scottish brogue, this missive brought "Johnny" up to date on the effort to defeat the Yazooists and closed by promising "Johnny" his "old stand" back as state auditor. The only reply to "A Traveller's" attempt to impugn the motives of Telfair and Wereat was an anonymous note published two weeks later, informing the public that the "letter" was in fact a forgery that would be dealt with at a later time, along with other Yazoo tricks.[72]

Wereat preferred to attack the Yazooists in the relative tranquility of the May 1795 state constitutional convention. A delegate from Bryan County, Wereat was unanimously elected temporary chairman on May 4 and played an important role in the body's deliberations. He helped draft the rules and acted as spokesman for two committees, one recommending constitutional revision and another proposing specific amendments. Wereat also was appointed to the committee to consider anti-Yazoo petitions submitted to the convention; this group recommended that petitions be transmitted to the next session of the General Assembly.[73]

The elections for the General Assembly in November 1795 returned a clear majority of anti-Yazoo legislators to both houses.[74] The acknowledged leader of the foes of speculation, James Jackson, had resigned from the United States Senate and returned to Georgia. He secured a seat representing Chatham County in the state House of Representatives, in order to direct personally the campaign for repeal of the Supplementary Act. When the General Assembly convened in January 1796, Jackson moved that a committee be appointed to investigate charges of "corruption" connected with the sale of the western territory; the committee was appointed, with Jackson its most prominent member.[75] This committee reviewed the anti-Yazoo petitions turned over to the legislature by the constitutional convention and also collected affidavits demonstrating that "fraud, corruption, and collusion" purportedly had accompanied the transaction. Using this evidence, Jackson's committee brought in a bill "rescinding" the Supplementary Act, providing for public destruction of records related to the sale, and authorizing repayment to purchasers of money deposited in the state treasury. The legislature passed the Rescinding Act by a large margin, and the newly elected governor, Jared Irwin, signed it immediately.[76]

The tactics employed by Jackson's investigating committee pushed John Wereat to center stage once more. Following passage of the Rescinding Act, Yazooists charged that Jackson had "suppressed" a portion of former state treasurer Philip Clayton's testimony before the committee. According to these critics, in his appearance before Jackson's "inquisition," Clayton alleged that he had overheard John Wereat say that he had been authorized by Jackson and others to offer up to $1 million for the western territory in the fall of 1794. In a letter to a Savannah newspaper, Wereat flatly denied ever having made the statement attributed to him by Clayton. Nevertheless, no one publicly refuted the report that Clayton had made the apparently false charge concerning Wereat before Jackson's committee, yet no such remark appears in Clayton's affidavit as published by the committee.[77]

At the time of the furor over the alleged "suppression" of Philip Clayton's testimony, John Wereat was savoring the life of a gentleman planter in Bryan County. His peace and tranquility were short-lived, for he soon found himself embroiled in a bitter family squabble that forced him once more into the public eye and dragged on for nearly six years after his death. The controversy erupted following Wereat's announcement, on December 17, 1797, that he was offering for sale a five-hundred-acre tract of land on the Great Ogeechee River that had once belonged to his brother-in-law, the Reverend John Collier. Collier's son, Thomas, who had served as deputy auditor under Wereat and been disgraced by accusations of corruption, promptly inserted a notice in a Savannah newspaper claiming that the land in question was not Wereat's to sell. He asserted that although his uncle had originally sold the land to the Reverend John Collier, executed the titles, and received payment, "those titles were in my brothers [*sic*—John Collier Jr.'s] possession at the time of his decease in Savannah. Mr. Wereat, administrator of his estate, thereby obtained possession, and still retains them; whether fraudulently or otherwise must be determined by a jury of Chatham County."[78]

Wereat replied a month later, charging that Thomas Collier's publication had been intended to injure his reputation. He termed Collier's assertion that he had "obtained possession of certain papers as administrator of your brother's estate," a "base falsehood," and claimed to welcome the investigation into the matter promised by his nephew. Wereat added that "any further publication you may think proper to make will be treated with silent contempt."[79] Collier fired what turned out to be the final shot in this newspaper war, an invective-laden missive maintaining—among other things—that Wereat consistently had practice "dissembling flattery … (for plunder) towards me and your sister's family."[80]

True to his word, Wereat remained silent, even after Collier sued him to recover the disputed tract of land. Although Wereat had chosen to ignore his nephew's accusation in public, he drew up a new will on April 1, 1798, providing that, upon his death, Thomas Collier was to receive but "One Spanish milled dollar." Moreover, Wereat stipulated that, even if his granddaughter and chief beneficiary, Elizabeth Fishbourne, died before reaching age twenty-one, "Thomas Collier shall receive no more than his dollar."[81] Collier's suit against Wereat was taken up by his sister and her husband, Jacob Isaacs, after both Collier and Wereat had died. It was finally dismissed in 1805.[82]

John Wereat died at his Bryan County plantation on January 25, 1799, at the age of sixty-five.[83] His death deprived the state of one who had served Georgia well from the outbreak of the American Revolution until his retirement as auditor in 1793. A reluctant leader of the conservative Whig faction during the war, he had gone on to help the fledgling state grapple with the manifold problems that accompanied independence. While it is tempting to describe him as an eighteenth-century bureaucrat, Wereat saw the matter in a different light. What he undertook on behalf of Georgia was neither a "profession" nor a "job"; it was, in his phrase, "the duty of every good Citizen."[84]

Wereat's involvement in the Yazoo sale, motivated by friendship and by a desire for financial gain, was unsuccessful. His decision to oppose the corrupt purchasers redounded to the state's benefit, though perhaps at some cost to Wereat's reputation. He was a conscientious public servant whose accomplishments deserve to be better known. Quiet and reserved by nature, Wereat preferred to avoid controversy; ironically, he found no peace short of the grave.

Chapter 8

Thomas Carr and the Camden County "War" of 1793

[**NOTE:** Delivering this paper proved to be an interesting experience. First of all, it was drawn from my dissertation, so I didn't actually have to *write* it before I presented it; I just had to come up with an introduction and conclusion to put it into a broader context. Secondly, I already had submitted the essay to the *Atlanta Historical Bulletin* before I set off on my cross-state trek to deliver the talk at Midway Church, built by Congregationalists in 1792 (and on the National Register of Historic Places since 1973), near Savannah, and I knew that it had been accepted for publication.

Still, the trip itself was quite an adventure. At the time, Westminster had a small boarding department, so part of our annual "parents' weekend" was the opportunity for parents of boarding students to meet their kids' teachers. At first, I didn't think this would present a problem, but it turned out that I was wrong: while the school was perfectly willing to let me deliver my paper on the coast, the powers that be also expected me back in Atlanta later that day to meet with a few of the parents of my boarding students! It made for a rich, full day, especially since Faith and our boys, who were then four and one, went along for the ride.

One thing I remember about the session at Midway Church was that all the presenters were offered the opportunity to deliver their papers from the wonderful pulpit in the old church. I can't remember what my colleagues decided to do, but I was reluctant to speak from a pulpit. I kept thinking of my grandmother's statement years earlier that she expected me to be either a minister or a teacher; the Midway jaunt offered me the chance to be both at once, but I couldn't bring myself to mount that pulpit. Instead, I stood at a table at floor level and spoke. Oh, and while I delivered the paper, Faith, Jim, and David remained outside, killing time on the grounds.

This essay was published in the *Atlanta Historical Bulletin* 20 (Fall 1976): 37–45.]

*****

In Georgia between 1789 and 1794, the activities of frustrated land speculators, the development of a breach between supporters and opponents of the Washington administration, and the continuation of long-standing feuds between strong-minded factional leaders helped to shape the conduct of political campaigns for statewide and national office.[1] Partisan strife at the local level, which was also an integral part of Georgia politics during the late eighteenth century, is harder to characterize. Perhaps the best example of such a struggle occurred in Camden County, south of Savannah, in 1793, when Thomas Carr attempted to rebuild his blighted political fortunes by moving there, armed with grants for thirteen thousand acres of land and appointment as a local magistrate.

Carr had previously resided in Richmond County in northeast Georgia, where he engaged in land speculation and politics. Beginning his career as a speculator in bounty land grants after the Revolution, he soon branched out into other forms of speculation, including participation in the Tennessee Yazoo Company in 1789–1790 and in a shadowy organization known as the Combined Society, whose objectives included formation, from lands to be secured from the General Assembly, of a new state along the Georgia frontier. Not only did Carr suffer financial reverses when these schemes proved abortive, but he also failed to win reelection to the state legislature in 1790, after having served two terms in that body as a member from Richmond County. His subsequent efforts at a political comeback, in 1791 and 1792, were unavailing. At that point, Thomas Carr decided to remove to the moss-hung desolation of Camden County.[2]

Camden County had a tradition of bitter political contests, despite its sparse population. In 1790, there were only eighty-one free, white males sixteen years of age or older in the entire county, out of a total of slightly more than three hundred persons. At the time of the first federal census, two men stood preeminently among the politically active residents of Camden: superior court judge Henry Osborne; and Jacob

Weed, Thomas Carr's brother-in-law, who commanded the county militia and served as a judge of the inferior court and a justice of the peace, as well as a member from Camden in the General Assembly. In 1791, Weed died, and Osborne was stripped of his office after being convicted by the state House of Representatives of suppressing returns from Camden and Glynn Counties during the hotly contested congressional election of 1790 between Anthony Wayne and James Jackson.[3] The coincidence of these two events created a vacuum in the county's leadership, and at once, longtime Camden residents as well as newcomer Thomas Carr attempted to rush in.

One of the most ambitious men among the likely successors to Weed and Osborne was Abner Williams, who had settled in Camden County about 1784. He was elected to the House of Assembly in 1788 and 1789 and to the state House of Representatives in 1790 and 1791. Williams commanded the First Company of the county militia, an important organization in Camden which, like neighboring Glynn, bordered the coveted Tallassee country and hence was seldom free from the possibility of skirmishes with the Creek Indians. He also held a civil appointment, that of county receiver of taxable property. In that position, he had aroused a storm in 1789 by accusing the county's numerous absentee landlords, most of whom were prominent politicians, of evading payment of taxes on their Camden holdings.[4]

At the end of 1791, Abner Williams's political future seemed bright. In December, he was a key prosecution witness at the impeachment trial of Judge Henry Osborne. His testimony not only helped seal the fate of a formidable rival but also called into question the conduct of four local magistrates who had authenticated the return of an illegal poll held by Osborne.[5] Three days after Osborne was stripped of his state and county judicial offices and barred from holding any other post in the state for thirty years, Governor Edward Telfair appointed Abner Williams judge of the inferior court and Camden justice of the peace.[6]

His appetite for political preferment not yet satisfied, Williams offered for Camden's state senate seat in October 1792 but was defeated by another rising politician, John King. Like Williams, King had received two offices in the county magistracy in December 1791. At this point, Thomas Carr entered the picture, allying himself with Abner Williams and another Camden resident, Simeon Dillingham, in an effort to have King's election overturned.

Williams, Carr, and Dillingham petitioned the senate in November 1792, outlining charges against King reminiscent of those raised against Henry Osborne in 1791.[7] The petitioners asserted that seventy of the approximately one hundred votes cast had been illegal because those casting them either had paid no tax during the preceding year or were not residents of Camden County. Moreover, they claimed that King and his friends "did employ boats to convey the aforesaid illegal voters to the place of Holding the Election."

On November 26, the senate committee on privileges and elections reported that the allegations made in the protest were serious enough to warrant an inquiry. The full senate agreed, set the second Monday in November 1793 as the date for the investigation, and authorized King and Carr to collect affidavits in the interim. King must have set to work immediately to have this decision reversed, for the following day, the senate voted to reconsider—and then to reject—the committee report, with Senate president Benjamin Taliaferro of Wilkes casting the tie-breaking vote in favor of quashing the inquiry. Two days later, the upper house struck another blow at Abner Williams when it confirmed new appointments to the Camden inferior court and county magistracy: Williams's name was omitted from both lists. The senate coupled this action with the usual resolution in such cases, repealing all previous appointments to those posts, including the ones given Williams eleven months earlier.

With his former ally, Abner Williams, thus discredited, Thomas Carr moved to carve out a position of influence for himself in Camden County. While in Augusta to present the petition challenging John King's election, Carr learned that the General Assembly was about to revise the state militia law in order to bring it into conformity with a measure recently adopted by Congress. Following passage of the revised militia act, Governor Telfair issued a proclamation notifying Georgians of the proposed rearrangement. On January 5, 1793, Carr wrote the governor, urging him to divide Camden into captain's districts, adding that "as I am so very well acquainted with the deferent [*sic*] Settlements, as to their Strength, beg leave to inform you of the boundaries which I should think to be most proper." Carr also offered to carry with him when he set out for Camden any orders from Telfair respecting the county militia.[8]

General James Jackson, whose militia division included the Camden County units, warned Governor Telfair late in March 1793 that "the Inhabitants of Camden I fear are too much divided to elect Field Officers."

He admitted that Abner Williams was the "eldest Officer" in the county and, hence, the logical choice to command the Camden units, but he also mentioned five other likely candidates for the post. Jackson declined to endorse any of them, however, as he knew "not who would be agreeable to the County; they have too much party to elect from my accounts."[9]

The members of Camden's legislative delegation did not share Jackson's reservations. Upon their return to the county at the close of the General Assembly session, the legislators informed the local magistrates of the passage of the new militia law. The justices of the peace promptly divided Camden into company districts and ordered the election of militia officers. James Seagrove, federal superintendent of the southern Indians, was chosen to command the companies. A number of residents, including Abner Williams and Simeon Dillingham, immediately sent a petition to Governor Telfair protesting that local authorities had "conducted the [election] in such Privacy that we have cause to Suspect they have sent on the Nomination of such men ... to be Commissioned as will be disagreeable to a Majority of the Free Inhabitance of said county." Telfair, evidently mindful of General Jackson's warning about the state of public opinion in Camden, dispatched General James Gunn to the county, apparently with orders to arrange for new elections.[10]

By the day set for the new election of field officers, excitement in Camden County had risen to a fever pitch.[11] The candidates for the post of lieutenant colonel commandant were Thomas Carr and Richard Carnes. Carnes had been elected to the Georgia House of Representatives in 1792 and, at the end of that session, also had been appointed Camden justice of the peace and judge of the inferior court. It is not clear whether Abner Williams, aware that he himself stood no chance of commanding the Camden regiment, overtly supported Carr for the post. Nevertheless, he evidently was a vocal opponent of Carnes, who, he no doubt felt, had supplanted him in the magistracy. As a result of Williams's conduct at the polls and of a dispute over the legality of the votes for one company district, which tipped the scales in favor of Thomas Carr, the election erupted into a clash between opposing bodies of armed men. During the affray, Abner Williams was shot and killed.

Carr was at the polls that day as both a candidate and a magistrate. He promptly issued warrants for the arrest of eight participants in the melee, including Camden senator John King and Thomas King. Most of those involved fled before they could be arrested, but the two Kings used their authority as magistrates to release one another on bond and then retired with a group of armed supporters to a nearby blockhouse, from which they bid defiance to the local constable.

Despite the violence that had marred the militia election and the protest from supporters of Richard Carnes, Governor Telfair allowed Carr's victory to stand.[12] Early in September, Colonel Carr began the ticklish job of asserting his authority over citizen-soldiers who were rent by dissention because of the events of July 10 and alive to the threat of an attack by the Creeks.

Carr's initial action was to dispatch his second in command, Major Abner Hammond, to Bullshead blockhouse on the Little Satilla River. There, Hammond was to meet the assembled militia officers, select the senior captain, and send him to take command of the Colerain horse troop from Captain John F. Randolph, who was to be arrested for his part in the assault on Abner Williams. One officer, Captain William Johnston, like Richard Carnes a member of the county's 1792 legislative delegation and newly appointed magistrate, refused to report to Bullshead as directed, so Carr ordered him arrested. Meanwhile, word of the new commandant's plan to take Randolph into custody had aroused the anger of the Colerain garrison.[13]

In his report of the situation to Governor Telfair, Carr painted a bleak picture of his first attempts to bring the Camden militia into line. The officer whom he sent to take command at Colerain had been met by a flat refusal of members of the horse troop to obey him. They alleged they had been told by Richard Carnes not to turn over their post to anyone unless ordered to do so by Carr's immediate superior, Brigadier General James Gunn. Thereupon, Carr attempted to cut off supplies to the Colerain garrison, which he described as being "in an actual state of Rebillion [*sic*]," but the local militia contractor refused to obey him. Angered by how his orders had been flouted and alarmed by the prospect of an alliance between Richard Carnes and General Gunn, Carr demanded to know if Governor Telfair had issued "private orders," either to Gunn or to the division commander, Major General James Jackson. If the governor had not sent such secret instructions, then Carr requested assistance in dispersing the mutinous troops, because they were "too strongly posted for me to attact [*sic*] with my unarmed force at present—and they had previous to my appointment collected nearly all the arms in the County ... I think those men (who are a Banditta) are keept [*sic*] together By designing Carecters [*sic*] for desperate purposes." [14]

Governor Telfair already had ordered the convening of a military court of inquiry to investigate the unrest in the Camden militia. This plan was frustrated when John and Thomas King emerged from their blockhouse to arrest two of the investigating officers for their part in removing Captain John F. Randolph from command of the Colerain troop.[15] Carr, outmanned and outgunned by the insurgents, next tried to negotiate, using Major Hammond as intermediary. By September 20, the Colerain garrison still refused to commit themselves, explaining that they expected to talk with their former commander, Captain Randolph, and inviting Carr to attend the proposed meeting in person to present his side of the controversy.[16]

Meanwhile, on September 15, General Gunn ordered Colonel Carr's arrest. Unaware of this order and still without a response to his letter of September 10 to Governor Telfair, Carr sent a copy of the earlier communication to Augusta, along with several other documents purporting to show that the mutineers were receiving encouragement from "John King and General Gunn In there [*sic*] electioneering plans so as to endanger the liberties of the Citizens of this County." He dispatched a similar letter to General Jackson, requesting him to order troops from another regiment into Camden to quell the mutiny. Although Jackson expressed sympathy for Carr's plight, he refused to act unless ordered to do so by the governor.[17]

By the end of September, events in Camden County were approaching a crisis. Colonel Carr and the troops loyal to him were running out of supplies, while the stream of foodstuffs to Colerain remained steady. The day agreed upon for the election of company officers was imminent, and electioneering grew increasingly frantic in both camps.[18] General Gunn also was moving toward a collision with Carr, ordering Captain Randolph, whom Carr had relieved of command, to take possession of the post on Little Satilla where the colonel was stationed. Furthermore, Gunn reportedly sent eight officers to Camden to convene a court-martial to try Carr for countermanding the orders of a superior officer.[19]

Randolph made one unsuccessful attempt to arrest Carr at Burnt Fort, but the colonel was not out of danger yet. An informant warned Carr that Randolph planned to lie in ambush for him somewhere between Burnt Fort and the settlement of Temple, and urged him "not to go any where with out being arm'd and with a few men along with you." Carr struck back immediately, waylaying a messenger carrying dispatches from Randolph to Gunn.[20]

At long last, Governor Telfair intervened, sending General Jackson southward to supervise militia elections in both Glynn and Camden Counties and convene a new court of inquiry in Camden. Informing the governor of his intention to depart on this mission, Jackson appeared to side with Carr against Gunn, complaining that the date set by Gunn for Carr's trial would hamper the work of the court of inquiry. Jackson also refused to consider Captain Randolph and Lieutenant Randolph McGillis, reputed ringleaders of the mutiny, as the "real Officers" of the Colerain garrison.[21]

Carr's position had become untenable even before Jackson embarked from Savannah. He received a copy of Gunn's arrest order on October 3, nearly three weeks after it had been written, but twelve days later the beleaguered colonel still had not received a copy of the charges against him. His letters to Augusta had not yet elicited a direct response from the governor, so Carr wrote to Telfair again, demanding a court of inquiry into both his own conduct and that of General Gunn, who, he declared, was "the Cause of some of the disorder which has taken place in this County" since Carr had assumed command of the militia.[22] The day after he penned this letter, however, Colonel Carr decided that he had shot his bolt. Professing his innocence of any wrongdoing, he nevertheless told Governor Telfair he could not receive a fair trial because General Gunn had appointed his own supporters as members of the military court. Claiming that he was unwilling to be "dragd and hald" about by Gunn and his "factious party," Carr submitted his resignation as commandant of the Camden regiment. He departed from Camden in some haste and returned to Richmond County.[23]

Carr was tried by court-martial not once but twice because Telfair's successor as governor, George Mathews, ordered the first verdict reconsidered. It is not clear what, if anything, was done to punish Carr's alleged misconduct, but when the defendant did not attend the second trial, the presiding officer remarked that "the Court was of opinion (*thro this neglect*) that … Col. Carr had little or no defence [*sic*] to make, at least not sufficient to exculpate him from the several charges."[24] Major Abner Hammond, Carr's former second in command, seems to have followed Carr into exile, for early in 1794 Adjutant General A. C. G. Elholm asked the Camden justices of the peace and the remaining militia officers to indicate the most senior company grade officer residing in the county, who was to be given temporary command of the militia. The magistrates, including John and Thomas King, supported the pretensions of a certain Captain Hebbard against those of Hugh Brown, a supporter of Carr during the late unpleasantness. Hebbard secured the appointment. Two months later, Captain John F. Randolph, the alleged leader of the mutineers, was restored to his command.[25]

The Camden County "war" was over. Thomas Carr, an ambitious but maladroit interloper, had met his match in the small band of determined men who refused to relinquish the influence that had come their way in the wake of the death of Jacob Weed and the disgrace of Henry Osborne. A measure of tranquility descended over the county. True, that aura of calm had been purchased at the cost of one man's life and ninety days of near anarchy, but in the context of Camden's turbulent partisan strife, the interlude was perhaps cheap at that price.

Chapter 9

"Oh The Colossus! The Colossus!": James Jackson and the Jeffersonian-Republican Party in Georgia, 1796–1806

[**NOTE:** The autumn of 1987 was a busy time. I had published a revised version of my dissertation as *Politics on the Periphery: Factions and Parties in Georgia* (Newark: University of Delaware Press, 1986). I also was writing the third, and final, installment of my biography of John Wereat; preparing a paper on Georgia and the federal Constitution that I would deliver in Jonesboro, Georgia, in September; and writing an article on James Jackson's effort to create a Jeffersonian-Republican Party in Georgia.

The Jackson piece originated as a lecture at a joint meeting of the Georgia and South Carolina historical societies in Augusta, Georgia, in October. In addition to presenting the essay at that meeting, I already was toying with the idea of publishing it in the relatively new journal for scholars in my "field," the *Journal of the Early Republic*. The Friday night reception was interesting, but I was more concerned to return to my motel room and go over the paper a few more times before the actual delivery on Saturday morning.

The talk went well, I thought. During the coffee break, I was approached by Professor Kenneth Coleman, author of *The American Revolution in Georgia* and doyen of studies of the Revolutionary period in Georgia, who asked if he could speak with me during lunch. My journal takes up the story:

> Coleman ... stated that he believed there was a need for a book on the history of Georgia between 1789 and 1820 (i.e., a sequel to his

> study of the Revolutionary era, which covered 1763–1789). He had planned to write such a tome, he said, but at the age of seventy-one, he was too old to undertake it. He wondered if *I* might be interested in doing so!
>
> Now, you have to read between the lines here. Coleman didn't say anything about my paper; he knew about my book but he didn't indicate that he'd read it, nor did he refer to my dissertation. And yet—he was implying that he thought I was equipped to do the sort of survey he had in mind.
>
> I was stunned. I stammered something to the effect that while of course I was interested, he needed to realize that I did not have the sort of time for research that college professors had. This led Coleman to ask whether I was interested in a college job … I told him that, while I would have killed for a college job in 1973, I really liked the [prep school] job I had … As we parted he told me to let him know if I was interested in the project; I thanked him for his support and told him I would.

This was an interesting conversation. First of all, Kenneth Coleman already had written at least a précis of such a book *himself*, part two of *A History of Georgia* (1977; 1991). Moreover, his book on the Revolution in Georgia was much broader than the title suggests, and I suspected that his idea for a sequel ran along those same lines, while I was more interested in pursuing the narrower theme of political faction/party development in the state, even though I would also need to include information on other topics to provide the broader context of the story I was interested in.

At any rate, basking in the glow of Coleman's positive comments, I published this essay in the *Journal of the Early Republic* 9 (Fall 1989): 315–334. It represents the epitome of my occasional efforts to break out of the category of "Georgia historian" and reach a broader audience. Despite my hopes, however, I don't believe that I received much (if any) feedback on it, positive or otherwise.

As a final note, I should mention that, when I delivered the substance of this chapter as a talk, it was organized thematically. As I pondered submitting it to a more "prestigious" journal, however, I began to rethink that scheme, which seemed to me to presuppose more knowledge about Georgia history on the part of readers than was perhaps realistic. Eventually,

I restructured the article along more traditional, chronological lines, and it was accepted.]

*****

On March 24, 1796, the *Georgia Gazette* published a satirical piece entitled "The Yazoo Dream" from a correspondent signing himself "Foote." According to this author, a disappointed speculator in Georgia lands might have described the victorious leader of the anti-Yazoo forces in the state legislature as follows:

> Oh the damned fellow! Oh the Colossus! the Colossus!—damn him, knock him down, stab him, skiver him—he is a little fellow, not five feet high, much like Robespierre; catch him, advertise him in every paper; he has not ability at all—but—he has—Murder! fire! brimstone!—he has burnt Yazoo!

The politician described by "Foote" was James Jackson, and his portrait, though crude, perfectly captures the view that Jackson's enemies had of him at the midpoint of his career.

Modern Georgians, if they know of Jackson at all, associate him with the defeat of Yazoo. Students of the rise of political parties in Congress during the 1790s acknowledge Jackson's contributions as an early, vociferous spokesman for what was to become Jeffersonian Republicanism. Yet James Jackson's significance for the emergence of political partisanship in Georgia, a direct result of the conjunction of the Yazoo sale and the rise of a national opposition political party in Congress, is usually neglected, even by Jackson's only twentieth-century biographer.[1] Taking advantage of the anti-Federalist, antispeculation consensus he inherited in the wake of the notorious Yazoo land fraud, Jackson painstakingly extended a coastal political faction statewide and transformed it into Georgia's Jeffersonian-Republican Party. The diminutive Jackson indeed became the "Colossus" of Georgia politics, dominating public affairs until his death in 1806 at the age of forty-eight.

Born in England in 1757, James Jackson was sent by his parents to Georgia in 1772. He resided in Savannah at the home of a family friend, John Wereat, and read law in the office of Samuel Farley. Jackson became an early supporter of American independence; according to his later recollection, he was "the first Boy in [Georgia] who bore arms against" the

British. He rendered distinguished service to his adopted state throughout the Revolution, rising to the rank of lieutenant colonel and commanding his own "legion" at the age of twenty-four. After the war, Jackson returned to Chatham County, where he practiced law, served in the legislature, and established himself as a planter. Appointed colonel of the Chatham militia regiment in 1784, he soon rose to command of the state's first militia division.[2]

A number of "versatile Georgians," who were elected regularly to the legislature, held commissions as local magistrates, and served in the upper echelon of the officer corps in the state militia, dominated Georgia politics in the decade following the War of Independence.[3] Jackson's political career flourished in this environment. He soon became the central figure in a Savannah-based political faction that included a number of other young men whose later careers were to be inextricably linked to his. Moreover, Jackson's militia duties and his service in the state legislature enabled him to establish political connections with important up-country officer-politicians like William Few, James McNeil, and Jared Irwin. Just as important as the allies Jackson cultivated in the 1780s were the enemies he made. Two of them, Thomas Gibbons and James Gunn, became Federalists and, thus, foes of Jackson in the 1790s, but the roots of their enmity lay in the preceding decade.[4]

Elected a member of the first Congress under the new federal Constitution, James Jackson quickly became a vocal critic of Secretary of the Treasury Alexander Hamilton's financial program. In May 1789, one spectator at a congressional debate noted that there was not "the least attempt to create a party, or to divide the House by setting up the Southern in opposition to the Eastern interest, except in Mr. Jackson, from Georgia, the violence of whose passions sometimes hurries him into expressions which have, or appear to have, such a tendency." A modern scholar, Lance Banning, describes Jackson as "perhaps the most fervid democrat in the First Congress," one of the earliest exemplars of what Banning terms "the Jeffersonian persuasion." In his speeches, Jackson warned that a strong federal government would endanger both individual liberty and state power; appealed to history to prove that a permanent funded debt weakened rather than strengthened a nation; asserted that the assumption of state debts would reward speculators at the expense of honest patriots; and claimed that the proposed Bank of the United States was monopolistic and unconstitutional.[5]

Jackson's fiery congressional rhetoric appears to have had only limited impact on his constituents. Although federal grand juries in Georgia generally echoed his views of Hamilton's system, Georgians who contributed to newspapers in Savannah and Augusta largely ignored Hamilton, expressing alarm instead over federal Indian policy and over the new government's attitude toward Georgia's western territory. In other words, while Jackson warned of the dangers in the brave new world of Federalism, articulate Georgians harped on the same issues that had bedeviled relations between the state and Congress under the Articles of Confederation.[6]

In 1791, General Anthony Wayne, an ambitious newcomer to Georgia politics and a firm supporter of President Washington's administration, defeated Representative Jackson in an election marred by rumors of glaring voting irregularities by Wayne's campaign managers. Jackson's quest for vindication lasted for over a year and was not completely successful, but it did provide an opportunity to develop further his flamboyant, pugnacious style of leadership. Jackson and his supporters traveled throughout the state's eastern congressional district, collecting affidavits implicating Wayne's managers in the fraudulent voting and placed this evidence before grand juries in the counties concerned. The Savannah newspaper published Jackson's affidavits and grand jury presentments critical of the January election, thereby keeping the affair before the public. In a campaign marred by violence, Jackson next won a seat in the Georgia House of Representatives, where he took a leading part in the impeachment, conviction, and removal from office of one of Wayne's managers, superior court judge Henry Osborne.[7]

In 1792, following Osborne's ouster, Jackson undertook a laborious and successful fight in Philadelphia to deprive Anthony Wayne of his congressional seat, but a tie-breaking vote by the Federalist Speaker of the House denied the seat to Jackson. Nevertheless, in November 1792, the Georgia legislature chose Jackson to succeed William Few in the United States Senate, a decision that the state's most prominent Federalist, Senator James Gunn, claimed "had been agreed on, many months previous to the meeting of the Legislature."[8] Jackson's skillfully plotted campaign against those who had stolen his congressional seat in 1791 established a pattern for exercising leadership and molding public opinion that he was to employ with even greater adroitness during the furor over the Yazoo land fraud of 1795.

*****

In the 1780s, the sale of Georgia's extensive western lands had seemed the answer to the state's manifold financial problems. The legislature had countenanced a variety of approaches to the disposition of the public domain, from sales to wealthy individuals, to cession of the lands to Congress, to grants to companies in 1789. None of these methods had worked, and speculative fever remained high.[9]

Another unsuccessful effort to purchase a portion of the state's western territory, spearheaded by federal district judge Nathaniel Pendleton, formed the immediate backdrop for the infamous Yazoo fraud. Pendleton's proposal struck a responsive chord among men of a speculative bent in Georgia and elsewhere. By mid-November 1794, a majority of the legislature once again reportedly favored sale of the lands to companies. The first law embodying this apparent consensus, passage of which allegedly was insured by an ample distribution of money and sub-shares of land by Georgia's Federalist senator James Gunn and other leaders of the purchasing companies, was vetoed by Governor George Mathews in December 1794, but a revised version, the so-called Supplementary Act, secured the governor's assent in January 1795.[10]

James Jackson resigned his seat in the Senate, returned to Georgia, and plunged into the battle to overturn Yazoo. Although charges of bribery and corruption tainted virtually all of Georgia's prominent Federalists, the campaign waged by Jackson and other foes of speculation to elect an anti-Yazoo majority to the next legislature was not fought along recognizable national party lines. In a private letter to James Madison, Jackson linked the Yazoo speculation to funding and assumption, the Bank of the United States, and John Jay's treaty with Great Britain as evil fruits of Hamilton's loose construction of the Constitution. In his pamphlet *The Letters of Sicilius* (1795), however, which served as the bible of the anti-Yazooists, Jackson's treatment of the alleged unconstitutionality of the sale was much more abstract. According to Jackson, legislators who had voted for the Yazoo Act had considered not the good of the state but their own private interests. The transaction had created a monopoly that would increase the burden of debt on the people of Georgia, produce violence, and prevent the peaceful enjoyment of property. Above all, Jackson contended, the Yazoo Act was calculated "to dismember the state, if not the union. And to fling the part dismembered into the arms of some European despot, or to give us some lordling among the speculating tribe."[11]

Voters returned Jackson and a full slate of his supporters to the legislature for Chatham County, and the foes of Yazoo prevailed statewide.[12] During the 1796 legislative session, Jackson played the major role in exposing the corruption that had helped secure passage of the Yazoo Act. He headed an investigating committee that collected evidence substantiating the charges of bribery. The Rescinding Act, which repealed the sale, embodied the anti-Yazoo arguments Jackson had advanced in his *Letters of Sicilius*. Finally, Jackson arranged for destruction of the records of the sale of the state's western territory.[13]

Jackson's hand also was evident in the important matter of replacing state officials implicated in the corruption of the preceding session. Opposition to Yazoo was the main criterion, but it is surely no coincidence that newly elected attorney general David Mitchell, Judge William Stephens, Treasurer John Berrien, Surveyor General Samuel Hammond, and Senator Josiah Tattnall were experienced members of Jackson's coastal faction. Judges Benjamin Taliaferro and James McNeil were up-country residents, but they too had aided Jackson in his fight against speculation. The new solicitor general had given evidence before the investigating committee Jackson had headed. Finally, the legislature elected Jackson's long time ally from Washington County, Jared Irwin, as governor.[14]

The election of Irwin to the governorship in 1796 revealed a tactic Jackson would gradually refine as he struggled to consolidate his hold over Georgia politics, the use of a primitive party caucus. Evidently, Jackson saw Yazooists everywhere, and, in order to field the strongest candidate for governor, he and his supporters convened just before the legislature was to meet to elect state officials. According to a hostile source, Jackson had left Savannah for Louisville early in January 1796, "fully determined to have made [Edward] Telfair governor," but, after arriving in the capital, "he judged it prudent to start some other person." When three of Jackson's associates refused to offer for the post, "fifty-seven members, from among the faithful, met privately in the woods the evening before the election, and there tried by ballot the strength of Telfair's and [incumbent Governor George] Mathews' interests, when it was found that the latter would by far out poll the former." Only at this point, the informant concluded, was Irwin "as a last resort … called to that important station."[15]

Violence had long been the final arbiter in Georgia politics. Like a number of his prominent contemporaries, James Jackson was a quick-tempered, truculent partisan. He had killed radical leader George Wells in a duel in 1780 and reportedly exchanged shots with Thomas Gibbons in 1786 and again in 1792. The passions unleashed by Yazoo produced two violent, no-holds-barred confrontations in the streets of Louisville and Savannah between Jackson and Yazooist Robert Watkins in 1796 and might also have led to a rumored duel between Jackson and Senator James Gunn.[16]

Jackson's associates could afford to be no less forceful than their leader when circumstances demanded. Thus, violence or the threat of violence became almost an integral part of Jackson's political organization. For example, when a speech in March 1796 by Republican congressman Abraham Baldwin castigating land speculators nearly led to a duel between Baldwin and Federalist senator James Gunn, Jackson exulted that "if I had not pushed [Baldwin] at Philadelphia ... and here with *the papers*—the speech would never have been made nor the correspondence [between Gunn and Baldwin] have taken place ... but enough—I am satisfied as it has turned out, it will answer the best of purposes."[17] On another occasion, a Jackson aide, George Troup, was so stung by criticism from a writer styling himself "Q" of one of his pseudonymous productions that he assaulted an editor of the Savannah *Columbian Museum* with a "loaded whip" in a futile effort to learn "Q's" identity.[18]

One of James Jackson's signal achievements was to polarize Georgia politics, though initially in a way that has continued to baffle historians who scan the columns of Georgia newspapers in search of references to "Federalists" and "Republicans." For example, only after they had nullified the sale of the western territory by securing passage of the Rescinding Act in 1796 did Jackson and his supporters work to take advantage of the involvement of most of the state's prominent Federalists in the sale by tarring every member of the opposition with the "Yazoo" brush. Thus, critics attributed Senator James Gunn's crucial vote for the highly unpopular Jay Treaty with Britain to his interest in Yazoo. Moreover, when residents in Augusta and Savannah formed committees to protest this treaty, a writer in the *Georgia Gazette* warned citizens of Savannah to subject members of such bodies to careful scrutiny in order to "guard against the persons on each committee who are embarked or any wise concerned in the Yazoo or Western Territory speculations, and to suspect that they have been active merely to curry favor in the next Election."[19]

Political divisions in Georgia most clearly resembled those in Congress during Jackson's governorship (1798–1801), when news of the so-called

XYZ Affair revived Federalist fortunes in Georgia and encouraged Jackson to use his office as a Democratic-Republican pulpit. At the height of the anti-French frenzy created by the XYZ dispatches, Governor Jackson received a letter from Georgia's senior Republican congressman, Abraham Baldwin, summarizing a pro-French account of the affair in a German newspaper. The governor inserted an extract of Baldwin's letter in the Savannah press. This was a serious blunder, for it provided Jackson's political foes with ammunition needed to mount a carefully orchestrated campaign against Baldwin that cost him his congressional seat in November.[20]

Nevertheless, this setback proved only temporary, for the following year, a party caucus chose Baldwin as the nominee for the United States Senate over the incumbent Republican, Josiah Tattnall. As Jackson explained it, had both Tattnall and Baldwin been nominated, the prize would have gone to Thomas Carnes, who retained considerable influence in the up-country despite his involvement in Yazoo. To prevent this, "friends" of Tattnall and Baldwin had "thought it best and prudent to have a meeting and run the person having the highest number," and Baldwin came out on top. Governor Jackson asserted that to have "split would have effectively lost all." Baldwin's elevation to the Senate also would placate those in the piedmont, who had begun to complain that low-country residents occupied a majority of Georgia's seats in the national legislature. Tattnall was a tidewater planter, while Baldwin resided in Wilkes; with the latter's election, the up-country held two of the state's four congressional seats.[21]

Governor Jackson delivered blasts at the Adams administration's conduct of foreign affairs in 1799 and 1800. In the latter year, confident that Jefferson would be elected president in 1800 and basking in the glow of a General Assembly with only seven "Adamites" among its members, Governor Jackson charged that "an influence exists in America, partial to British rule and ready for a monarch." He warned that Americans must "keep a watchful eye over our republican rights and constitutions," but he assured his audience that he himself would never abandon Republicanism: "The richest monarch of Europe is too poor to purchase my principles, or to shake my firm adherence to the constitutions of our country."[22] Rather than heap praise on Thomas Jefferson in 1800, Jackson supporters also linked the outcome of the presidential election to the fate of the western territory. Correspondents reminded voters that they must either give their suffrage to "*tried* republicans only" or face the prospect of seeing President

Adams and Senator Gunn reelected and "the work of two conventions and five legislatures tumbled down with one stroke."[23]

An ironic measure of Jackson's success in politicizing Georgia was the increasingly one-sided partisanship of the state's press. Little that Jackson did or said escaped the eyes of anonymous critics in the Augusta and Savannah newspapers, but until 1799, the absence of a firmly Republican paper hampered efforts by the governor's supporters to defend him. In January of that year, however, Ambrose Day began to publish the *Louisville Gazette.* Although the motto of Day's sheet was "Reason and Truth Impartial Guide the Way," most of his contributors wrote on behalf of James Jackson. When James Hely entered into partnership with Day in April 1800, the printers changed the name of the newspaper, adding "Republican Trumpet" to the masthead, and they chose a new creed, "Liberty is Our Motto—and Truth Our Guide." By the autumn of 1800, it was clear that, for the editors of the Louisville paper, James Jackson and Thomas Jefferson embodied "Truth" in its purest form.

In the summer of 1800, a correspondent in the pro-Federalist, anti-Jackson *Augusta Herald* accused the Louisville newspaper of "endeavouring to circulate calumny against the highest officers of the American government" and hinted that Day and Hely were merely figureheads, with Governor Jackson himself setting their editorial policy. Even if Jackson wrote nothing for the *Republican Trumpet* himself, there was probably some truth to this charge, for two of Jackson's aides-de-camp, George Troup and Thomas Charlton, as well as Secretary of the Executive Department Thomas Johnson, contributed essays to the Louisville sheet in defense of the Republican cause in general and of Jackson in particular.[24] The Louisville printers responded in kind, asserting that William J. Hobby, a New England native who had parlayed his uncompromising Federalism into the postmaster's position in Augusta, actually wrote the *Herald's* editorials.[25]

The twin dangers of Yazoo and sectionalism once again threatened the Jackson coalition in November 1800, when the legislature was to elect a successor to Senator James Gunn. According to Governor Jackson, during the first week of the General Assembly, "the host of Lawyers, the Aristocratic set of Augusta," who were in Louisville to attend the circuit court, had "persuaded the Western members a back Countryman ought to be the person" chosen. This strategy temporarily split Jackson's supporters, since his low-country allies opposed the selection of a second upcountry man for the Senate. Every Republican candidate agreed to withdraw in favor of the governor, but Jackson claimed he refused to offer for the post until, "on sounding and finding that [Yazooist Thomas] Carnes would take [the Senate seat] from [the Governor's choice, John] Milledge our Democratic and Antiyazoo Friends determined to run me whether or not and elected me 50 votes out of 67."[26]

The retirement of Senator James Gunn, the state's leading Federalist and a prime mover in the Yazoo fraud, symbolically sealed the triumph of James Jackson's anti-Yazoo campaign. Moreover, Thomas Jefferson's victory in the presidential election of 1800 instantly strengthened the hand of Jackson, Georgia's most prominent Democratic-Republican. Elevated to the Senate in place of Gunn, Jackson became the chief dispenser of federal patronage among the state's Jeffersonians. While Jefferson himself insisted that Georgians nominated for office be "of perfect integrity, and of republican principles," Jackson and his Senate colleague Abraham Baldwin balanced these qualifications with more practical considerations, such as the importance of family "connections," the need to satisfy the increasingly vocal demands of backcountry Republicans for a larger slice of the patronage pie, and the opportunity to advance the careers of younger party members.[27]

That Jackson believed William J. Hobby to be his real nemesis in the office of the *Augusta Herald* is clear from the campaign he undertook in Washington, following Jefferson's election to the presidency and his own elevation to the US Senate, to have Hobby removed as postmaster in Augusta. Buttressed by anti-Hobby polemics in the columns of the *Republican Trumpet*, and despite Hobby's vociferous denials of Jackson's charges, the postmaster lost his office in January 1802 amid a bitter controversy that became a cause célèbre in both the state and national Federalist press.[28]

Of greater long-term significance than Jackson's attempts to silence Federalist critics was his and his supporters' effort to establish friendly newspapers in Georgia's major towns, Savannah and Augusta. On September 8, 1800, Jackson's Chatham County ally John Milledge urged Savannah attorney Charles Harris to continue working toward establishment in the port of "an independent and firm press." Milledge recommended that "a small number of us in [Chatham] County must have stated meetings for the sole purpose, of devising ways for the support of a republican press" so that "truth may be known in our land." These efforts eventually bore fruit in August 1802, with the launching of the Savannah *Georgia Republican*, edited by James Lyon and Samuel Morse. Lyon and Morse were feisty editors who proved equal to those at the Federalist *Columbian Museum* in outraging the political opposition. Nevertheless, by early 1804, their tactics had become offensive to a number of Jackson's supporters, who withdrew their advertising in retaliation. Evidently, this turn of events caused Jackson concern, for in November 1804, James Hely, one of Jackson's "Louisville Trumpeters," moved to Savannah to set up the *Southern Patriot*.[29]

Although sometimes denounced as a "Jacobin sheet" by Jackson's opponents, the *Augusta Chronicle*, under the long editorship of John E. Smith, had tempered its Republicanism. Smith died on February 1, 1803, and almost immediately, local Republicans sought Jackson's aid in finding a suitable replacement. By mid-March, Jackson had reached agreement with Dennis Driscoll, a former editor of the *American Patriot* of Baltimore. As the senator explained in a letter introducing Driscoll to Governor John Milledge, the printer had been "compelled to abandon" Baltimore "for supporting the principles you and myself have ever avowed." In Jackson's opinion, this circumstance would operate in Georgia "not as an objection; but a recommendation." To procure Driscoll's services in promoting Republicanism in Augusta, Jackson promised him financial assistance in purchasing the *Chronicle*, "as well as as much of the publick work, as is consistent with your duty." Driscoll took over the *Chronicle* before the end of the year and lived up to Jackson's expectations of a Republican editor, especially after Federalist William J. Hobby officially joined the rival *Herald* in July 1804.[30]

After Jefferson's election to the presidency, violence marred Jackson's efforts to use federal patronage to further the careers of his supporters. Working together, Federalists in Savannah and Washington tried to discredit Georgia appointments and, through them, the new president's patronage policy. For example, in the spring of 1802, when an anonymous writer in the *Washington Federalist* viciously attacked the commander of Georgia's federal revenue cutter, Henry Putnam, and federal district attorney David Mitchell, Jefferson and members of Georgia's congressional delegation discussed various remedies, including recourse to libel suits.[31] Mitchell and Putnam, like Jackson, preferred direct action to legal niceties. In August 1802, Mitchell shot and killed William Hunter, a Federalist merchant in Savannah, in a duel. Henry Putnam also searched for the source of the rumors about his career and evidently discovered it in the person of Thomas Gibbons, whom he publicly horsewhipped in the streets of Savannah. By the end of 1802, Jackson could inform the president grimly that "the Republicans hold their own even at the expense of a little blood in this State & I have no doubt will continue to do so."[32]

There were more ways to serve James Jackson and Thomas Jefferson than shedding blood or spilling ink on behalf of Republican principles. Consider, for example, the case of Jackson's brother Abram, captain of the governor's bodyguard in Louisville and his personal secretary, as well. He later served as Speaker of the Georgia house from 1802 to 1806. In the fall of 1798, angered by rising criticism of Governor Jackson emanating from Alexander M'Millan's Augusta *Southern Centinel*, Abram took matters into his own hands and attempted to discredit M'Millan.

On September 6, 1798, Abram Jackson wrote to Henry Caldwell, solicitor general of the Middle Circuit, then in Burke County to attend court, asking him "to speak to the Grand Jury *those who can be relied on* and use your exertions to procure a presentment against M'Millan and his party for the unmerited attack on the *chief magistrate* of the state." Someone intercepted the letter and sent it to M'Millan, who published it along with biting commentary. This drew Governor Jackson into the fray to deny "that ever my brother was ordered or desired by me to write to Mr. Caldwell the letter which has been published."[33] Regardless of the governor's denial, in mid-October 1798 the Jefferson County grand jury, meeting in Milledgeville, the state capital, presented the *Southern Centinel* as a "public nuisance" and its editor as a "public grievance." One year later, M'Millan's sheet ceased publication, helped into journalistic oblivion by Governor Jackson's refusal to pay the editor for services supposedly rendered the state.[34]

Another important cog in James Jackson's political machine, Savannah attorney Joseph Welscher, appears to have been the sort of "popular leader" who would have been at home in Sam Adams's Boston. In 1795, Welscher led an anti–Jay Treaty demonstration in Savannah that climaxed with the burning of effigies of John Jay and Georgia's Federalist senator James Gunn, one of only two southern senators to vote to ratify the treaty. The following year, after Jackson had been snubbed by most of the lawyers attending the federal court session in Savannah and had engaged in a violent street brawl with Yazoo supporter Robert Watkins, Welscher spearheaded efforts to exact revenge. He led a group of Jackson's supporters who serenaded the visiting attorneys at their boarding house with a variety of "republican songs," and he helped organize a meeting to draw up resolutions backing Jackson.[35] Although Jackson surely held Welscher's skills as a mass leader in high regard, even he admitted, analyzing the lawyer's fitness for nomination to a state judgeship early in 1798, that Welscher, "tho [*sic*] possessed of talents wants respectability in the eyes of the people, perhaps unjustly."[36]

Among those at Welscher's beck and call were the artisans of Savannah. According to one writer, the president of the Savannah Association of Mechanics, tailor Balthazar Shaffer, was Jackson's "Privy Counsellor." Shaffer's name headed the list of signatures on an October 30, 1795, letter to Jackson from "a considerable portion of the Citizens of Chatham County," asking him to resign from the United States Senate to lead the fight in Georgia against Yazoo. Another artisan who signed the October letter, John Carroway Smith, presided at the meeting called the following spring to protest the treatment of Jackson by the visiting lawyers. A letter sent at the end of 1800 by the town's Republicans to senator-elect Jackson praising his conduct while the governor included the signatures of Balthazar Shaffer and another artisan, Thomas Glass. Needless to say, Jackson took care to attend the annual dinner of the Mechanics' Association.[37]

Because so many of the movers and shakers of Georgia politics also held high rank in the militia officer corps, musters of citizen-soldiers rapidly became partisan gatherings in the wake of the Yazoo fraud. For example, the commander of the Columbia County regiment, Colonel Jesse Sanders, favored his troops with an anti-Yazoo "harangue" and then gave them the opportunity to sign petitions urging the repeal of the Yazoo Act and a congressional investigation of the Jay Treaty. Seven months later, Colonel Sanders enlivened a Fourth of July muster with a heated oration denouncing land speculators for their opposition to the Rescinding Act.[38] Subsequent events helped to polarize militia units still further. By the first years of the new century, Federalists controlled the elite "Volunteer Corps" in both Savannah and Augusta.[39] Nevertheless, the Chatham Artillery, led by three aides-de-camp of General James Jackson, fired a cannon in honor of Jefferson's election and pledged their Republican faith over drinks on the Fourth of July under Jackson's satisfied gaze. Likewise, when the Chatham Hibernian Fusileers celebrated their anniversary in March 1801, they raised their glasses in praise of President Jefferson and Senator Jackson.[40]

It was the crowning irony of Jackson's career that the land question, which had given him the opportunity to build a Jeffersonian party in

Georgia, was also the issue that helped to undo much of his work. Jackson realized land hunger was the Achilles' heel of his organization, so he made it his special preserve. As a delegate to the state constitutional convention of 1798, for instance, Governor Jackson saw to it that the substance of the Rescinding Act was engrafted on the revised frame of government.[41]

Before 1800, Jackson and his allies also prevented Yazooists from transferring their claims against Georgia to the national government, where the dominant Federalists might have given them a sympathetic hearing.[42] After 1800, with Jackson in the Senate, Jefferson in the presidency, and Republicans in control of Georgia, a speedy settlement to the question of the fate of the Yazoo lands seemed likely. Negotiations moved too slowly, however, for Jackson, one of the Georgia commissioners appointed to arrange a land cession.

On March 27, 1802, in a move of calculated desperation, Jackson warned one of the federal commissioners, Albert Gallatin, that public opinion in Georgia was in "great ferment" over the evident reluctance of the national government either to pay the state for the Yazoo lands or to return them. Then, in an appeal to Gallatin's party loyalty, Jackson expressed the fear that further delay would "give the Federalists in [Georgia], an ascendancy in the next election [for the General Assembly] & if the Fed's get the advantage it is ten to one but they repeal our powers [to arrange a cession]." Jackson certainly exaggerated the prospects for a Federalist revival in Georgia, but his dire warning had the desired effect. On April 24, 1802, the negotiators signed an agreement transferring to the federal government Georgia's claim to the Yazoo lands. In return, the United States agreed to pay Georgia $1.25 million and extinguish as quickly as possible the remaining Indian claims within the state. The goal toward which Jackson had been working since Jefferson's election, the transfer of the state's western land claims, and the related headaches, to a Republican national administration, had at last been realized.[43]

And yet, in 1803 and again in 1806, as Jackson's supporters in the General Assembly debated the question of disposing of territory obtained through treaties with the Creeks, the land question continued to be divisive. Republicans in the legislature agreed on the method to be used, a lottery, but they disagreed bitterly over whether the land should be sold to raise revenue or granted at little or no cost in order to ensure as broad a distribution as possible. This squabble unleashed once more the forces of sectionalism Jackson had struggled for so long to subdue.[44]

Moreover, with Yazoo dead and Federalism routed in Georgia after 1800, the sense of urgency that had made the party caucus a key mechanism for selecting candidates for important offices disappeared, giving way to a decentralized nominating process, which also increased sectional strains. In some cases, county leaders chose slates for the legislature, and Jackson's lieutenants in each section of the state agreed on candidates for congressional races. In an attempt to reduce the dangers of sectionalism to the emerging Jeffersonian consensus, Jackson's supporters apparently worked out a tacit division of responsibility for the nomination of party candidates for major offices: after 1801, piedmont Republicans received a majority of seats on the state's congressional delegation, while the party regularly conferred the governorship on Jackson's low-country lieutenants. Jackson himself seems to have had the final word in selecting a tidewater resident to complete the Republican congressional slate.

Yet these arrangements did not always work smoothly. Ambitious up-country men like John Clark grew more willing to challenge Jackson's allies for control of the Republican machine or to run their own campaigns independently of it. In the absence of a serious Federalist threat to Republican hegemony, the mantle of "republicanism" became a protean garment that could be twisted by their supporters to fit even former Yazooist Matthew McAllister or those like Peter Early, whose political creed, according to the *Republican Trumpet*, "whether federal or republican seems not to be accurately ascertained."[45]

Had James Jackson lived, perhaps none of these developments would have weakened the organization he and his lieutenants had constructed. An instinctive Republican in the First Congress, Jackson seemed almost more Jeffersonian than Jefferson, and his zeal for the cause helped immeasurably to move Georgia into the anti-Federalist camp between 1789 and 1794. The Yazoo fraud, and Jackson's key role in overturning it, proved decisive in completing the transition to Republicanism. Rumors of bribery outraged many Georgians, and implicated the state's most prominent Federalists as the chief agents of corruption. Using rhetorical techniques developed while opposing Hamiltonian measures, and leadership skills honed against Anthony Wayne and his campaign managers in 1791–1792, Jackson defeated the Yazooists. To replace those discredited by their involvement in Yazoo, Jackson insisted on opposition to speculation as a prerequisite for office and employed a caucus of like-minded legislators further to ensure that those nominated for major posts were firmly wedded to the cause. Because routing the Yazooists also shattered Federalism in the state, Jackson was in a commanding position to erect something permanent on the ruins.

Jackson's organization embraced most of Georgia by the end of 1796, but his opponents, whether Yazooists, Federalists, or both, were a tenacious lot unwilling to surrender without a struggle. To combat their efforts at vilification, Jackson and his supporters established firmly Republican newspapers in Louisville, Savannah, and Augusta. As a result, the tenets of "Republicanism," as espoused by Jefferson and interpreted by Jackson, became staple elements in Georgia's political discourse. An era of violent partisanship arrived with a vengeance.

Jackson justified one of his brawls with Robert Watkins on the grounds that Watkins had made a remark which "flesh & blood of such texture as mine would not bear."[46] This quick temper, coupled with his frenetic leadership style and his position as Georgia's most visible Jeffersonian, made Jackson a lightning rod for attacks by the opposition and no doubt contributed to his lurid image in the Federalist press. Nevertheless, Jackson's success as a party organizer depended heavily on the efforts of a cadre of strong-minded lieutenants and a growing body of party regulars. Rewarding these supporters and keeping them unified in the face of sectional pressures and clashing ambitions taxed even Jackson's powers of persuasion, not to mention the patronage at his disposal. With his demise in 1806, factionalism reasserted itself, as some Republicans followed the general's hand-picked successors, William Harris Crawford and George Troup, while others cast their lots with a pugnacious up-country Republican, John Clark.[47]

But the power of the senator's organization remained formidable in the summer of 1803, when still another Jackson supporter killed yet another Federalist in a Savannah duel. Commenting on this latest political bloodletting, an anonymous resident of the port drew the obvious moral: "Republicans are not to be trifled with in this part of the world."[48] That Republicans were not to be trifled with in Georgia was largely the work of James Jackson. Perhaps nothing indicates more clearly Jackson's significance as creator of Georgia's Jeffersonian-Republican Party than the fact that it did not long survive his death intact: a political leader could be replaced, but a "Colossus" could not.

Chapter 10

James Gunn, Georgia Federalist

[NOTE: With the skills at scholarly drudgery inculcated by my grad school professors and blessed with an understanding spouse, I was able to maintain a fairly regular schedule of publishing during my career. After all, my chances to secure a college teaching position might well hinge on how prolific I was in keeping my name before possible employers, or so I was told. From early in my grad school years through the mid-1980s, my efforts in that area ran to book reviews for various journals, as well as a number of articles, some derived from my dissertation but others adapted from public lectures I had given in various venues. Then, in the early 1980s, I began to consider revising the dissertation for publication as a book, which eventually saw the light of day in 1986.

Once the book was published, I began considering a sequel, carrying the story of party development in Georgia across several more decades. On the other hand, there didn't seem to be any hurry to plunge into another large research project. But, if not preparing to write a new book, then what would I do to keep my historian's skills honed? Book reviews, of course, were always possible, but what about articles? I had ideas for possible articles about several of the major characters in my book.

One of the most obvious of these was James Gunn, the "villain" of *Politics on the Periphery*, because he had been the prime mover of the infamous Yazoo land fraud that played such a large part in Georgia politics and, thus, in my research. Probably in the mid to late 1980s, I actually outlined a long biographical piece on Gunn. I eventually decided to publish it in two parts, the first covering Gunn's career in state politics between his arrival to Georgia at the end of the Revolution and his election in 1789 as one of the state's first US senators under the federal Constitution, the second treating him as Georgia's most prominent Federalist and the organizer of the Yazoo fraud.

Creating an outline for this project was one thing, but writing it was quite another. I finally got off the dime in the early 1990s, by which time I had begun to consider seriously applying for a sabbatical from Westminster to stimulate research on a sequel to *Politics on the Periphery.* Curiously, though, it was that growing possibility that also fueled my determination to finish projects remaining from the dissertation research, especially the Gunn biography. The first part, it turned out, came fairly easily, and was published in the *Georgia Historical Quarterly* in 1996. The concluding section was a tougher row to hoe, however, because I struggled with how to treat Gunn's involvement in Yazoo without simply repeating the same stuff I had said about it in the book—and in the 1989 article on James Jackson in the *Journal of the Early Republic.* The final segment of the Gunn biography did not appear until 2010, after I had been researching my second book for almost a decade and a half! (Obviously, one of the advantages of teaching in a "prep school" rather than in a college or university is that no one cares if you *ever* publish anything, so there is no pressure to do so!)

I have revised the two essays and combined them here into a single narrative of Gunn's career in Georgia.]

* * * * *

A number of years ago, historian James Broussard maintained that trying to describe Georgia Federalists was "a bit like writing about Bigfoot or the Abominable Snowman … We see their tracks; we know more or less where they live; we can even name some of them; but we do not yet understand them."[1] Perhaps the most prominent member of this small but hardy band was James Gunn, who arrived in Georgia in 1782, an impecunious twenty-nine-year-old former Continental Army officer whose service had been marred by scandal. Seven years later, Gunn was chosen one of Georgia's first US senators under the new federal Constitution, and his rapid ascent in public life sheds light on Georgia's political culture in the formative years of the early republic.

Georgia was a land of opportunity after the Revolution. Americans from throughout the colonies had seen service there, and, when the war ended, many headed for the southern bastion of the new nation. As a result, Georgia's white population nearly tripled, from an estimated eighteen thousand in 1775 to almost fifty-three thousand in 1790.[2] Most of the white newcomers were undoubtedly more interested in making a living than making a name for themselves, but for the comparative few who nursed political ambitions, including James Gunn, Georgia also provided fertile soil.

Between 1777 and 1782, James Gunn rose to the rank of captain in the First Continental Dragoons, a unit that participated with other Virginia troops in the campaign to force the British to evacuate Savannah.[3] It was there that the controversy arose that—at least in Gunn's opinion—besmirched his wartime career.

In 1780, the Virginian found it necessary to procure a new mount by drawing on his regiment's stock of "public horses," replacement animals considered as property of the army. While this practice was common among units of mounted troops, when Gunn subsequently traded his "public horse" to another officer for two horses and a slave, his bargaining skills led to an investigation by the inspector general. The case eventually came to the attention of General Nathanael Greene, the American commander in the South. Greene, who believed that Gunn was guilty of "improperly disposing of public property," appointed a board of officers to examine the captain's conduct.[4]

In his testimony before the board of officers, Captain Gunn contended that his new mount had become his personal property, citing two other instances in his own regiment when officers had acquired public horses and then traded them away. Two defense witnesses testified that they knew of the cases referred to by Gunn, and one of them added that he had never heard the regimental commander disapprove of the practice. After considering the testimony, the board ruled that Gunn had been "justifiable in exchanging or disposing of the horse as it was a custom precedented [*sic*] in the Regiment and the Commanding Officer never disapproving the same." According to one source, upon learning of this ruling, "Gunn, in defiant tone, called upon [General Greene] to approve the sentence."[5]

After reviewing the board's decision, however, General Greene rejected it, arguing that "nothing appears more repugnant to reason and common justice than priviledges [*sic*] claimed upon precedent originally wrong." Furthermore, Greene asserted that he had recently learned that, contrary to the claims of Gunn and his witnesses, in the instances cited in the captain's defense the officers involved had not "converted public horses to their own private use." Greene referred the matter to the Continental

Congress, which, two months later, supported his actions and ordered that "General Greene be directed to order Captain Gunn to replace the horse he sold with another equally good." There, presumably, the matter rested for the duration of the war.[6]

Georgia showed its gratitude to General Greene for his part in delivering the state from the British by awarding him a plantation, Mulberry Grove, on Cumberland Island, where he settled with his wife, Catherine. Though neither his Revolutionary record nor his future prospects were as bright as those of Greene, James Gunn too made Georgia his adopted home after the war and threw himself energetically into its economic and political life.

Within a short time after the British evacuation of Savannah in the summer of 1782, Gunn purchased a house and lot in the port and two plantations, Clifton Plantation and Cashall-Hall.[7] That Gunn was able to acquire so much property so quickly can be explained, at least in part, by the minimal credit requirements in Georgia at the time. But rumormongers also attributed it to the fact that Gunn's new young wife, the former Mary Jane Wright, brought with her to the marriage "a pretty fortune."[8]

James Gunn clearly was determined to turn his Revolutionary War service to his advantage in the postwar world. An original member of the Georgia Chapter of the Society of the Cincinnati, Gunn eventually succeeded General Anthony Wayne as chapter president in July 1792. Gunn also put his military experience to practical use as an officer in the Georgia militia; by May 1786, he was a colonel in the first Chatham County Regiment.[9]

Following the evacuation of Savannah, one of the major issues roiling the political waters in Chatham County was the treatment to be meted out to "Tories," a term used to describe several groups of people: Georgians who had either remained loyal to the Crown during the Revolution or been forced by circumstances to accept British protection (most had already been targeted by the state's Confiscation and Banishment acts of March 1779 and May 1782); a small number of British merchants who had been permitted by state authorities to remain in Savannah temporarily to supply necessities to the victorious Whigs and to settle their own affairs; and former residents of other states who had come to Georgia after having been banished from their homes for "treasonable" activities.

Vocal residents of Savannah were so concerned about threats posed by these groups that they organized the anti-Tory Chatham County Association in the autumn of 1783. James Gunn advertised his Whig credentials by serving as a member of the association's standing committee of thirteen, which was to receive and evaluate reports of "Tory" activities.[10] At the first legislative election following the organization of the Chatham County Association, Gunn was chosen one of Chatham's representatives in the House of Assembly, a position to which he would be reelected for most of the rest of the decade. Gunn had no sooner taken his seat in the assembly than he was also appointed a justice of the peace for Chatham and a commissioner of the northwest road.[11]

As a state legislator, James Gunn continued his efforts on behalf of good Whigs and against the machinations of Tories and their sympathizers. For example, in January 1784, when the House of Assembly moved to humiliate the former governor and fervent Whig Lyman Hall—who had angered legislators by his outspoken activism during his governorship—by denying him the assembly seat to which had recently been elected, Gunn was one of only three Chatham representatives unsuccessfully to oppose the motion.[12] A year later, Gunn joined other Chatham legislators to defeat efforts to readmit three local Loyalists—Thomas Gibbons, Thomas Young, and Dr. Andrew Johnston—to citizenship without penalty. That the former Virginian's stance on the Tory issue was more extreme than most of his Chatham colleagues seems clear from events later that same day. Chatham representative James Jackson was not content to deny Thomas Gibbons's painless readmission to citizenship. When Gibbons, a Savannah attorney, threatened to overturn the state's Confiscation and Banishment Act in court, Jackson moved to bar him from the practice of law for a period of fourteen years. Although the motion passed, only James Gunn among the Chatham delegation joined Jackson in supporting it.[13]

Married to a wealthy wife and firmly established as a planter, militia officer, magistrate, and rising politician, James Gunn perhaps should have been contented, but he could neither forgive nor forget the blow he believed General Nathanael Green had dealt his honor in 1782.[14] In the spring of 1785, with Continental military service and the constraints of rank behind him, Gunn challenged Greene to a duel "upon the footing of equality of Citizens." When Greene rejected Gunn's challenge, "Gunn sent him word that he should attack him wherever he met him. "'Tell him,' said Greene, 'that I shall always carry pistols!"[15]

Perhaps aware that, to an ambitious, hotheaded man like James Gunn, his refusal to fight a duel amounted to an admission of either guilt or cowardice and thus might prove as satisfactory as a willingness to exchange shots, Nathanael Greene appealed to a higher authority. On April 25, 1785, Greene set out his case for refusing Gunn's challenge in a letter to his former commander, George Washington. Washington supported Greene, arguing that, regardless of the validity of Gunn's claims, his attempt to gain satisfaction "was to the last degree dangerous," because a commander should not be subject to a private challenge from a subordinate over actions taken while on public duty. Had the duel actually been fought, Washington declared, it would have established an unfortunate precedent that "would unquestionably have produced a revolution."[16]

Gunn and Greene apparently never encountered one another in the streets of Savannah before Greene's death on January 19, 1786. Nevertheless, Gunn's abortive challenge to Greene, who was regarded by many Georgians as a hero, might well have had one untoward consequence for the ambitious former Virginian. In the next election after the contretemps, Gunn was not returned to the legislature. Since he would be reelected to serve in the sessions of 1787, 1788, and 1789, perhaps voters in the autumn of 1786 denied Gunn a seat to send a message: even in Georgia, truculence had its limits.

In his letter to General Washington, Nathanael Greene had characterized James Gunn as "without reputation or principle. Indeed he is little better than a public nuisance being always engaged in riots and drunken [brawls]." Yet, in view of Gunn's rapid rise in politics and the militia, Greene's low opinion of him was not widely held among low-country residents. On the other hand, that there was more than a grain of truth in the retired general's acid description of the former Virginian is clear from an examination of certain aspects of Gunn's militia service. And in these episodes, it seems, lay the origin of the split between James Gunn and James Jackson that shaped—and warped—Georgia politics for almost fifteen years.

*****

Controversies surrounding the leadership of the Chatham County militia grew almost inevitably out of sectional tensions in Georgia during the latter half of the 1780s. The House of Assembly, dominated since the end of the Revolution by the up-country, dealt a series of blows to low-country pride.[17] The first of these was the temporary removal of the state capital from Savannah to Augusta in 1786, pending construction of a more centrally located seat government, to be called Louisville. In the summer of that same year, amid clashes between backcountry settlers and their Creek Indian neighbors, the legislature placed Georgia on a wartime footing. To pay for the mobilization of the militia, the assembly authorized the emission of bills of credit, to be redeemed through sale of vacant lands. Low-country merchants and mechanics had been dreading the prospect of paper money since the end of the War for Independence, and now, with their fears confirmed, they organized to oppose it.[18]

The same session of the assembly also revised the state militia law. Low-country residents, seeing that measure as yet another insult aimed at them from Augusta, attacked the militia law on several grounds. Public meetings adopted resolutions critical of the law's provisions that militiamen who did not turn out when ordered must pay a fine of £15 or provide a substitute and that units on active duty were to be subject to the same regulations as federal troops. The October session of the Chatham County grand jury complained that the law allowed commanders to pay for supplies with a certificate rather than with currency. This power, the grand jurors protested, "may be attended with great inconvenience and distress to the citizens of this state, more especially when so large a sum of paper money is ordered to be emitted for the aforesaid purposes."[19]

Moreover, the performance of the Chatham militia won few plaudits in the autumn of 1786. One observer asserted that Savannah residents were so nonchalant in the face of the crisis with the Creeks that "officers cannot raise a common guard for the defense of the town, and … the county is in nigh the same situation." The lack of readiness of the Chatham troops led one of their officers, Benjamin Fishbourn, to moan, in a letter to his Revolutionary commander, General Anthony Wayne, "Oh God, Militia—what did Baren [*sic*] Stuben say *Damn the Militia—damn you—and god damn myself.*"[20]

Although the Chatham militia might have been reluctant to mobilize against what they perceived as a distant threat from the Creeks, they were more willing to take the field against danger closer to home. In the spring of 1787, an anonymous correspondent to the *Georgia Gazette* showered accolades on Colonel James Gunn for his leadership of a combined force of Chatham and South Carolina militia in a raid against a "banditti of runaway slaves" who had established a camp in Patton's Swamp. The troops killed six of the runaways, drove the rest from the field, destroyed twenty-one houses, and seized seven boats. According to one observer, Gunn's

> decisive effort ... to break up the Camp, and destroy the confidence and strength of the runaways, cannot fail of producing the best effects, as they had got seated and strongly fortified in the midst of an almost impenetrable swamp, and opening a general asylum, which no doubt would have been embraced by many [runaway slaves] on the approach of hot weather. Indeed running away had already become more prevalent than usual.[21]

Despite Gunn's success in the raid against the runaway slave encampment, state officials—among them General James Jackson, whose militia command included the Chatham County units—continued to press low-country residents to cease their opposition to the new militia law. On this issue, Colonel Gunn enlisted on the side of the beleaguered citizens of Chatham. The dispute came to a head in the autumn of 1787, when a writer signing himself "Cassius" used the Augusta newspaper as the forum for a devastating textual criticism of Jackson's brigade orders.

"Cassius" assailed General Jackson mercilessly, claiming that his "stings are so venomous, that you have been known for years in the Legislature, by the name of the *Chatham Wasp.*" He concluded that, "You turn General over us, and cannot issue a brigade order, and you have turned the citizens of [Savannah] too, but it was out on guard to keep up a military show to support your consequence and justify your pluming yourself in regimentals on Sundays."[22] Jackson quickly identified "Cassius" as James Gunn and ordered him arrested and court-martialed for belittling the orders of a superior officer. The state executive council countermanded Jackson's arrest order until the threat of war with the Creeks subsided. Relations between Jackson and Gunn continued to deteriorate, and, a year later, the general again ordered the colonel's arrest, once more evidently without success.[23]

Both Gunn and Jackson were hot-tempered, high-handed, and unwilling to back away from a fight. Clashing ambitions certainly played a part in setting them at odds, as did their different perspectives on the proper role of the Chatham militia. That a break between them was imminent was obvious even before Gunn penned his "Cassius" letter. The incident in question, which occurred at a raucous Fourth of July celebration in Savannah in 1787, not only reveals the growing animus between Gunn and Jackson; it also furnishes the most detailed instance of Gunn's penchant for drunken, riotous conduct.

After a morning spent celebrating American independence, the officers of the Chatham militia gathered at a coffeehouse for an afternoon of drinking and fellowship, with James Gunn and William Stephens presiding. After the celebrants had "been in their cups" for quite a while, some of those present called for a song from Captain Joseph Welscher.[24] Welscher replied that the only song he knew might prove offensive, for "it was an old English song made before the war." Having been assured that the tune would not give offense, Welscher began to sing, but he had not gotten very far before James Gunn, his much-vaunted American patriotism apparently intensified by drink, joined several others in groaning loudly. Welscher reiterated his desire not to offend anyone, and he reminded Gunn that he had already apologized for the song. When Gunn replied, "Damn the song and you too, you damned stinking puppy," the two men almost came to blows, but some of Gunn's friends got the colonel cooled off so that he simply demanded that Welscher leave. Welscher refused to do, and he was supported by William Stephens, on whom Gunn next turned his anger, only to be calmed once again by his friends.

Gunn eventually left for home, but Welscher continued celebrating until the party broke up around eleven thirty at night. At that point, so drunk that he could hardly stand, Joseph Welscher also staggered homeward, on a path that led by Gunn's house. As the captain passed the colonel's residence, Gunn called out that he wished to speak to him. Gunn's wife, frightened that her husband would "beat or kill" Welscher, immediately sent a servant to rouse a neighbor, John Berrien. When Welscher approached Gunn, the colonel stated that he had been waiting for him, and he snatched Welscher's sword away. Gunn asserted that Welscher had insulted him in public, which the captain denied, only to have his denials answered by the stings of Colonel Gunn's whip. The drunken, battered Welscher was spared further abuse by the timely arrival of John Berrien, who separated the two men and sent them to their homes.

Two days later, Welscher formally challenged Gunn to a duel, but Gunn refused, claiming that Welscher had already rejected similar overtures from him. According to Welscher, this flurry of unanswered challenges led Gunn to conclude that "he was justified in taking no further notice of the business but by arresting me; when that was got over, should my insults be offered him he would horsewhip me in every place he met me." Welscher asserted in the press that his own character, not Gunn's, had been impugned, and, in language strangely similar to that used by Gunn against Nathanael Greene two years earlier, he demanded satisfaction: "If Col. Gunn is superior to Captain Welscher, it does not therefore follow that Mr. Gunn is superior to Mr. Welscher—the one is a gentleman, and what is the other more."

Gunn ordered Welscher court-martialed on two counts of conduct unbecoming an officer: his actions on the Fourth of July; and his role in a similar drunken dispute nine months earlier with one James Simpson that, according to Welscher, had been a private matter unrelated to militia service. Welscher pleaded not guilty to both charges. The military court acquitted him on the first charge but found his conduct toward James Simpson "highly censurable" and recommended that Welscher's brigade commander, General James Jackson, issue an official reprimand in his brigade orders.

Gunn had the proceedings of Welscher's court-martial published in the *Georgia Gazette*, and in his letter to the paper's editor, he hinted broadly that James Jackson himself was behind Welscher's activities. According to Gunn, Welscher was "too contemptible and insignificant to attract further attention from me—but *as his conduct is secretly fanned*, though ostensibly disapproved, the regiment will have it in their power to judge from these proceedings, and determine for themselves." As for the "secret fanner" of Welscher's actions, Gunn hinted that the key to identifying him was the fact that Welscher had not been charged earlier for his role in the affair with James Simpson: "Had Gen. Jackson given me the information [about the earlier dispute] which is contained in his Brigade Order [reprimanding Welscher], Capt. Welscher should have been arrested at that time—but as that, and many other circumstances *equally* dishonorable, did not come to my knowledge 'till lately, I cannot be justly charged with delaying the business, or now bringing it forward, from any motives but *such* as are consistent with the *duty* I owe the regiment." Gunn concluded with another veiled thrust at Jackson, asserting that "I found Capt. Welscher an officer in the regiment when I got a command in it—by what means he obtained his first appointment might afford amusement for a speculative inquiry."

James Gunn's knack for keeping himself in the public eye did nothing to diminish his popularity. In December 1788, he was the top vote-getter among three candidates chosen to represent Chatham County in the upcoming state constitutional convention, and he finished fourth among fourteen successful candidates for the Chatham seats in the 1789 House of Assembly.[25] In both 1787 and 1788, the assembly elected Gunn to represent Georgia in the Continental Congress, though he declined to serve in both instances. The arc of James Gunn's political career in his adopted state climaxed on January 17, 1789, when he was chosen one of Georgia's first US senators under the new federal Constitution.

Surviving evidence from before the election does not even mention Gunn's candidacy for the Senate. Up-country men Abraham Baldwin, William Few, and George Mathews were believed to covet a seat in the Senate, as was low-country resident Edward Telfair, who lived in Burke County but had business interests in Savannah and Augusta. Telfair himself indicated that there were "four or five [Senate] candidates" from Chatham County.[26] Although not named specifically by Telfair, General Anthony Wayne also actively sought one of the state's Senate seats. Like his wartime commander, Nathanael Greene, Wayne had been presented with a low-country plantation by the Georgia legislature. By the fall of 1788, he estimated that he had sunk "10000 Guineas" into his new plantation and was deeply in debt. The general also had property in Pennsylvania; between 1782 and 1788, he traveled back to his prewar home frequently, even holding political office there in 1783, 1784–1785, and 1787.[27]

Unfortunately, extant explanations for Gunn's election to the Senate come from hostile sources. Both Wayne and one of his low-country allies, James Seagrove, ascribed Gunn's victory to the "*intrigues* &ca" on his behalf by Ruben Wilkinson, whom Seagrove described as "from our back Woods—low and illeterate [*sic*] as possible, but Served our *Honorable Senator Gunn* in geting [*sic*] him votes at the Election." Another observer with strong reasons for despising Gunn, Nathanael Greene's widow, Catherine, charged that Gunn "found means to purchase to voats [*sic*] of the common people (which the assembly is composed of) and which have made him Senator."[28]

While nothing in Gunn's previous career suggests that he was above resorting to bribery, a comparison of his position and that of Anthony Wayne in January 1789 is also instructive. Wayne was absent from Georgia for long periods of time, while Gunn preferred to remain in Savannah nursing his political influence, even to the point of declining to attend the Continental Congress in 1787 and 1788.[29] In 1789, Gunn had behind him an almost unbroken record of service in the state legislature and the Chatham militia, and as justice of the peace. Although Anthony Wayne was elected to several offices in Pennsylvania during that period, he had thus far proved incapable of establishing a place for himself in the politics of low-country Georgia. Perhaps seeking refuge from his creditors, Wayne returned to Georgia early in 1788 determined to secure election to the new federal Senate. To strengthen his hand, Wayne felt that he should travel to Augusta as a state legislator. He ran for the assembly from Chatham in the autumn of 1788 but was defeated by "the tory interest in Savannah and it's [*sic*] vicinity," or so he believed. Wayne began to consider a move to Wilkes County in the up-country. Moreover, following his defeat in the Chatham election, there was even talk of having Wayne represent up-country Franklin County in the state constitutional convention in place of an elected delegate who had resigned.[30]

These ploys, if they had succeeded, might have called into question General Wayne's place of residence in Georgia. A more immediate threat was spread, according to Wayne, by "the *Tories* & the friends of those who are candidates for the *Senate*," who claimed that the general's postwar sojourns in Pennsylvania meant that he was not a citizen of Georgia at all, a charge that Wayne hotly denied.[31]

If Anthony Wayne attended the legislative session of January 1789, he did so as a private citizen, just another anxious office-seeker. James Gunn, on the other hand, was in Augusta as both a member of the assembly and a delegate to the state constitutional convention, and he had demonstrated impressive public support in winning both posts. Wayne had played a prominent military role during the Revolution, but, perhaps because of the press of his affairs in Pennsylvania and his struggle to establish himself as a planter in Georgia, he seems to have eschewed service in the Georgia militia. Gunn, whose wartime record had been modest at best, had nevertheless thrown himself wholeheartedly into the affairs of the state militia and had risen rapidly through the ranks.

Finally, when the House of Assembly turned to the election of two senators on January 16, 1789, its members adopted a policy that helped to doom Anthony Wayne's candidacy. Aware of the role that sectionalism had already played in Georgia's post-Revolutionary history, the assemblymen moved to minimize its impact on the election of US senators. An up-country man, Florence Sullivan of Wilkes, moved that one of the senators must have been a resident for at least three years of one of the low-country counties (Chatham, Effingham, Burke, Liberty, Camden, or Glynn), while the other must hail from the up-country (Richmond, Wilkes, Franklin, Greene, or Washington). Sullivan's motion was seconded by a low-country man, Edward Telfair, and passed by the House.[32] The assembly did not proceed to elect senators that day, however. While the skeletal assembly minutes give no details of the debate on Sullivan's resolution, subsequent events suggest that the legislators had second thoughts about going on record as favoring a strict sectional division of the state's two Senate seats.

When the House reconvened the next day, Florence Sullivan moved that the previous day's resolution regarding the election of US senators be reconsidered, and the assembly agreed. Chatham representative Jacob Waldburger then moved to rescind the resolution. His motion was seconded by another low-country man, John Hardy of Liberty County, and the House rescinded Sullivan's resolution by the overwhelming margin of 60–13. Having removed the sectional criteria, the assembly proceeded to elect to the first United States Senate two men who fit those criteria to a tee, William Few of Richmond County and James Gunn from Chatham.[33]

So, while unwilling officially to establish a sectional precedent for senatorial elections, the members of the assembly nevertheless tacitly recognized the importance of an equal division of those important new officials between the state's contending regions in 1789. It was this decision that both blasted Anthony Wayne's hopes of representing Georgia in the federal Senate and thrust James Gunn onto the national stage. Even if Wayne's popularity was stronger in the piedmont than along the coast, as some observers believed, he could not claim that he resided in the up-country; thus, if he were to be elected at all, it would have to have been as the low country's senator. This he was unable to do, because of James Gunn.[34]

Gunn might have been only a captain of dragoons during the War for Independence, but in postwar Georgia politics, his grasp of strategy and tactics was superior to that of the more renowned Anthony Wayne. During the 1780s, Wayne had been content, or forced by circumstances, to rest on his Revolutionary laurels, while James Gunn, with nothing to lose and much to gain, had kept himself constantly in the public eye, occasionally even going to embarrassing lengths to do so. Wayne—and other observers, as well—had underestimated Gunn in January 1789, but they had not been the first to do so. Nathanael Greene, in pursuit of a higher principle, had overturned the board of officers' ruling favorable to Gunn, only to have Gunn, whose anger at this perceived stain on his honor had continued to smolder, challenge him to a duel three years later. James Jackson must have welcomed Gunn's support in his campaign against former Loyalist

Thomas Gibbons in 1785; yet, two years later, he felt the lash of Gunn's invective over both the conduct of Joseph Welscher and Chatham County's attitude toward the revised militia law.

Clearly, James Gunn was unwilling to permit either his status as a newcomer to Georgia or the scandal of the "public horse" to stand in the way of his political ambition. By 1789, his forceful personality and his sometimes shady character had carried him to the highest level of Georgia politics. As Gunn prepared to leave Georgia for the wider arena of the United States Senate, he took with him at least one lesson learned over the previous seven years in his new home: the importance of being truculent.

* * * * *

During his two terms in the Senate (1789–1801), Gunn moved from a stance of opposition to key measures proposed by George Washington's administration, including parts of Treasury secretary Alexander Hamilton's financial plan, to support for the more bellicose faction of the Federalist Party during the Quasi-War with France. Although the skeletal surviving Senate records hold few clues to the Georgian's thinking on these issues, it seems clear that he irrevocably cast his lot with the Federalists no later than 1795, when he was one of only two southern senators to vote in favor of the controversial Jay Treaty with Great Britain. Nevertheless, it also is likely that Gunn's support for that treaty was less the product of his view of the pact's merits than of his belief that, by voting to approve Jay's handiwork, he would stave off a congressional investigation into Georgia's infamous Yazoo land fraud, of which he had been the prime mover.

Probably because he represented a frontier state and had served in both the Continental Line and the Georgia militia, Gunn frequently was assigned to Senate committees dealing with military affairs, land, and frontier conditions. Like every member of the new Congress, Gunn quickly became involved in scuffling over local patronage appointments.[35] One of the Georgians Gunn hoped to reward was Reuben Wilkinson, whom he nominated for the collectorship of Savannah. Wilkinson reportedly had been a key figure in Gunn's victory for the Georgia Senate seat, but he also had been suspended from the Savannah collectorship, which had previously been a state office, for what his successor, Benjamin Fishbourn, called "Mal-Practices."[36] When Fishbourn himself was nominated as naval officer of Savannah by President Washington, Gunn and fellow Georgia senator William Few joined to block the appointment, forcing the embarrassed President to appoint Lachlan McIntosh instead. Fishbourn had been an aide-de-camp to Anthony Wayne during the Revolution and had supported the general in his unsuccessful campaign for one of Georgia's Senate seats, so Gunn and Few probably blocked Fishbourn's nomination because they viewed him as a Wayne man and not as someone beholden to either of them.[37]

Early in his first term in the Senate, James Gunn seemed (like Georgia Representative James Jackson) suspicious of the new administration's measures, although he was not inflexible. For example, between mid-May and late June 1789, Gunn moved from opposing the establishment of excise taxes to supporting them. When he saw that the Impost Bill would work hardships on the southern states, Gunn told a correspondent that "it is one of those things that can not be avoided, I thought a few weeks past that I never would be a friend to an Excise Law, Its [*sic*] a hateful tax, but the great portion that will fall on the northern States will be some compensation for the unequal manner in which the Impost Bill will operate." Gunn also opposed giving the president the power to remove heads of cabinet departments without the advice and consent of the Senate.[38]

Perhaps because of his militia service in Georgia, Gunn was suspicious of establishing a powerful regular army. In September 1789, for example, he supported a motion in the Senate to add to the House's proposed Fifth Amendment to the Constitution a paragraph characterizing standing armies in peacetime as "dangerous to Liberty;" demanding that military power be subordinated to civilian authority; requiring a two-thirds vote in both houses of Congress to raise regular troops in time of peace; and limiting military enlistments to one year.[39]

By the spring of 1790, Gunn was fuming about the "bare faced Conduct of [Rufus] King and [Oliver] Ellsworth in Supporting every Measure proposed by the Secretarys [*sic*]. Indeed their Toolism [*sic*] is sufficiently evident to every Body." Talk like this, as well as Gunn's continued opposition to the inappropriate use of federal force, had Pennsylvania senator William Maclay, a determined foe of strengthening the central government, quoting Gunn's views favorably in his diary and promising to "arrange matters so that [Gunn] will be taken notice of" when he visited Philadelphia.[40]

Gunn also voted against several key parts of Hamilton's financial plan, apparently fearing how much the Treasury secretary's grand design would strengthen the executive branch. On July 16, 1790, he opposed combining funding and assumption into "one system" and a few days later voted against establishing a national debt for the new republic. On January 20, 1791, Gunn supported a motion to reconsider the terms of incorporation of the Bank of the United States so that its charter would expire in 1801 rather than 1811, but the motion was defeated, 16–6. When he wrote to Georgia governor Edward Telfair a few days later, Gunn reported that the "objects of deliberation at present are the Bank and excise Laws … [T]he great Object of the Bank Bill is to consolidate the monied Interest of America and Strengthen, in an astonishing degree, the Executive department of the General Government, and an excise was necessary to discharge the Interest of the Assumed debt."[41]

In a sense, Gunn's ambivalent early votes on the power of the new central government reflected popular opinion in Georgia. In 1788, a state convention had ratified the federal Constitution unanimously, believing that a stronger national government would shield the state from dangers along its exposed frontier. Yet, as Hamilton's plans unfolded, some Georgians, following the lead of Georgia congressman James Jackson, drew back in alarm at the financial strength envisioned for the new government by its architect. Moreover, if the space devoted to criticism of specific measures of the Washington administration in the Georgia press is any indication, the major grievances nursed by Georgians between 1789 and 1794 had the same basis as former complaints against the Confederation Congress—the questions of sovereignty over the western territory and over Indian affairs.[42]

In August 1790, the administration negotiated the Treaty of New York with the Creek Indians, greatly angering many in Georgia. While the pact confirmed an earlier treaty by ceding to Georgia lands east of the Oconee River, it also returned to the Creeks the so-called "Tallassee Country," lands lying between the Altamaha and St. Marys Rivers that had been ceded to Georgia by a group of Creek chiefs in the disputed Treaty of Galphinton in 1785. The most galling provision of the New York treaty to Georgians was that it guaranteed indefinitely to the Creeks all the lands within the limits of the United States lying west and south of the boundaries established by the document, thereby seeming to threaten the future expansion of the state. Not surprisingly, both of Georgia's senators, Gunn and Few, voted against the treaty. In a letter to Alexander Hamilton on November 11, however, Gunn promised to try to persuade the Georgia legislature to adopt a moderate tone in protesting the treaty, and the relatively mild wording of the protest probably bears the imprint of Gunn's considerable political influence.[43]

By late 1791, Senator Gunn seemed eager to ingratiate himself with Secretary Hamilton. According to one jaundiced account of his conduct at a dinner in December, Gunn observed to Hamilton, "with that plain freedom he is known to use, 'I wish, Sir, you would advise your friend [Rufus] King, to observe some kind of consistency in his votes. There has been scarcely a question before the Senate on which he has not voted both ways. On the representation bill, for instance, he first voted for the proposition of the Representatives, and ultimately voted against it.' 'Why,' said Colonel Hamilton, 'I'll tell you as to that, Colonel Gunn, that it never was intended that bill should pass.'"[44]

Gunn's rivalry with James Jackson, which had originated in Georgia in the period between the end of the Revolution and the launching of the new federal government, heated up in the early 1790s. Perhaps it was a measure of the superiority of Jackson's organizational skills or the result of the weakness of the faction headed by Gunn, but Gunn usually delayed his departure for the nation's capital so that he could attend the annual session of the Georgia legislature. Between the initial session of the First Federal Congress and the second session of the Third Congress, he delayed his return to Congress anywhere between one and three months. For example, in November 1792, Jackson reported to his ally John Milledge that Gunn had been in Augusta during the legislative session and had been backing George Mathews for the United States Senate seat occupied by William Few. Because Jackson believed Few had no chance of being reelected, he claimed, he had allowed his own name to be placed in nomination, and he was chosen to succeed Few on November 30.[45] Gunn described what had occurred rather differently in a letter to General Anthony Wayne, explaining that he had delayed returning to Philadelphia because he needed to remain in Georgia until the legislature adjourned. He asserted that "Jackson premeditated a blow, which it was my duty to resist, and it ended in his disgrace, for he carried nothing, but his election [to the Senate], and that had been agreed on, many months previous to the meeting of the Legislature."[46]

By the end of 1793, Gunn apparently was aiming for the governorship. In early November, Jackson wrote his friend Milledge in Augusta about rumors he had heard regarding the approaching gubernatorial election. Jackson advised that, if Gunn offered for the post, Milledge should "struggle hard against any one else," because, if Gunn were chosen governor, Jackson expected Milledge to be chosen to replace Gunn in the Senate.[47] Near the end of December, Seaborn Jones of Augusta wrote to Georgia congressman Thomas P. Carnes, explaining that Gunn's plan to seek the governorship had failed. Carnes replied that, "you tell me that Gunn has been sick & that (if he intended to have been Governor) he was unfortunately [sick] two or three days before & after the meeting of the Legislature [.] I cannot say with certainty that Gunn wished for the Office, but my mind has a strong bias affirmatively." Carnes added that he was enclosing "cash to the amount of Six-hundred dollars, to do what is necessary on my part towards the completion of our Scheme—Engross as much Land as possible ... I have wrote to every body I could think of about Augusta." Thus, it seems likely that Gunn did indeed seek the governorship that fall, in hopes of using the office to support the sale of Georgia's western territory to companies of speculators.[48]

There already had been several unsuccessful efforts to separate Georgia from her western land claims since the end of the American Revolution, but by early 1794, land speculators were optimistic once more.[49] In addition to the allure of lands extending west to the Mississippi River (including present-day Alabama and Mississippi), various speculators were also trying to profit from peddling lands in the "pine barrens" of Effingham, Liberty, Glynn, and Camden counties in the southeastern part of the state. By mid-November 1794, two weeks into the annual session of the General Assembly, Representative David Mitchell of Chatham County told Judge Nathaniel Pendleton, who had come to Augusta to further a land scheme, that a large majority of the legislators favored the sale of the western territory and that a bill embodying this desire would be passed by both houses.[50]

So obvious was the speculative fever late in 1794 that one partner in a land company informed his company's agent in Augusta that the "extent and variety of the applications which will be made to the present session of the [Georgia] Assembly, will not a little embarrass the members, and, I fear, increase your difficulties."[51] Another observer wrote in disgust that "nothing is going on here but Land Speculation, which is conducted altogether by northern Sharks, together with a few Georgians who only act as lackeys." Far away in Philadelphia, Senator James Jackson was also well aware of the prevailing spirit in the Georgia capital, where, he wrote, "speculation, Oblivion & so on, I suppose will go together—well let them go."[52]

Speculators thronged the streets and shops in Augusta searching for money to invest, even as anonymous writers circulated printed handbills warning the public against "the arrival of prodigious sums from Amsterdam, in return for speculation in Glynn and Camden [counties]." To one writer in an Augusta paper, "Cassius," who was probably James Gunn, all the money arriving in the capital simply meant that the state legislature must "get clear of the bone of contention [the western territory] on the best terms you can." "Cassius" went on to recommend that "if parts [of the western lands] is disposed of to companies or individuals, you will have a full treasury and be immediately enabled to extinguish the Indian claims on a considerable part of the residue—This done, and bestowed gratis on the citizens of Georgia, in proportion to the number of free born persons in each family, must be an act of the strictest justice."[53]

Gunn was an organizer of one of the speculative groups, the Georgia Company. On November 28, 1794, about two weeks after he had been handily reelected by the legislature to the Senate, Gunn informed associate justice of the United States Supreme Court James Wilson that the various competing companies of speculators had arranged a compromise and thus had removed a stumbling block to the successful completion of their purchases. Their proposals were being considered by a joint committee of twenty-two, fourteen of whom were in favor of selling, but Gunn worried that none of the fourteen had the "capacity to place the Subject in a point of view to be understood by the ignorant." Gunn told Wilson that a majority of the legislators favored the sale and asserted that "we have taken measures which will ensure Success, But, my good Sir, they are to be executed by men whose want of Talents may ruin every thing."[54]

Just what were the "measures" Gunn had taken to ensure the successful purchase of Georgia's western territory by the speculators? Gunn applied lessons he had learned while watching Alexander Hamilton cultivate support for his financial plan: Gunn, like Hamilton, worked assiduously to attach men of wealth and influence to his scheme by appealing to their self-interest. In articles of agreement drawn up on January 1, 1795, before passage of the Yazoo Act in its final form, Gunn and his associates in the Georgia Company made this strategy explicit. The partners stated that they had found it "expedient to dispose of a considerable quantity" of the lands they hoped to secure "to diverse persons, for the purpose of raising a fund to effect the purchase of the same; and the said parties have also found it necessary to distribute to a variety of citizens of this State certain sub-shares or quantities thereof, in order that the benefit of such purchase, if any there be, should be as generously diffused as possible."[55]

To dispose of "money shares" costing one thousand pounds each, the proceeds from which were to be used as the down payment on the purchase, Gunn turned to a number of affluent Savannah merchants. In addition, Justice Wilson held shares valued at £25,000, and South Carolina congressman Robert Goodloe Harper owned a share of seventy-five thousand acres and a sub-share of fifty-six thousand acres. Gunn also might have had as a silent partner the wealthiest man in Georgia, and his sometime political ally, Savannah mayor Thomas Gibbons.[56]

With a single exception, every member of the Georgia General Assembly who voted for the Yazoo Act also held sub-shares in one or more of the enterprises, as did two other assemblymen who did not vote on the question of the bill's passage. Each of the companies set aside sub-shares for those members who "thought it right to sell the lands." The allotments were to be sold on the same terms as those for persons buying them after the bill was signed into law, except that, according to one source, the legislators "were not to pay any money therefore in advance." In the interim, senators and representatives who saw no conflict of interest in accepting the proffered shares could raise the purchase money by disposing of their holdings, either on their own or by selling them back to members of the speculating groups.[57]

The organizers of the Yazoo sale were careful to provide for a number of Georgians in key positions. State treasurer Philip Clayton held sub-shares in the Georgia Company for one hundred and twelve thousand acres. Both of Georgia's solicitors general were involved in Gunn's Georgia Company, and two of Governor George Mathews's personal secretaries held positions in the speculative hierarchy. Although he eventually voted against the bill, Mathews's son-in-law, state senator Samuel Blackburn, allegedly backed the sale in debate. Finally, two of those who had vigorously opposed the sale of the Yazoo lands in 1789, Seaborn Jones and John King, chose to cast their lots with the proponents of the sale in 1795. In addition to Gunn himself, three other Georgians occupying federal offices also supported the Yazoo cause. Federal district attorney Matthew McAllister was one of Gunn's partners in the Georgia Company, and Representative Thomas P. Carnes procured shares in both the Georgia Company and the Tennessee

Company, as did several members of his family. While Judge Nathaniel Pendleton—whose unsuccessful efforts in 1793 helped lay the groundwork for the later sale—denied any financial interest in the transaction, he did admit writing the bylaws of the Georgia Mississippi Company, some of whose members had been associated with the judge in 1793.[58]

Securing adherents in the General Assembly evidently was not intended merely to expedite passage of the Yazoo bill. Legislators were by virtue of their offices men of influence in their localities, and associates in the different companies expected support for the sale by willing legislators to dampen dissent among their constituents. To further this end, speculators also distributed sub-shares to other prominent Georgians, particularly those whose actions might carry weight in the up-country. Recipients of the landed largesse included longtime politicians as well as perennial aspirants for public favor. Former congressman Francis Willis had an interest in Cox's Tennessee Company. Militia leaders and veterans of the state's many Indian campaigns like Samuel Jack and John Appling received sub-shares, as did Elijah and John Clark of Wilkes County, along with one of Elijah's sons-in-law, Micajah Wilkinson. With an eye toward the inevitable newspaper war, Gunn saw to it that Alexander M'Millan, printer of the *Augusta Southern Centinel*, received twenty-eight thousand acres of Georgia Company land. If representative Robert Watkins of Richmond County supported the sale while remaining aloof from the prospective purchasers, at least two of his relatives, Thomas and Anderson Watkins, had no such scruples, the former being an associate in the Upper Mississippi Company, the latter a shareholder in the Tennessee Company. Another recipient of the Upper Mississippi Company's largesse was superior court judge George Walton, one of Georgia's signers of the Declaration of Independence and a former governor of the state.[59]

Even if this judicious division of the Yazoo spoils helped to ensure passage of the bill, there were other potential stumbling blocks that Gunn could not overlook. A majority of the legislature elected in 1794 might be unwilling, either from principle or from self-interest, to overturn the sale, but their successors, who were to be chosen on November 2, 1795, could conceivably be of a different opinion. Therefore, the Yazoo Act stipulated that final payment was due from the purchasing companies on or before November 1, 1795. Delegates to a state constitutional convention, which was to meet in May 1795, had been chosen at the same time as the members of the Yazoo legislature. Gunn probably realized that, if popular resistance to the sale of the western territory were fomented by agitators like James Jackson, an appeal might be made to this convention to nullify the purchase. When the fifty-six delegates assembled at Augusta, at least twenty had a financial interest in the Yazoo purchase.[60]

Statements given before a legislative committee investigating the Yazoo sale suggest other things Gunn probably did to ensure that the sale passed through the assembly and received the governor's assent. According to one legislator, Peter Van Allen, for example, land was allotted to each member of the legislative majority, "who were not to pay any money therefore in advance, and were particularly indulged, until the whole of the purchase money was payable at the treasury, in consequence of their vote and support of the law for selling the land."[61]

John Sheppard, a member of the Yazoo legislature who opposed the sale, testified that state treasurer Philip Clayton offered him seventy pounds, "at the request of General Gunn," if he would go home and not vote on the measure. At the ensuing session of the legislature, James Jackson used Sheppard's affidavit, as well as one from Robert Raines, as the basis for resolutions of impeachment against Clayton, claiming that Clayton, at the instigation of Gunn, had tried to bribe two members of the state senate, Sheppard and Henry Mitchell, to go home during the legislative session rather than vote against the bill.[62]

Another member of the Yazoo legislature, Robert Flournoy, implicated James Gunn in offering seventy-five thousand acres of western lands to himself and to state senator Henry Mitchell for supporting the measure. In fact, claimed Flournoy, Gunn had asserted "that no member of the Legislature should or could expect to have a share [of the Yazoo lands] if he did not vote for the bill." James Simms, a representative from Columbia County, told Jackson's investigating committee that Gunn had offered him fifty thousand acres of land for each member of the state senate he was able to convince to vote for the Yazoo sale. Henry G. Caldwell reported that Gunn had told him that he had given superior court judge William Stith $13,000 for his help in securing passage of the act.[63]

In the aftermath of the Yazoo sale, Gunn acted quickly to complete the transaction and to protect it in the nation's capital, while James Jackson tried to block completion of the sale. In the US Senate, for example, Jackson reported to a Georgia ally that he had successfully rebuffed an effort by Gunn and New York senator Aaron Burr to establish the right of the Yazoo speculators to the lands they had purchased. Shortly thereafter, a grand jury in Richmond County condemned Gunn's decision to absent himself from Congress in order to pursue his private interests in Augusta during the Yazoo session of the legislature.[64]

When Senator Gunn did return to the national capital to further his speculative venture, he also let it be known that his vote might be available when the time came for the Senate to pass judgment on John Jay's Treaty with Great Britain. New York senator Rufus King urged Alexander Hamilton to use his influence to persuade Gunn to vote for the treaty. Hamilton replied that, while his influence with the Georgian was "overrated," it would give him "real pleasure to be able to promote his accommodation or advantage; as my opinion intirely [*sic*] coincides with yours." A few days later, Gunn voted in favor of the Jay Treaty, one of only two southern senators to do so, while his senatorial colleague from Georgia, James Jackson, opposed it.[65] When news of Gunn's vote reached Georgia, a public meeting in Savannah carried effigies of Jay and Gunn in a cart, hanged them to a gallows erected on the South Common, and then lit a fire under them, "which soon consumed them in the presence of a numerous company of spectators."[66]

Gunn, trying to use Rufus King's good offices to dispose of the Yazoo lands, informed the New Yorker that he had heard the tale of the effigies being hanged and burned in Savannah, and that "it is honorable to be insulted by the most infamous." Less than two weeks later, Gunn thanked King for his help, adding that "through your assistance I have made an arrangement for Completing my last payment to the State, and should have made a handsome profit, But for the dishonorable interference of Some of my associates." Gunn's final payment to Georgia was $200,000; he then sold the lands to James Greenleaf for a $25,000 profit.[67]

According to Senator William Plumer of New Hampshire, writing six years after Gunn's death, Senator William Branch Giles of Virginia told him that Gunn had declared to Senator John Brown of Kentucky "that he had strong reasons, which he could not resist, to vote for the ratification of that [Jay] treaty—That those reasons, & not the conviction of his own mind, compelled him to do it. That the strong reasons were assurances from Rufus King that if he would vote for the treaty—their [Federalist] party would ratify & confirm the *Yazou* [*sic*] *claim.*—This fact said Giles I can prove.—But, added Mr. Giles, Gunn was deceived by the smooth language & sybtle [*sic*] insinuations of Mr. King—for King never made such assurances—for he was opposed to the Yazou [*sic*] claim—He only made insinuations which the ardent mind of Gunn appreciated beyond their true meaning—Gunn was deceived."[68]

James Jackson resigned from the Senate and returned to Georgia, where he led a successful campaign to elect an anti-Yazoo majority, including himself as a representative from Chatham County, to the next session of the General Assembly. Though the term *Federalist* was not employed in the newspaper warfare that ensued, Georgians were reminded over and over again that among leading Yazooists were prominent "friends of government," in addition to Senator Gunn, like Supreme Court justice James Wilson, South Carolina congressman Robert Goodloe Harper, and Georgians Thomas Glascock, Matthew McAllister, Thomas Carnes, Nathaniel Pendleton, and George Walton. The legislature investigated the circumstances surrounding the sale, with Jackson serving as spokesman, and concluded that "fraud, corruption, and collusion" had accompanied the transaction. Using this evidence, the committee brought in a bill declaring the Yazoo Act null and void; providing for the public destruction of records connected with the sale; and authorizing repayment of money deposited in the state treasury by the purchasers. The lower house passed this so-called Rescinding Act on February 1, 1796, by a vote of 44–3.[69]

Despite rumors and threats of impeachment of state officials like Treasurer Philip Clayton tainted by Yazoo, the legislature adjourned late in February 1796 without impeaching anyone; legislators simply refused to reelect officials involved in the sale. On the other hand, the General Assembly did criticize Senator Gunn for his role in the passage of the Yazoo Act, resolving that, because he "did attempt to corrupt and unwarrantably influence some of the Members" to vote for the sale, Gunn had "lost the confidence of this Legislature." Hence, the Georgia congressional delegation was instructed to work to amend the federal Constitution so that "the Legislature of any state [could] recall a Senator in Congress … whenever the same may be deemed necessary."[70]

Commenting on this resolution in the Federalist *Gazette of the United States*, James Gunn asserted that it had been included in a motion offered by Jackson himself, and thus its passage had been "dictated by a malevolent leader of a disappointed faction." The charges against him, the senator argued, were based on affidavits taken not "by a judicial process, and the opportunity of a cross interrogation; but by a secret committee, of which Jackson was chairman." Gunn emphasized Jackson's role in the no-confidence motion "because his enmity to me, on this ground, is well known. It is also well known, that there has been a ferment in Georgia for some time past; that [Jackson] had put himself at the head of a prevailing party, and has abused the public confidence." Gunn claimed he would welcome a fair legislative investigation into the purchase, since he believed he would be exonerated.[71]

Either because of this resolution or because of a speech by Georgia Representative Abraham Baldwin on March 2, 1796, against land speculators, Gunn demanded from Baldwin the right to peruse "any paper from the State of Georgia intended for public use" in his colleague's possession. When Baldwin refused, Gunn challenged him to a duel, only to have another congressman accuse Gunn of a breach of privilege. After Gunn apologized for his conduct, the House Committee on Privileges ruled that "any further proceedings thereon are unnecessary." When he learned of this exchange, James Jackson averred that he had practically had to force Baldwin to make the speech against speculators that had so riled Gunn, but he concluded smugly that he was "satisfied as it has turned out, it will answer the best of purposes."[72]

Tradition has it that Gunn and Jackson fought a duel over all of this. In a letter to Milledge, Jackson vowed that he would "fight [Gunn] if he demands it, but if he takes any other measure I am resolved to take his own steps with him."[73] By the end of 1796, Gunn was working with South Carolina Federalist congressman Robert Goodloe Harper to secure a cession of the Yazoo lands to the federal government. Nevertheless, at least one of Gunn's Georgia associates demanded that a Philadelphia correspondent "ask Gun[n] why he has neglected his friends, he ought to have been in Georgia."[74]

By mid-1797, according to James Jackson, Gunn had been "released by the premature death of his wife from the bonds of matrimony and will no doubt be soon, a beau Garcon in the gay rounds of the seat of Government." Jackson also related a salacious bit of gossip, though admitting he could not vouch for its veracity. He wrote that the late Mary Jane Gunn, "tired and weary of life and the miseries she had endured," had taken poison, adding that the "deed it is said was hastened by [Gunn's] insisting to come into the same room where she had confined herself from the time of his arrival, declaring she never would bed with him again."[75]

Even in the wake of his wife's death, Senator Gunn could not ignore his duties as chief dispenser of federal patronage in Georgia. For example, James Seagrove wrote Gunn recommending William Mowbray as collector of the port of St. Marys. Seagrove assured Gunn that "every thing go's [*sic*] on favourable in this Country—I believe we shall send such Men to the next Legislature as you will approve of; and also to the [state constitutional] convention [of 1798]." Whatever his qualifications were for the collector's post, Mowbray had received at least fifty-six thousand acres of land in Gunn's Georgia Company during the Yazoo sale. Writing to Treasury secretary Oliver Wolcott, Gunn referred to Mowbray as "a good friend to government," recommended by "some of the most respectable men in that quarter." President John Adams appointed Mowbray to the collectorship in March 1798.[76]

Georgia governor James Jackson was undoubtedly referring to Senator Gunn, who would soon be returning to the state to take his seat as a Camden County delegate to the May 1798 constitutional convention, when he commented late in February that all the Yazoo speculators were not in jail: "One of the biggest [is] about to leave his Seat to recorrupt the people." During the convention, Gunn refused to vote on several amendments proposed by Governor Jackson regarding land in general and Yazoo in particular, and on May 30, Gunn and Richmond County delegate (and fellow Yazoo speculator) Thomas Glascock refused to sign the new constitution, "they having leave to decline signing the Constitution agreeably to request."[77]

Gunn and Glascock refused to sign the new frame of government because, they claimed, those sections of the document related to the Yazoo sale amounted to an ex post facto law. When the delegates would not allow their protest to be included in the convention's journal, Gunn and Glascock published it in the Augusta *Southern Centinel*.[78] Because both dissidents were high-ranking militia officers, their refusal to sign the new state constitution—and Governor Jackson's angry reaction to that action—set off a controversy that dragged on for several years, with neither Gunn nor Glascock having the opportunity to defend his beliefs but with both men also continuing to hold their ranks in the militia.[79]

By late 1798, James Gunn had moved into the camp of the strongly anti-French, pro-war Federalist faction in the national capital. In the wake of news from France about the XYZ Affair, public opinion temporarily redounded in favor of President Adams, and Gunn initially seemed optimistic about a Federalist revival in Georgia. On October 1, he forwarded to Adams a fulsome address from Glynn County and noted that "I add with pleasure that Several of the Grand Juries in Counties which have long been under the influence of Jackson have declared their willingness to Support the Supreme Executive and Sir I am persuaded that there is little probability of either *Baldwin* or *Milledge* being returned to the next Congress." About a week later, a group of Federalists gathered in Savannah to show their approval of Adams's policy toward France and Gunn's conduct in the Senate.[80]

As tension mounted over French seizures of American shipping, the Federalists moved to create a provisional army, and James Gunn was one of the candidates for a post in it. Alexander Hamilton, who was to serve as inspector general of the provisional army under the command of former president George Washington, asked Gunn how he would feel about joining the new force. "If we are to be seriously engaged in military operations," Hamilton wrote, "tis not a compliment to you to say that you are one of those men who must be in the field." Gunn replied that "trained up in the honorable pursuit of a military life, I frankly confess my regard for you as a commander, and my passion for military service." Still, Gunn also claimed that he was "disgusted with every thing connected with public life" and was determined "not to be commanded by *some men* now in commission." Nevertheless, he entreated Hamilton "to believe that it will give me infinite pleasure to do you all the service in my power." Hamilton responded that he was "very glad to ascertain the military ground upon which you are willing to stand. If things progress, I trust there will be no obstacle to your occupying it."[81]

A few weeks later, however, Gunn no longer believed Federalist fortunes in Georgia would revive in the wake of the XYZ Affair. According to Massachusetts Federalist Theodore Sedgwick, writing to Rufus King, "Gunn gives us no hope of a reformation in Georgia, but [Abraham] Baldwin, who has lost his election as a member of the house, will I fear be chosen [for the US Senate]."[82] Gunn was also, at the same time, apparently supplying Republicans with information about Federalist plans in the upcoming presidential election. According to Thomas Jefferson, Republican senator W. C. Nicholas of Virginia told him that "Gunn, who goes with [the Federalists], but thinks in some degree with [the Jeffersonian Republicans]," contended that the Federalists were willing to break up the Union if a Republican should be elected president in 1800.[83]

As chairman of the Senate's special committee on defense, Gunn continued to work with Secretary of War James McHenry and Alexander Hamilton to organize legislation needed to create a provisional army.[84]

Despite these efforts, and regardless of Hamilton's supposed high opinion of his military ability, Gunn's dream of concluding his public career in a blaze of martial glory was doomed to disappointment. General Charles Cotesworth Pinckney informed Federalist congressman Robert Goodloe Harper that "with regard to what you mention respecting the Secretary's wishes relative to Genl. Gunn, of whose military talents I have a very high opinion, ... neither a Brigadier nor Colonel of Cavalry is to be appointed from Georgia, but merely a Colonel of Infantry ... From the manner in which your letter is expressed, I take it for granted that Genl. Gunn would not wish to be brought forward as a Colonel of Infantry."[85]

Gunn had been "disgusted" with public life in December 1798; a year later, he told Seaborn Jones that he intended "to quit this ground," presumably because he recognized that, thanks to James Jackson's success in overturning the Yazoo sale, he stood no chance of being reelected to the Senate.[86] If Republicans in Georgia were aware of Gunn's determination to leave the Senate, they ignored it, choosing instead to bandy his name about during the 1800 campaign as a kind of Federalist/Yazooist bogeyman to energize the party faithful. For Georgia Republicans, the question of Gunn's reelection became highly symbolic: to retire him from office would seal the triumph of the anti-Yazoo campaign. The thoroughly anti-Yazoo and increasingly Republican legislature chose Jackson to succeed Gunn in the Senate.[87]

During the presidential election campaign of 1800, Gunn favored John Adams's running mate, Charles Cotesworth Pinckney, for president, probably because Gunn opposed Adams's controversial effort to settle the nation's differences with France short of all-out war. In May, he informed John Rutledge Jr. of South Carolina that "Mr. *Adams*, and his Dear friend Mr. *Jefferson* have been *twice closeted* together since Saturday last, and it is Generally understood to be [agreed?] on between [them] that Genl. Pinckney is not to be the President—A. declares Mr. J—the only man in American qualified to fill the appointment, Except himself." A few days later, Gunn advised Rutledge to "make the *question* Genl. Pinckney against any other man, and say but little about Federal, or anti-Federal."[88]

In the aftermath of the presidential election, Gunn wrote Hamilton, urging him to reunite the Federalists. He recommended "the policy of the federal party *extending the influence of the Judiciary*" before the expiration of Adams' term, or else see the Republicans do so when the new Congress assembled. Gunn argued that "men of sense in every State, must go into the State legislature, and mind for *future events.* With the aid of some judicious management, the federal party will unite in every quarter, and, *in future* men of *sense* will be preferred, and the bloated pride of an individual treated with disdain."[89]

Early in December 1800, the Convention of Mortefontaine, ending hostilities between the United States and France, was presented to the Senate by President Adams. In a letter to Hamilton, Gunn described the convention as "detestable. The independence of our country humbled to the dust." The Georgia senator added that if, as current rumor had it, both Jefferson and Burr received seventy-three votes in the Electoral College, it was "probable that the federalists will have to choose among rotten apples." Gunn dug in his heels on both the French Convention and the election of the president, informing Hamilton that, while a rejection of the agreement with France "would excite some unpleasant feeling in America," ratification "would be dishonorable." Turning to the tangled dispute over the next president, Gunn opined that Congress would not elect Burr, adding that he believed "the democrats have taken their ground with a fixed resolution to destroy the government rather than yield their point. I feel that some of our friends have committed themselves by writing improperly to Burr. We know the man, and those who put themselves in his power will repent their folly." The French convention failed of ratification on January 23, 1801. Sentiment swung the other way after the vote, however, with Hamilton urging that it would be "better to close the thing where it is than leave it to a Jacobin Administration to do much worse." The Senate reconsidered the convention, and, after making a few changes, approved it on February 3, 1801, with Gunn voting for the settlement.[90]

Knowing that he would leave the Senate in March 1801, and aware that a Republican would be the next president, James Gunn acted upon his earlier sentiments to Hamilton that the Federalists needed to secure control of the judiciary in order to perpetuate their ideas in a Republican world. On February 21, 1801, he wrote to President Adams, recommending Thomas Gibbons of Savannah for the federal judgeship in the eastern district of Georgia. Gibbons was the leader of a Savannah Federalist clique, a sometime ally of Gunn, and a longtime foe of James Jackson, but Gunn termed him "well qualified" and "a Gentleman of great professional abilities." Gibbons received the appointment, much to Jackson's chagrin, but eventually the new president, Thomas Jefferson, saw to it that Gibbons, and Adams's other "midnight appointments," were not allowed to take their posts, a decision that eventually produced the landmark Supreme Court decision of *Marbury v. Madison* (1803) establishing the doctrine of judicial review.[91]

Following the expiration of his second Senate term, Gunn returned to Georgia, where he died on July 30, 1801, only four days after arriving in the capital of Louisville. According to one source, Gunn's death "was owing greatly to a draught of cold water after the taking of medicine, and what is strange, the doctor and several gentlemen were in the room, and not one observed his death till some time after he expired." He was buried with the honors of war in what is now the Old Capitol Cemetery.[92]

So controversial had James Gunn become that even death did not immediately remove him from the public eye. Contributors to James Jackson's organ in the state capital offered a sarcastic obituary for "General Yazoo." A week later, in the Federalist sheet in Savannah, an account of Gunn's funeral ended with the hope that he was "now beyond the reach of friendship, or of hatred; nor can his ashes be affected by censure or by praise. May he rest in peace."[93]

Early in September, two of Jackson's journalistic defenders leveled yet another charge at the departed Gunn. Asserting that they did "nothing more than a justice to the memory of Brigadier-General Gunn," they asked that the editor of the *Columbian Museum* insert an excerpt from an obituary that had appeared in the firmly Republican *Aurora* in Philadelphia: "General GUNN appears to have shaken off this mortal coil at a season when his services could no longer be useful. The Editor of the *Aurora* will bear testimony of the usefulness of general GUNN; and acknowledges that *to him* the public was indebted for the exposure of the memorable *Caucuses* and many other intrigues of the *Tories* in Congress."[94]

*****

A study of James Gunn's career in Georgia reveals much about the character and personality of one of the state's most controversial politicians during the Early Republic. Physically imposing and quick-tempered, Gunn brooked no interference with his political ambitions.[95] Between 1782 and 1789, he unsuccessfully challenged retired General Nathanael Green to a duel, for what he considered a slight on his honor during the Revolution; assailed Georgia Revolutionary hero James Jackson in the press; horsewhipped a militia subordinate—and Jackson ally—in a drunken brawl at the end of a particularly raucous Fourth of July celebration; and defeated several better-known candidates, including General Anthony Wayne, for one of Georgia's United States Senate seats in January 1789.

In some ways, the emergence of James Gunn as Georgia's most prominent Federalist was not surprising. He was an arrogant, ambitious man who saw himself as a member of the political, social, and economic elite and had scant patience with those he considered beneath him. Despite a lackluster record during the Revolution, Gunn was proud of his service in the Continental Army, and after moving to Georgia at war's end, he became active in the Society of the Cincinnati, succeeding General Wayne as head of the Georgia chapter in July 1792.[96]

Regardless of the ideas he brought with him to Georgia, Gunn's early political career was shaped by other factors, as well. He staked out a position in the rough-hewn political culture of the young republic's southernmost state in the years after the Revolution as a planter, high-ranking militia officer, magistrate, and politician; each of these activities reflected local or state—rather than national—forces. Gunn became a political opponent of James Jackson in the context of Georgia politics, for example, so few politically savvy Georgians were probably surprised when, upon entering the United States Senate, Gunn aligned himself on the opposite side from Jackson on some major issues. Yet, at first, the new Georgia senator also opposed, or at least harbored misgivings about, several proposals advanced by the administration, including the creation of a standing army and Treasury secretary Hamilton's financial plan.

As the new government created by the federal Constitution began to operate, however, Gunn first showed himself a "friend of government," then became a Federalist, and, by the late 1790s, was an avid supporter of the more bellicose faction of the Federalist Party at the time of the Quasi-War with France.[97] James Gunn, who had opposed a standing army in 1789, became an important cog in the Federalist effort to create a provisional army a decade later and even hoped to win a post in the new organization. What solidified his commitment to Federalist politics was his role as chief architect of the Yazoo land sale. Gunn had learned from watching Hamilton how economic self-interest could be harnessed to political ideology. He combined this lesson with his military experience to devise a strategy by which he hoped to secure passage of the Yazoo Act and enable purchasers to dispose of their lands. Although illness apparently kept him from being elected governor of Georgia in 1793, as part of his plan to further the sale of the state's western territory, Gunn was still able to push the act through the legislature in 1794, marshalling his forces like the militia general he was and using methods judged by the succeeding legislature to have been corrupt.

In the aftermath of the Yazoo sale, Gunn paid scant attention to the fortunes of his fellow Georgia Federalists, preferring to arrange for the sale of *his* Yazoo lands to northern speculators, using the assistance of Federalist leaders like New York senator Rufus King to grease the skids for the sale. Apparently in return for King's good offices, Gunn became one of only two southern senators to vote for Jay's Treaty, which was so unpopular, especially in the South, that it was ratified in the Senate by only a single vote. In 1799, a Virginia Republican described Gunn to Thomas Jefferson as a senator who voted with the Federalists much of the time but also agreed with the Republicans on some issues. A sarcastic obituary of Gunn in the Republican Philadelphia *Aurora* suggested that there was some truth in that characterization of the Georgia senator.

James Gunn shared certain aspects of Federalist ideology, but the motive force for his actions following passage of the Yazoo Act in 1795 was his desire to dispose of his share of the western lands at a substantial profit before Georgia had time to reconsider the sale. He was successful, though he also complained that, because of interference from some of his associates, he had not received as much money as he had hoped. Moreover, while Gunn was busy locating buyers for Georgia Company lands, his longtime rising Republican rival, James Jackson, managed both to have the Yazoo Act rescinded and to construct a formidable anti-Yazoo—and anti-Federalist—majority in that body, which doomed Gunn's chances for election to a third term in the Senate. Perhaps out of disappointment over this development, or because, like many Federalists, he genuinely feared revolutionary France in the late 1790s, Gunn threw himself energetically into efforts by one faction of his party to create a provisional army as a shield against the French and their American sympathizers. This effort also failed, and former senator Gunn returned to Georgia in 1801, where he died within a few days of his arrival. A politician of marked ability but few scruples, James Gunn, Georgia Federalist, was the architect of his own destruction.

Chapter 11

The Yazoo Land Fraud and the Politics of Up-Country Georgia

[**NOTE:** I had begun research on what I hoped would be the sequel to my first book in 1996. My progress was steady but slow. I remember wondering if there were any way I could jump-start some of the research; as it turned out, there was. My old friend, Professor Edward Cashin of Augusta College and State University mentioned me to an acquaintance of his, Dr. Sophia Bamford, who was organizing a lecture series about the history of the "dead town" of Petersburg in the Broad River Valley of northeast Georgia. Dr. Bamford contacted me and asked if I would be willing, in April 2002, to offer a paper on the politics of the area. She suggested something on the "Politics of Petersburg," I countered with "The Yazoo Land Fraud and the Politics of Up-Country Georgia," Dr. Bamford agreed, and I was off.

The up-country was the section most agitated by land hunger during the late eighteenth century, and, for that reason, securing the support of up-country men was central to US senator James Gunn's strategy to push the Yazoo Act through the legislature. Moreover, in the wake of the Yazoo business, control of the up-country also was a key plank in the platform of the leader of the anti-Yazoo forces, James Jackson. Jackson chose William Harris Crawford as the leader of his faction's forces in the up-country. And Crawford's rise cannot be understood apart from the opposition furnished by young General John Clark, who not only had received some Yazoo lands but also refused to kowtow to James Jackson when it came to his political future. In other words, it seemed to me that focusing on the impact of Yazoo in the up-country might furnish an opportunity to begin making the transition from the years of Jackson's political supremacy in Georgia to the more contentious decades following his death in 1806.

In June 2002, I wrote a brief account of this adventure for the History Department *Newsletter*, published under the title "George's Ego," thanks to newsletter editor Jere Link (though, as you'll see, I had no problem with that title):

Tignall [Georgia] is about 125 miles east of Atlanta, in Wilkes County, only a few miles from the Savannah River. The "town" consists of a couple of gas stations; a combination police station/city hall; a café open daily from 6:00 am to 2:00 pm; a small grocery store; a couple of nondescript shops; an auto repair place; and the site of the lecture, the North Wilkes Library, a converted bank building at the far end of town. As compact as Tignall is, we were nearly late because we got caught behind the town school bus, which seemed to stop every hundred feet or so in the three block "downtown area." That Tignall still exists is due primarily to Dr. Sophia Bamford, an 88 year-old retired physician and the organizer of the lecture series of which my talk was a part. Dr. Bamford, a Tignall native, returned to her hometown after a distinguished medical career in the Boston area. She was determined to keep Tignall alive by stirring up interest in the region's history, and her strategy apparently has worked. This year's lecture series was the seventh she has put together since returning from Boston—and, so she tells me—her last.

Between 50 and 60 people attended the lecture, and the average age in the room had to be upwards of 60. Still, members of the audience were there because they *wanted* to be, which meant that, believe it or not, interest in the topic was high. The Q & A session following the talk was lively, as was the conversation at the reception afterwards.
The essay is published here for the first time.]

* * * * *

The Yazoo land fraud was one of the most significant events in the post-Revolutionary history of Georgia and the nation. The bizarre climax to a decade of frenzied speculation in the state's public lands, the Yazoo sale of 1795 did much to shape Georgia politics during the Early Republic. James Jackson skillfully used popular outrage at the corruption accompanying the sale both to overturn the transaction and to construct the state's first true political party. Nationally, efforts by disappointed Yazoo speculators to obtain compensation from Congress helped split the nation's ruling party, the Jeffersonian Republicans, and led to a landmark Supreme Court decision. Finally, the terms under which the state eventually disposed of the disputed territory to the national government strained relations between Georgia and Washington for a generation.

* * * * *

Georgia was too weak after the American Revolution to defend its vast western land claims, comprising the modern states of Alabama and Mississippi and referred to as the "Yazoo lands" because the Yazoo River flowed through part of them. The legislature listened eagerly to proposals from speculators willing to pay for the right to establish settlements. In the early 1780s, Georgia supported two unsuccessful projects to create counties in the western territory and in 1788 tried, again without success, to cede a portion of those lands to Congress. In 1789, the legislature sold about twenty-five million acres to three companies, only to torpedo the sale six months later by insisting that payment be made in gold and silver rather than depreciated paper currency.[1]

Pressure continued to build on legislators to act. A group of speculators headed by Georgia federal district judge Nathaniel Pendleton tried in 1793 to purchase a portion of the state's public domain but failed to persuade the legislature. By mid-November 1794, however, a majority of that body reportedly favored sale of the western territory. Governor George Mathews vetoed the first law embodying this apparent consensus in December, but a revised version secured his assent on January 7, 1795. This "Yazoo Act" transferred an estimated thirty-five million acres to four companies for $500,000. To bring off this speculative coup, the leader of the Yazoo forces, Georgia's Federalist US senator James Gunn, arranged to distribute money and land to legislators, state officials, newspaper editors, and other influential Georgians. Cries of bribery and corruption accompanied the measure as it made its way to final passage. Angry Georgians protested the sale in petitions, grand jury presentments, and street demonstrations. Despite the swelling opposition, the Yazoo companies completed their purchases and set about disposing of their landed booty.[2]

Learning of the circumstances surrounding passage of the Yazoo Act, Georgia's leading Jeffersonian Republican, US senator James Jackson, resigned his seat and returned home, determined to overturn the sale. Making skillful use of county grand juries and newspapers, Jackson and his allies gained control of the legislature in a tumultuous campaign. After holding hearings substantiating the corruption charges, Jackson dictated the terms of the 1796 Rescinding Act, nullifying the Yazoo sale. He also arranged for the destruction of records connected with the sale; ensured that state officials tainted by Yazoo were denied reelection and replaced by his own anti-Yazoo, pro-Jefferson supporters; and, in 1798, orchestrated a revision of the state constitution that included the substance of the Rescinding Act.[3]

By the mid-1790s, party lines had begun to solidify in Congress between Federalists and Jeffersonians but had not yet had much impact in Georgia. An early supporter of Jefferson, James Jackson used the fact that the most prominent "corrupters" of the Yazoo legislature were Federalists to march Georgia into the ranks of the Jeffersonian Republican Party. During his governorship (1798–1801) and his last term in the US Senate (1801–1806), Jackson and his allies established Jeffersonian newspapers in the state capital, Louisville, and in Augusta and Savannah, and adroitly wielded patronage to transform what had been a coastal political faction into a statewide political party.[4]

To prevent those claiming lands under the Yazoo purchase from receiving a sympathetic hearing in a Congress dominated by Federalists, Jackson and his lieutenants blocked any cession of the western territory until the Republicans were in control. In 1802, after the triumph of the Jeffersonians in the presidential and congressional elections of 1800, commissioners from Georgia, including Jackson, transferred the land, and the Yazoo claims, to the federal government: the United States paid Georgia $1.25 million and agreed to extinguish the remaining claims of Native Americans to areas within the state as quickly as that could be done on peaceful terms.[5]

* * * * *

The ramifications of the Yazoo fraud in Georgia were tremendous, especially in the up-country, where land hunger had been endemic for decades. One of the four successful groups of Yazoo speculators in 1795, the Georgia Mississippi Company, was comprised of Augusta residents, including veteran Richmond County legislator and militia leader General Thomas Glascock. Moreover, virtually all the up-country legislators who voted for the Yazoo Act had accepted either sub-shares in the purchase or money from the organizers.

Judge William Stith of Warren County figured prominently in the passing out of favors to legislators. Up-country congressman Thomas Carnes, who had received land from at least two of the purchasing companies, and Richmond County legislator Robert Watkins, the only member of the lower house to vote for Yazoo without accepting either money or land (though several of his relatives did), were staunch defenders of the sale throughout the late 1790s. George Walton of Richmond County, one of Georgia's signers of the Declaration of Independence, a former governor, and veteran jurist, joined Carnes and Watkins in penning newspaper essays defending Yazoo and attacking the motives of those who rescinded the sale. In order to ensure the support of influential Georgians who were not in the General Assembly, the prospective purchasers distributed sub-shares to prominent men throughout the state. Among the up-country recipients were Elijah Clarke and his son John, and Alexander M'Millan, proprietor of the *Southern Centinel*, one of Augusta's two newspapers.[6]

Yet the involvement of prominent up-country men in Yazoo and its defense did not seem to weaken their influence in the region. Watkins and Glascock continued to represent Richmond in the General Assembly, and both men were elected to the 1798 constitutional convention. Walton was returned to the bench by the legislature. According to James Jackson himself, the political strength of Carnes and William Stith remained formidable in the piedmont, and it was all he and his supporters could do to keep them out of the US Senate, the national House of Representatives, and the governor's chair between 1798 and 1801.[7]

The legislature appointed brothers Robert and George Watkins to compile a new digest of Georgia laws. When they dared to include the Yazoo Act in their compilation, however, Governor Jackson refused to pay them and saw to it that William Harris Crawford and Horatio Marbury were put in charge of the project. The resulting Marbury and Crawford digest did not include the Yazoo Act; the defiant Watkins brothers had their volume, Yazoo Act and all, printed out of state.[8]

Even most of the up-country men who joined James Jackson in opposing the Yazoo sale were not averse to land speculation. Either they opposed only the corruption that had lubricated the sale or, if one believes their Yazoo critics, they were disappointed at their inability to force themselves into the companies organized by successful purchasers. William Few of Columbia County and General John Twiggs of Richmond County, who allegedly organized a raucous demonstration in the streets of Louisville in an unsuccessful effort to influence Governor George Mathews to veto the sale, had been members of the Georgia Union Company, a late-blooming organization whose bid for the western territory had been rejected by the legislature because they offered too little, too late. Another opponent of Yazoo, Richmond County legislator James McNeil, had dabbled unsuccessfully in land speculation in an effort to block the 1789 Yazoo sale. Among Jackson's up-country allies, the one who seemed least interested in land speculation was Congressman Abraham Baldwin, a native of Connecticut who resided in Wilkes County.[9]

Surely the most determined supporter of Yazoo and, thus, the most vigorous opponent of James Jackson in Georgia, was Richmond County's Robert Watkins. The ink had hardly dried on the Yazoo Act before Watkins leaped to its defense in Alexander M'Millan's *Southern Centinel*. He later used the columns of Augusta's other newspaper, the *Chronicle*, to attack the arguments in Jackson's pamphlet, *The Letters of Sicilius*, the Bible of the anti-Yazooists in the campaign to overturn the sale.[10] The pugnacious Watkins was one of only three representatives to vote against the Rescinding Act in 1796. In February 1797, the Richmond legislator introduced a bill that would have ceded the western territory (and, of course, the Yazoo claims) to the federal government; the measure was defeated overwhelmingly.[11]

As a member of the 1798 state constitutional convention, Robert Watkins signed the revised frame of government only under protest, arguing that adding the Rescinding Act to the Georgia constitution amounted to an ex post facto law impairing the obligation of contract. Convention delegates Thomas Glascock and James Gunn, who had been leaders among the Yazoo purchasers, refused to sign the constitution. Because Watkins, Glascock, and Gunn were high-ranking militia officers and, thus, required to defend Georgia and its constitution, an angry Governor James Jackson convinced the legislature to require all militiamen to subscribe an oath promising to support the revised state constitution. The ensuing loyalty oath controversy kept the state's military arm in turmoil for several years.[12]

Robert Watkins did not confine his opposition to James Jackson to the halls of the legislature or the convention. After the adjournment of the General Assembly in February 1796, for example, he accosted Jackson in the streets of Louisville and asked him "how he could reconcile it to his own feelings to have headed a vile party during the [legislative] session to the general injury of the whole state, and in unfounded attacks upon the reputation of a number of good men." That kind of question, Jackson later recalled, "flesh & blood of such texture as mine would not bear." In the ensuing scuffle, the two men fought with whips, pistols, bayonets, and fists before they were separated.[13]

Jackson and Watkins clashed again several months later, this time in the streets of Savannah. Most of the lawyers in the seaport to attend the federal court session reportedly snubbed Jackson, but Jackson considered Watkins's conduct particularly galling, for when he accosted the Augusta attorney near the bay, Watkins merely laughed in his face. Jackson brooded over this insult for about an hour, complaining to his friends and vowing his "determination of caning Watkins the first place he should meet him" and then set out to find his antagonist. When the two men finally met, they took up where they had left off in Louisville, pummeling each other with fists and sword canes. According to an eyewitness account by a Watkins partisan, the Augustian was "drubbing [Jackson] pretty soundly when they were parted by the magistracy."[14]

Even as Robert Watkins was doing his best to oppose Jackson in Georgia, Congressman Thomas Carnes and Senator James Gunn were working assiduously, if unsuccessfully, in Congress to smooth the way for the Yazoo speculators.[15] Meanwhile, the state legislature, spurred by Chatham representative James Jackson, passed the Rescinding Act and a series of resolutions designed to punish those who had worked to secure passage of the Yazoo bill. One of the resolutions charged that, because Senator Gunn "did attempt to corrupt and unwarrantably influence some of the Members" of the 1795 legislature to vote for the Yazoo Act, he had "lost the confidence of this Legislature." Hence, the Georgia congressional delegation was instructed to work for an amendment to the federal Constitution "authorizing the Legislature of any state to recall a Senator in Congress therefrom whenever the same may be deemed necessary."[16]

Either because of this resolution or because of a speech by Congressman Abraham Baldwin on March 2, 1796, castigating land speculators, Senator Gunn demanded the right to peruse "any paper from the State of Georgia intended for public use" in Baldwin's possession. When Baldwin refused, Gunn challenged him to a duel, only to have one of Baldwin's fellow congressmen accuse the senator of a breach of privilege. After the Georgia senator and his "friend" in the affair, Senator Frederick Frelinghuysen of New Jersey, apologized for their conduct, the House Committee on Privileges ruled that "any further proceedings thereon are unnecessary."

When he learned of this exchange, James Jackson commented that "if I had not pushed [Baldwin] at Philadelphia ... and here ... with *the papers*—the speech [of March 2] would never have been made nor the correspondence [between Gunn and Baldwin] have taken place— ... but enough—I am satisfied as it has turned out, it will answer the best of purposes."[17]

Since state officials were elected annually, most of those implicated in the great land fraud were swept from office by the anti-Yazoo legislature in 1796 and replaced by men opposed to the sale. For example, Peter Van Allen, a New York native who had settled in Petersburg to practice law, had testified against the Yazoo speculators before Jackson's legislative investigating committee; Van Allen was chosen one of the state's solicitors general. As Jackson consolidated his control of Georgia in the wake of the Rescinding Act, he insisted that appointees and legislative hopefuls combine opposition to Yazoo with a firm commitment to Jeffersonian Republicanism. This policy not only allowed Jackson to reward experienced politicians but it also enabled him to attach political newcomers to his party, including a rising young attorney from Lexington, William Harris Crawford. As Jackson wrote to an ally in 1801, "We must take some of those Friendly young men by the hand."[18]

Jackson also was not averse to encouraging dissension among his foes. For example, in March 1795, as he rallied his allies to assault the forces of Yazoo, Jackson urged General John Twiggs to "humour [*sic*] young Genl [John] Clark," who had recently quarreled publicly with Senator Gunn over the latter's refusal to deliver a promised share in the Georgia Company to Clark. Like his father Elijah, John Clark was a powerful figure among the transplanted North Carolinians of the Georgia up-country, and trying to neutralize his influence on the Yazoo question made good political sense to Jackson. As he wrote at the time, "all is fair play & if we heartily go to work we will upset their dirty work."[19]

James Jackson's desire to establish Republican newspapers in the state's major towns also affected the up-country. At the time of the Yazoo fraud, there were two papers in Augusta, the *Chronicle*, which clung to the old-fashioned notion that an editor should be impartial on controversial issues, and the *Southern Centinel,* whose editor, Alexander M'Millan, had received a sub-share of twenty-eight thousand acres of Yazoo land from the Georgia Company and who opened his columns mainly to bitter foes of Jackson. During his governorship, Jackson helped to drive M'Millan out of business by refusing to pay him for services supposedly rendered the state.

Up-country men opposed to the governor did not lack an outlet for their political venom, however, for several months before M'Millan closed up shop, George F. Randolph and William J. Bunce established the pro-Yazoo, anti-Jackson *Augusta Herald.*[20]

The *Herald* was soon engaged in a no-holds-barred struggle with the governor's newly established sheet in the capital, the *Louisville Gazette & Republican Trumpet.* Jackson and his associates were convinced that the *Herald* had a "secret editor," New England expatriate William J. Hobby, who had parlayed his uncompromising Federalism into the federal postmaster's job in Augusta.[21] Once elected to the US Senate in 1801, Jackson persuaded Postmaster General Gideon Granger that Hobby was mixing political partisanship with his federal duties, and the Augusta postmaster was removed from office. Although his firing freed Hobby to join the *Herald* officially, Jackson was able to checkmate his editorial efforts to some extent by procuring the services of an experienced Jeffersonian editor, Dennis Driscoll, to take over the rival *Augusta Chronicle* in 1803.[22]

Disputes growing out of the socio-economic differences between the coast and the up-country had been a constant feature of Georgia politics since before the Revolution. This sectionalism was something James Jackson could not afford to ignore as he extended the Jeffersonian-Republican Party across the state. Thus, even though Jackson and his associates killed Yazoo, they also attempted to satisfy the land hunger of frontier residents by exerting constant pressure on the national government to secure additional land cessions from the Indians. This policy was to become both bipartisan and permanent in the decades ahead.

Up-country men also chafed because most members of the state's congressional delegation hailed from the coast. As one piedmont resident wrote sarcastically in 1798, "It is certainly a great stretch of political indulgence, to us poor ignorant backwoods people, that any man above Chatham or Effingham [counties], could be found having sense enough to go to Congress." In deadly earnest, he added that "From numbers and respectability," up-country residents were "justly entitled, to an equilibrium in the political balance. Our complaisance to the eastern members has been so great, that for some years they have had three members in Congress, and the back country but one; whereas the scale ought to be reversed."[23] In response to such complaints, James Jackson and his up-country supporters apparently worked out a division of responsibility: after 1801, up-country Republicans received a majority of the state's congressional seats, while the governorship was conferred regularly upon Jackson's low-country lieutenants.

*****

Perhaps the most significant effect of the Yazoo land fraud on the politics of up-country Georgia was the role it played in the emergence of the rivalry between William Crawford and John Clark, creating political factions that would dominate the state for almost four decades.[24] Crawford rose rapidly in Jackson's Republican Party, becoming the leader of the up-country Jeffersonians. His associates included a number of Broad River Virginians, men like Charles Tait, an Elbert County lawyer, and William Wyatt Bibb, a Petersburg physician with political aspirations.

Although John Clark is usually portrayed as the champion of "democratic" frontier farmers, sort of a Georgia version of Andrew Jackson, the inner circle of the faction he headed was composed of lawyers and professional men, many with roots in North Carolina, who yearned for public office but refused to acknowledge the supremacy of James Jackson. Clark's brother, Elijah Clarke Jr. was a perennially unsuccessful candidate for Congress. The general's brothers-in-law included Duncan Campbell; John Griffin; and William J. Hobby of the *Augusta Herald*, whom Republicans suspected, probably correctly, of serving as the unlettered Clark's ghostwriter during his frequent newspaper wars. Other notables in the Clark faction were John M. Dooly, like Clark the son of a noted Revolutionary partisan, and, after Jackson's up-country allies had frustrated his hopes for a seat in Congress, Petersburg attorney Peter Van Allen.

Although rivalry between the Virginia and North Carolina cliques was a traditional feature of politics in the Broad River Valley by the 1790s, Yazoo lifted it out of this regional context and incorporated it into an emerging state party system. John Clark had procured shares in at least two of the Yazoo companies, which put him at odds with Jackson's insistence that political preferment be extended only to those opposed to the great land fraud. On two occasions in November 1801, following his first election to the General Assembly, Clark seemed to side with the disappointed speculators on issues before the legislature.[25] Furthermore, numbered among Clark's relatives and supporters were men who were tainted, at least in Jackson's opinion, by Yazoo or Federalism, or both. Thus, almost from the first, William Crawford, Jackson's chief up-country lieutenant, set his face against the political pretensions of Clark and his supporters.

The rivalry between Clark and Crawford turned violent in 1802, when Crawford killed a Clarkite—and former Jackson supporter—Peter Van Allen, in a duel.[26] In 1803 and again in 1804, Crawford successfully backed his old friend Charles Tait for a judicial appointment against the claims of Clark's brother-in-law John Griffin. During these campaigns, Clark and Crawford engaged in such a heated correspondence in the press that a duel was averted only by the decision of a "court of honor" appointed by Governor John Milledge.[27]

Matters came to a head in 1806, when Judge Tait witnessed a deposition that seemed to implicate John Clark in passing counterfeit money. Clark demanded Tait's impeachment, but a committee of the legislature, for which Crawford served as spokesman, exonerated the judge. The full house adopted the committee report, and Clark, convinced that Crawford and Tait had conspired to damage his reputation, challenged Crawford to a duel. The two men met in December 1806 at the High Shoals of the Apalachee; in the exchange of shots, Crawford was wounded. Clark challenged Crawford again in July 1807, but Crawford refused to meet him. Clark vented his anger by flogging Judge Tait in the streets of the new capital, Milledgeville.[28]

Following James Jackson's death in 1806 and William Crawford's election to the US Senate in 1807, leadership in Georgia's Republican Party passed first to David Mitchell and eventually to Jackson's Chatham County protégé, George M. Troup, developments that produced no perceptible diminution of partisan strife. Clark's influence, which had been concentrated at first in the up-country, spread gradually over the entire state until, after the War of 1812, Georgia had its first two-party system, which looked so different from the one developing in the rest of the country that understanding it baffled contemporaries and continues to puzzle modern historians.

* * * * *

James Jackson's success in arranging for the cession of the Yazoo lands to the federal government in 1802 did not remove the issue from either Georgia or national politics.

Northern speculators who had acquired land from the Yazoo companies pressed Congress for payment, but for over a decade, congressmen sympathetic to Georgia—led by the eccentric Virginian John Randolph of Roanoke—rebuffed them. Randolph's stubborn insistence that Jeffersonian Republicans who supported compensation for the Yazoo speculators must themselves have been "corrupted" produced a schism in the nation's ruling party, with Randolph and his fellow "Old Republicans" moving into bitter opposition to the administration and its supporters. Among the claimants seeking satisfaction from Congress were New Englanders who had purchased lands from agents of the Augusta-based Georgia Mississippi Company. Members of this group, frustrated by Randolph's tenacious delaying tactics, eventually sued for redress. In the case of *Fletcher v. Peck* (1810), Chief Justice John Marshall ruled that the Rescinding Act had been an unconstitutional violation of the right of contract. Finally, in 1814, Congress resolved the issue, providing $5 million from the proceeds of land sales in Mississippi Territory to be shared by the claimants.[29]

A more tragic legacy of the Yazoo fraud grew out of the state's 1802 cession of its disputed western territory to Congress. As cotton culture spread across Georgia, federal officials proved either unwilling or unable to extinguish quickly enough for land-hungry Georgians claims of the Creeks and the Cherokees to lands within the state. Anger over this, to Georgians, unacceptable delay helped fuel the development of the "state rights" philosophy for which Georgia's leaders became notorious as they prodded Washington to complete the process of Indian removal. Developed by George M. Troup and honed by his gubernatorial successors, Georgia's approach to "state rights" was alleged by some contemporaries to be little different from John C. Calhoun's more famous philosophy of Nullification. A cursory glance at the state's stormy relationship with the federal government in the 1820s and 1830s suggests that this charge had some validity.

In 1825, the Troup administration negotiated with a faction of the Creeks led by Troup's cousin, Chief William McIntosh, a flagrantly corrupt treaty that transferred remaining tribal lands to Georgia. When President John Quincy Adams disavowed this Treaty of Indian Springs and said he would use the army if necessary to make his decision stick, the angry Troup insisted that the treaty was valid and threatened that Georgia would meet force with force. The crisis blew over only after the Adams administration negotiated new treaties in 1826 and 1827 that procured the Creek lands desired by the state.[30]

With the Creeks banished from Georgia, the turn of the Cherokees had come. Georgia governors George Gilmer, John Forsyth, and Wilson Lumpkin exerted constant pressure on the Cherokees to surrender their lands. This time around, the state had a powerful, unswerving ally in Washington, President Andrew Jackson, so Georgia's chief executives were able to ignore efforts by the US Supreme Court to defend the rights of the Cherokees. The last of the Cherokees were removed from Georgia in 1838. In a sense, then, in addition to everything else it did, the Yazoo fraud led to the "Trail of Tears."[31]

* * * * *

While all this was going on, Troup Party politicians had continued to use the Yazoo label as a partisan club to bludgeon supporters of John Clark. For example, in 1821, purportedly responding to a reader's bafflement at all the references to then governor Clark's involvement in Yazoo over twenty-five years earlier, a Troup newspaper in Milledgeville published a detailed account of the infamous transaction. Since this version of events was based on a sketch originally prepared by James Jackson about 1803, it was hardly objective, but it did serve to inform readers who had no personal memory of Yazoo of what had occurred and why those long-ago events should lead them to vote for George Troup instead of John Clark. (Despite this appeal to history, however, Clark defeated Troup for the governorship.)[32]

The use of *Yazoo* as a term of opprobrium did not end in 1821 or 1825 or even 1830. Georgia newspapers include heated references to the fraud and its perpetrators as late as 1835, *forty* years after the sale. That virtually all those involved on both sides of the Yazoo question had either retired or died by that date made no difference.[33]

By that time, too, the political landscape in Georgia had changed almost beyond recognition: Indian removal was all but complete; the low country had become a political backwater; what had been referred to, sometimes sneeringly, as the up-country was at the center of economic and governmental influence in the state; and there was a new frontier, one wrested by whites from Georgia's original inhabitants. While many factors were responsible for this remarkable transformation of Georgia in general and the up-country in particular, surely one of the most significant was the Yazoo land fraud.

12

The Case of the Smuggled Africans and the Disgrace of David Brydie Mitchell

[**NOTE:** In each of the major research projects I've undertaken, I've "discovered" a Georgian I had not known about and then set out to understand him. While working on my dissertation, for instance, I encountered John Wereat, and I eventually produced a "biography," comprising three journal articles, now combined in this volume. One of the Georgians I met in the next generation of political leaders was David Brydie Mitchell. While I already knew that Mitchell had been a cog in James Jackson's political machine, what caught my attention this time was his spectacular fall from political prominence. While serving as federal agent to the Creek Indians, Mitchell was removed from office for smuggling illegally imported Africans into Georgia through the Creek Nation. I wondered how he could have done such a thing. And, more importantly from my perspective, was his disgrace related in some way to the evolution of Georgia political parties?

Little had been done about the entirety of Mitchell's life, except for a master's thesis that "covered the waterfront," but superficially. The author's account of Mitchell's removal as Creek agent was brief and defensive, and it did little to weave either Mitchell's rise to political power or his downfall into the larger picture of Georgia politics. Once I began looking into Mitchell's treatment at the hands of historians of Native America, I found a consensus so negative that I questioned whether the Georgian could have been so corrupt and, at the same time, so inept, as he was portrayed.

Eventually, I accumulated several bulging folders of material that I hoped would help me understand what made David Mitchell tick. I began writing about him in 1997, and as I plodded along on the larger project, I revised and reorganized what I thought of as a potential "article" on Mitchell, though that did not materialize. Still, the account of Mitchell's career presented here includes the results of many years of research, reflection, and revision.]

*****

The political culture in Georgia after the American Revolution welcomed all sorts, but those who flourished tended to be versatile, able to combine plantation agriculture with the practice of law, along with service in the legislature, the militia, and the county magistracy.[1] Certainly James Jackson, who created the Jeffersonian Republican Party in Georgia, fit this bill, as did his frequent rival—and the state's most prominent Federalist—US senator James Gunn.[2] Moreover, members of Jackson's Jeffersonian Republican machine could afford to be no less versatile—or truculent—than he, especially if they nursed statewide or national ambitions.

One of the most determined and successful of James Jackson's political followers was David Brydie Mitchell. A native of Scotland, the sixteen-year-old Mitchell arrived in Savannah in 1782 to claim property left to him by his uncle. He studied law under William Stephens and by 1789 had become both an American citizen and a member of the bar. Mitchell also was active in the Georgia militia, rising to brigadier general in 1803 and major general three years later.[3]

Mitchell entered politics in 1794, winning election to the Georgia House of Representatives from Chatham County. Like a number of ambitious younger Georgians, he saw his career take off in 1796 when he joined James Jackson in the crusade against organizers of the infamous Yazoo Land Fraud and was elected state attorney general. Chosen a judge of the eastern division of the superior court in 1798, Mitchell served there until 1801.[4]

Thomas Jefferson's victory in 1800 meant that James Jackson, leader of the new president's party in Georgia, became the state's chief dispenser of federal patronage. One of those he promoted was David Mitchell, who was named federal attorney for the state's eastern district. Like several Georgians nominated by Jefferson, Mitchell shortly found himself the target of a smear campaign by Georgia Federalists hoping to discredit the new president's appointments. In April 1802, a newspaper in the nation's capital published an extract of a letter from an anonymous "gentleman in Savannah," accusing Mitchell of conduct that was, according to the Washington editor, "so immoral and debauched that it is impossible to describe it in words sufficiently chaste for the public eye."[5] President Jefferson and Senator Jackson discussed appropriate legal remedies for Mitchell and other Georgia appointees being attacked in the public prints, but Mitchell went in search of the author of the letter and evidently found him; a few months later, a Savannah paper tersely reported that Mitchell had shot and killed William Hunter, a Federalist merchant in Savannah, in a duel.[6]

At the same time Mitchell was establishing his bona fides as a member of Jackson's Jeffersonian Republican organization, John Clark—who subsequently became Mitchell's most determined rival—was becoming a formidable force in his own right. The indifferently educated son of Revolutionary hero Elijah Clarke (they spelled their last names differently)—and a commanding figure himself because of his escapades during the American Revolution and as a militia leader afterward—John Clark was a rough-hewn up-country leader. "Democratic" or not, John Clark, like David Mitchell and other movers in Georgia politics, was much concerned with his "honor" or reputation. [7]

* * * * *

Following Jackson's demise in March 1806, his Republican political machine passed into hands of his lieutenants: the old guard, John Milledge and David Mitchell; William Harris Crawford, the most prominent of the younger up-country Republicans; and the fast-rising coastal Republican George M. Troup. However, Milledge retired from politics by 1809; Crawford left the state for a career of national significance; and Troup served in the national House of Representatives from 1807 to 1815, and in the Senate, 1816–1818. Despite references by contemporaries and later historians to the rivalry between the "Crawford" or "Troup" party and the "Clark" party, to the extent that Republicans *in Georgia* had a leader, that man was David Mitchell.[8]

Mitchell was elected governor in 1809 and again in 1811.[9] Governor Mitchell angered John Clark and his supporters when he refused to appoint the general to command the state militia in the Creek War, choosing a Republican, John Floyd, instead. Mitchell later defended this decision by noting that "in the field, brains and money are both indispensable to a commanding general and of the former it is thought Clark is miserably lacking."[10] Clark apparently nursed his wounded pride and craved revenge, probably because "Men of honor always held a grudge." According to a contemporary source, the angry Clark even intended to chastise Mitchell physically for this perceived slight, but his plan failed.[11]

*****

Governor Mitchell's popularity plummeted during his second term, and his refusal to appoint Clark to command against the Creeks contributed to this development.[12] Mitchell also had been appointed by President Madison as American representative to Spanish East Florida during that province's so-called Patriot War. The administration was playing a double game, publicly distancing itself from the Florida Patriots but privately urging Mitchell to prevent the occupation of Florida by any other power. Mitchell sent units of the Georgia militia to Florida, to no avail, and the administration seemed ready to drop the whole Florida initiative, despite Georgia senator William Crawford's warning that public opinion in Georgia was "very high on this subject" and wished the territory held.[13]

No one emerged from this diplomatic double-dealing with his reputation intact, including Governor Mitchell, but he retained enough support in the legislature by 1815 to defeat incumbent Republican governor Peter Early in a runoff, winning the governorship for the third time. Early had angered many Georgians by vetoing the Alleviating Act, a measure popular with debtors but opposed by creditors because it eased terms for repaying loans, a process complicated by the financial consequences of the Embargo of 1807.[14]

*****

In the summer of 1816, Secretary of War William Crawford informed President Madison of the death of Creek agent Benjamin Hawkins and began to speculate on a successor.[15] Crawford told Madison he had discussed the Creek Agency with Governor Mitchell and believed him the right man for the job, and he predicted that, if the appointment were made, it would be approved by "a majority of the state."[16]

Governor Mitchell eventually accepted the post, but reluctantly. At first, he objected that being Creek agent was not commensurate with his current position, and, because he did not wish to be separated from his family, he would only accept if he were not required to live in the Creek

Nation. Crawford replied that both President Madison and Georgia senator William Bibb agreed Mitchell must live in the Nation if he accepted the post. Otherwise, the appointment would smack "too much of a sinecure," according to Madison, and Bibb warned that if, as agent, Mitchell lived outside the Nation, every "unfriendly act committed by any part of the Creeks would be charged to his absence and inattention." Both Bibb and Crawford argued that, if he settled his family in the vicinity of the Ocmulgee River, Mitchell could both reside among the Creeks and visit his family frequently.[17]

Mitchell pleaded for more time to make his decision, arguing that he must remain governor at least through the adjournment of the legislature to ensure a smooth transition for his Republican successor, and Crawford agreed.[18] Shortly thereafter, Mitchell asked for another delay because of rumors of war with Spain. Crawford replied that the president had once more agreed to Mitchell's request, but he dismissed the idea that war with Spain was imminent. Perhaps beginning to lose patience with the reluctant Georgian, Crawford said he would "be perfectly reconciled" to whatever decision Mitchell made and that, in offering him the post, he had simply hoped "to evince to you the high estimation I entertain of your talents and patriotism."[19]

According to one biased observer, despite Mitchell's initial hesitancy to accept the agent's post, he said that he had served the people of Georgia long enough; now it was time to serve his own interests.[20] Moreover, in a letter to Mitchell in late October 1816, while the governor was throwing excuses for delay at Crawford and the president, Savannah Republican William Bulloch remarked that he had not been aware (until Mitchell had told him) that the Creek agent's post could be so lucrative. And his subsequent efforts to profit from a family-run store in the agency, as well as charges that he skimmed money from the tribal annuity, both suggest, though they do not prove, that his motives for accepting the agent's job were at least in part mercenary. His partner in the agency store was Creek chief William McIntosh, and McIntosh's oldest daughter, Jane, married Mitchell's son William on August 14, 1818.[21]

* * * * *

As federal agent to the Creeks, David Mitchell had one paramount responsibility, at least in the minds of white Georgians: to secure additional land cessions from the Creeks, with the ultimate goal of eliminating them from the state. As one observer commented upon learning of his appointment, "*I know* [Mitchell] well and cannot entertain a doubt but that in all his decisions he will lean to the side of Georgia—the State in which he is *popular*, and where the *popular* cry is—*exterminate the savages.*" And, sure enough, by early June, a Milledgeville newspaper reported the upcoming sale of newly acquired Creek lands and described Mitchell as "pretty sanguine" he could secure from the Creeks a much desired strip between the Ocmulgee River and the territory they had recently ceded.[22]

Mitchell had no sooner taken over as Creek agent than he ran afoul of the US factor in the area, Daniel Hughes, who kept up a steady stream of letters to his superiors complaining of Mitchell's business practices; his alleged scheme to monopolize trade with the Creeks through the store he had opened in the Nation and that his son ran; and, in December 1817, his involvement in smuggling Africans for the purpose of selling them in Georgia. Another issue between them was the sale of alcohol within the Creek Nation: Mitchell issued an order on June 14, 1818, prohibiting this, complaining that the Creeks were getting drunk at Hughes's factory.[23]

General Edmund Gaines, commander of American troops in the area, and his superior, General Andrew Jackson, were determined to invade Florida and seize it for the United States, and they viewed Chief William McIntosh's Creek warriors as crucial auxiliaries. When he first took office, Mitchell learned that President Madison had barred American forces, including Native American auxiliaries, from entering Spanish territory. Until Madison permitted them to cross into Florida in pursuit of hostile Seminoles, Mitchell refused to allow McIntosh and the allied Creeks to be mustered into federal service, choosing instead to try to negotiate a settlement with the Seminoles. Mitchell's attitude reinforced General Gaines's perception that the agent was an obstructionist and also angered General Jackson. Moreover, Mitchell did not believe that blame for Indian-white violence on the Georgia-Florida frontier lay solely with the Indians, and he said so as early as March 1817. Six months later, agent Mitchell blamed Gaines for the attack on the Seminoles at Fowltown on December 2, 1817, a blunder he believed had initiated the Seminole War.[24]

* * * * *

One of the first things Mitchell did as Creek agent was distribute supplies.[25] He arranged for William Bowen, who had worked with his predecessor, Benjamin Hawkins, and as assistant factor to Daniel Hughes, to purchase $10,000 worth of trade goods, which were distributed in July 1817. Following this assignment, Bowen decided to open a store in Milledgeville, and he set off in search of financial backing for the venture. In Augusta, he arranged for letters of credit from two firms with offices there and in Savannah. Bowen next traveled to Savannah, where he learned that cargoes of sugar and coffee had recently arrived at Amelia Island, Florida.

Armed with financial backing, Bowen made his way to Amelia Island, where, according to his later account, he found prices too high and decided to abort the mission. Waiting for a ship back to Savannah, however, he discovered that a privateer had arrived with a cargo of Africans that could be had for a reasonable price, and he bought about one hundred of the slaves with credit originally intended for the purchase of sugar and coffee. Bowen took about sixty of the Africans with him toward Georgia, but the outbreak of the Seminole War and lack of provisions for the Africans led him to carry his charges only as far as the Creek Agency, early in December 1817.

Once he reached the agency, Bowen and his assistants put the Africans in the lower end of agent Mitchell's field, built houses for them, and set them to work. Once Mitchell returned on December 8, he and Bowen apparently discussed the Africans. Bowen next set off for Amelia Island to fetch the remaining slaves he had purchased. On the return trip, Bowen gave one of his assistants, a Creek Indian named Tobler, a letter to Mitchell suggesting that the agent was aware of the slave-smuggling operation, in case Tobler encountered any trouble from American authorities while moving the second group of Africans through the Creek Nation. Bowen then left Tobler with the Africans and headed for Savannah, where he persuaded his backers to approve his using their letters of credit to purchase slaves rather than sugar and coffee.

However, Tobler lost Bowen's letter en route, and it was discovered by a Creek woman and turned over to William Moore, a disgruntled former blacksmith at the agency looking for a way to get back at Mitchell, who had fired him. Moore, apparently aware of John Clark's lust for revenge against Mitchell, took the letter (and "copies" of two other letters Moore claimed to have found in the agent's desk) to Clark, who decided to use them against Mitchell, and, more importantly, through guilt by association to blacken the reputation of William Crawford, Clark's bête noire and Mitchell's longtime political ally.

A couple of weeks after the arrival of Tobler and the second group of Africans at the Creek Agency, David Mitchell allowed William Bowen and his business partner, Jared Groce, to depart for Alabama Territory with forty-seven of the smuggled slaves, after they had given bond to transport them out of the United States. Witnesses subsequently testified that, following the arrival of the Africans at the agency, some were marked with colored tape or string indicating which belonged to Mitchell and which to Bowen. The marshal of the Creek Nation told another witness that "the money which the Creeks ought to have received through the agent was paid by [Mitchell] for the Africans."

In analyzing this testimony, Attorney General William Wirt suggested that perhaps half the smuggled Africans comprised Mitchell's reward for his acquiescence in the transaction. Four days after Bowen and Groce departed for Alabama, McQueen McIntosh, surveyor for the district of Brunswick and the port of Darien, having heard that smuggled Africans were being illegally transported through the Creek Nation, arrived at the agency. When he learned that Bowen and Groce had left a few days earlier, McIntosh set off on their trail and overtook them before they reached Alabama Territory. He reported that, in addition to the forty-seven slaves found with Bowen and Groce, he had taken forty-one Africans into custody at the Creek Agency.[26]

* * * * *

In a letter to Governor William Rabun in January 1818, ostensibly concerned with the progress of his campaign against the Seminoles, General Edmund Gaines expressed "surprise and indignation" at newspaper reports "that the hostile Indians desire peace, and are willing to lay down their arms!" On the contrary, he asserted, there was no chance of peace until "those Indians are severely chastised." The general located the source of the opposition in "some evil disposed white persons" in the Creek Nation, "actually engaged in smuggling Negroes into the United States from East Florida." He claimed that "a considerable number" of slaves had been taken to the vicinity of the Creek Agency and that it was the responsibility of "the Agent [Mitchell] to detect or explain this apparent violation of the law." General Gaines predicted grimly that, because troop movements and Indian hostilities would "have a strong tendency to render this abominable traffic difficult and perilous," he expected "to be honored with the ill-will of every one engaged in it."[27]

Mitchell responded on February 13, 1818.[28] He began by describing benefits that would accrue to Georgia from the recent Creek treaty he had negotiated. He also reported that Chief McIntosh and his 1,500 friendly Creeks were eager to support General Gaines's campaign against the Seminoles, which indicated that Mitchell had received word that President James Monroe had lifted Madison's ban on American forays into Florida. Turning to the last paragraph of Gaines's letter, Mitchell claimed that, while he did not believe Gaines would willfully mislead the public, he had apparently received "reports or communications of some sort, unworthy of his confidence." The agent asserted that he had only released half of the Negroes Gaines referred to when the two men had posted security that they would take them out of the United States and that he planned to do the same with the remainder. Mitchell argued that he was confident the Africans were not for sale in Georgia but had instead already been purchased by several large landowners in the Alabama Territory. In sum, Mitchell maintained that Gaines had been misinformed and that his letter appeared to be "well calculated to excite a prejudice in the public mind against myself . . ., whether intended or not."

* * * * *

The crime of which Mitchell was accused, smuggling Africans into Georgia, was hardly novel in 1817. It apparently was systematic, supported by larger planters as a way to supplement their domestic labor force and carried out by unscrupulous traders in search of easy money.

General Gaines's charge that Mitchell was involved in a scheme to illegally bring Africans into Georgia through the Creek Nation, in violation of the 1808 law banning American participation in the international slave trade, initially produced only a brief flurry of comments in the press, including Mitchell's published denial in February 1818. In response, Governor Rabun urged the legislature to appoint a committee "to study 'this abominable traffic' and adopt measures to 'prevent this species of speculation.'" The committee estimated the number of smuggled slaves at three hundred and stated that any Africans apprehended could be sold under a law passed by the legislature in 1817.[29] In 1820, the legislature directed the governor to inform the American Colonization Society (as provided in the December 1817 Georgia law) as soon as the courts ruled in Georgia's favor. If the Colonization Society was not willing to repatriate the Africans, then the governor should sell them.[30]

Especially in view of what would happen later, the low-key response to General Gaines's charge of slave smuggling against Mitchell is, at first glance, surprising. It seems likely that Gaines's letter initially was an attempt to punish Mitchell for refusing to enlist the Allied Creeks in General Jackson's army for the invasion of Florida. But, once Mitchell learned that President Monroe had rescinded Madison's ban on raids into Florida and allowed the Creeks to be enrolled, Jackson and Gaines set off for Florida, and Gaines's anti-Mitchell crusade temporarily was held in abeyance.

* * * * *

At first, Mitchell believed that "the imputation about his hampering of military preparations [against the Seminoles] was the much more serious charge" being leveled against him by Jackson and Gaines. Yet, once he learned that General Jackson had begun bandying the slave-smuggling charge about, Mitchell turned to William Crawford for help but received little encouragement from the Treasury secretary. Jackson later charged that the Scotsman Alexander Arbuthnot had encouraged the Seminoles to wage war on the United States, but "in fact, [Arbuthnot] specifically praised David Mitchell's peace initiative, something that could not have enhanced the agent's reputation with Jackson and Gaines."[31]

Between the publication of Mitchell's letter in mid-February and the start of the fall political campaign, the Milledgeville papers were silent on charges aimed specifically at the agent. The *Savannah Republican* did publish a long piece on the illegal slave trade, arguing that American seizure of Amelia Island was worthwhile, if only because it put a stop to its use as a port of entry for slaves imported from Africa. This writer asserted that "a regular chain of posts" from St. Marys to the Georgia interior allowed such slaves to be carried "to every part of the country."[32]

Papers in Milledgeville also published stories examining American participation in the international slave trade, which had been illegal in the United States for a decade. On April 28, the *Reflector* reprinted a story from the *Baltimore Patriot* claiming that Spain had imported nearly one thousand Africans a week into her New World colonies over the past five months, yet most of them would end up in the United States. The author argued that Congress should make the smuggling of African slaves "a criminal instead of a finable offence." From late summer to fall, 1818, a writer styling himself "Philanthropist" published a series of essays expatiating on the horrors of the slave trade and urging the state legislature to prohibit the further introduction of *all* slaves, whether legally or illegally brought into Georgia, on the grounds that allowing the practice to continue would "deteriorate the morals of our citizens."[33]

By late July 1818, the state had arranged for the sale at public auction of the first group of Africans brought into the state by William Bowen. Then, on August 4, the *Georgia Journal* reported that Miguel de Castro had entered a claim against the Africans, asserting that he owned the brig from which they had been taken by privateers and then sold to persons who had moved them to East Florida, where they were purchased and smuggled into Georgia through the Creek Nation. A local judge stopped the sale temporarily. The situation had been clarified a week later: the sale would be held as scheduled, regardless of Castro's claim. On August 18, the *Reflector* juxtaposed two interesting items: Treasury Secretary Crawford arrived in Milledgeville on Sunday, August 16, and, the next day, sixty-three of the Africans were sold for more than $41,000.[34]

On September 8, 1818, the editors of the *Georgia Journal*, lamenting the apparent lack of public interest in the approaching congressional elections, reintroduced the topic of African slaves, citing remarks from an unnamed northern paper asking whether sufficient vigilance was being used to guard against the illegal importation of Africans. The *Journal* editors wrote that "there is reason to believe" such smuggling happened "frequently" in Georgia, and that among those involved in the practice were "some of our principal citizens, particularly one in a responsible trust, and who has enjoyed the public confidence to a high degree ... It is also hinted that he stands accused, before the government of other acts of delinquency." They asserted that a careful investigation of the accusations was needed for the good of all concerned.[35]

In keeping with prevailing journalistic canons, the *Journal* had not named Mitchell as the subject of these "suspicions," but it is hard to believe that any politically astute reader would have been unaware of his identity. Nevertheless, one week later, a correspondent to the *Reflector*, who signed himself "One of Thousands," dared the *Journal*'s editors to name the person referred to in their editorial.[36] The *Journal*'s only response was to publish two affidavits about the African slaves in their September 29 issue. The first, by Ludowick Ashley, claimed that he and a companion had met Bowen's Creek associate, Tobler, along the St. Marys River late in December 1817. He had with him forty slaves, which, Tobler claimed, belonged to him. A few days later, according to Ashley, he had encountered William Bowen in East Florida, and Bowen had stated that "General Mitchell was his friend." The second affidavit, from Mitchell himself, included a pass he had issued to William Bowen and Jared Groce through the Creek Nation. According to Mitchell, Bowen and Gross had produced a bill of sale for the detained Africans, who, they claimed, had been purchased in Camden County and were intended for settlement in the Alabama Territory, not Georgia. The two men had bound themselves to carry the forty-seven slaves out of the state.[37]

By late September 1818, then, it was clear that David Mitchell was the prominent Georgian allegedly involved in smuggling Africans into the state, but, in view of the silence of both Milledgeville papers on the subject for the rest of the year, it was equally clear that the charges had not yet hurt the Creek agent.

* * * * *

One way to interpret the denouement of Mitchell's career as Creek agent is to place it in the context of General Andrew Jackson's "settling scores" following the end of his Florida campaign.[38] Although the real cause of Jackson's and Gaines's enmity toward Mitchell was his effort to prevent the Creeks from aiding them on the Florida incursion, "the best way to bring down Mitchell was to accuse him of breaking the law ..., so they concentrated on allegations that Mitchell had been involved in slave smuggling from Florida." Gaines took the lead, but the scheme faltered when an army officer stationed in Georgia, who was in the best position to implicate Mitchell on the slave-smuggling charge, refused to play along. There followed a "new allegation against the agent [that] conveniently surfaced in June [1818]," when Benjamin Smith accused Mitchell's son William of purchasing, for five dollars a head, cattle from Florida that General Jackson had given William McIntosh to replace animals lost in Creek War. When he learned of this, Jackson dashed off angry letters to McIntosh and Mitchell demanding the return of the cattle, and he sent a copy of the charges to Secretary of War Calhoun. Mitchell replied hotly that he had no knowledge of Jackson's intentions in turning the animals over to William McIntosh; denied he had any part in the transaction; claimed that the number of cattle was much lower than Jackson said; and sent a copy of his letter to Calhoun.

Meanwhile, in Washington, the US Senate established a committee to investigate General Jackson's role in the Seminole War, especially his invasion of Florida.[39] In late November 1818, Mitchell held a conference with the Creeks at Fort Hawkins to distribute the tribal annuity, announcing afterward that he had decided to visit Washington "with the view principally of settling my Accounts."[40] When Mitchell arrived in the capital, it became clear that what he hoped to "settle" was his dispute with General Gaines. Appearing before a US Senate committee in February 1819, Mitchell again charged that Gaines's attack on the Indian settlement at Fowltown had sparked the outbreak of the Seminole War. His testimony evidently helped persuade the committee that the general was guilty as charged, despite Gaines's assertion that he had not allowed him to give his side of the story.[41]

* * * * *

On November 11, 1818, Governor William Rabun told the legislature he had appointed Colonel Charles Williamson to dispose of any slaves brought illegally into Georgia. Thus far, he wrote, proceeds from the sales had totaled $34,736.18, but, since Williamson had not been authorized to take possession by force of smuggled slaves, there were still "several hundred held by individuals in different parts of the state, without any legal claim whatsoever." Rabun urged legislators to act to clear up the situation. The next day, the solons resolved that the governor appoint someone to take possession of any African Negroes smuggled into the state and hold them until given further instructions.[42]

Rabun's last message to the legislature, delivered posthumously in November 1819, noted that, in December 1818, he had directed Colonel Williamson to auction off the remaining smuggled Africans. Williamson had no sooner advertised the sale than a deputy tried to seize the slaves on a warrant from Miguel de Castro, who had failed to block the earlier sale in August 1818. Convinced that "the name of De Castro [*sic*] was only borrowed to cover the mysterious designs of some of our citizens who have long been engaged in this abominable traffic," Rabun "refused to give them up to the marshall [*sic*], but finally agreed to suspend the sale, and hold [the Africans] subject to the decree of the district court, where the case is still pending." Moreover, he reported, he had also agreed to let the American Colonization Society ship the Africans back to their homeland once the district court decided the case in Georgia's favor.[43]

The Colonization Society's agent, the Reverend Cowles Meade, arrived in Georgia early in May 1819. Then, on June 1, the *Georgia Journal* published a letter from Rev. Meade to his superior, R. B. Caldwell, on the success of the effort to prevent the sale of the Africans in Milledgeville.[44]

At this time, there also were a few items published in defense of slavery and the slave trade. Just after the sale of the first group of Africans at auction, the *Reflector* published a long essay by "Amadis" of Putnam County on "the Negro Traffic." He defended both the slave trade and slavery and, in an obvious reference to the Georgia legislature, criticized state laws concerning the importation of slaves, an issue he believed belonged to the national government.[45] Almost a year later, after Rev. Cowles Meade had crowed in the *Georgia Journal* about his success in preventing the auction of the second group of Africans so that the ACS could transport them back to Africa, "Limner" argued that slavery existed out of necessity in all societies, and, if black slavery were abolished, white slavery would have to replace it.[46] The *Georgia Journal* also published "Thoughts of a Yankee, on Slavery in the Southern States," defending the "peculiar institution" in terms that foreshadowed the later "pro-slavery argument."[47]

* * * * *

Despite the report of the Georgia legislative committee in 1818, nothing was done about the slave-smuggling charge against David Mitchell during William Rabun's governorship. John Clark was aware of the charge against the Creek agent but was in no position to do much about it until he was elected governor in the fall of 1819. Behind the scenes, however, Clark was in the process of forming an anti–William Crawford alliance with Andrew Jackson that would drag the issue back before the public and, in the end, play an important role in securing Mitchell's dismissal.

On April 20, 1819, General Jackson wrote Clark, asking for help gathering information that might discredit Crawford, who, Jackson was convinced, was trying to ruin his reputation over his notorious foray into Florida during the Seminole War. By the time Jackson wrote to him, Clark (or, more likely, his brother-in-law William J. Hobby, the Augusta newspaper editor) was already at work on a pamphlet assailing Crawford, using the slave-smuggling charges against Mitchell, Crawford's longtime political associate, as part of the indictment. Clark promised to send Jackson a copy of the pamphlet as soon as it was published. According to Jackson's biographer Robert Remini, this exchange of letters "only revealed two embittered, petty men—men more to be pitied than condemned—quite incapable of doing Crawford serious harm." While the politically astute Crawford was indeed able to avoid damage from the scheme, Mitchell was not to be so fortunate.[48] In October 1819, shortly before his victory over George Troup in the governor's race, Clark began to publish in the Milledgeville newspapers the evidence he had been compiling against Mitchell. These documents, together with Clark's victory in the gubernatorial election and the publication of his pamphlet in the fall of 1820, ignited a firestorm of controversy that did not abate for almost a year.[49]

In January 1820, shortly after he took office, Governor Clark wrote Secretary of State John Quincy Adams, enclosing the resolution on investigating the illegal slave trade passed by the legislature during William Rabun's governorship but not sent to Washington before his death. Secretary Adams believed Governor Rabun had obscured the charges against Mitchell as much as he could and that Crawford had done the same.[50] Adams might have learned this from Attorney General William Wirt, who was investigating Mitchell for President Monroe, or he might have picked up the information in the course of his official duties. According to Adams's diary, during Wirt's investigation, not only the attorney general but also President Monroe and Secretary of War Calhoun revealed that they believed Mitchell guilty as charged. Wirt submitted his report early in 1821, President Monroe approved it, and in February, Calhoun informed Mitchell that he was being removed as agent to the Creeks.[51]

David Mitchell continued to gather evidence to demonstrate his innocence. He began publishing documents in the Milledgeville press in May 1821, and he eventually published his own hefty pamphlet, arguing that he was the blameless victim of a deep-dyed plot organized by his inveterate enemy, Governor John Clark.[52] Mitchell also did not let the loss of the agent's post interfere with his mercantile activities among the Creeks. On January 12, 1822, General Jackson informed Secretary of War Calhoun that Mitchell was still William McIntosh's partner in a store at the Creek agency and that they were "swindling the [Creek] nation completely," collecting both real and fictitious debts from the tribal annuity. He demanded that Calhoun order the new Creek agent, John Crowell, to put a stop to this practice.[53]

Later in 1822, Andrew Jackson prepared a memorandum of events that had convinced him Monroe's administration was rife with corruption. One item was "The case, of the opinion of the atto. Genl U.S. [*sic*] on which M. was removed."[54] This apparent reference to Mitchell's disgrace raises a question: why was Jackson disgruntled about Wirt's report, which had, after all, led to Mitchell's dismissal? The general probably was angry because Wirt's indictment was of Mitchell only, not of William Crawford, whom Jackson despised. In his correspondence with Jackson, Governor John Clark had seemed to promise that his pamphlet would link Crawford to Mitchell's slave-smuggling operation, and he did take a rhetorical roundhouse swing or two at the Treasury secretary in its pages, but public reaction, including not least the tenor of Wirt's report, suggested that his blows had failed to connect. To Jackson, Mitchell, though guilty, was a small fry; Crawford was the big fish, and Wirt had been unable, or unwilling, to land him.

*****

David Mitchell remained sensitive to charges reflecting adversely on his tenure as Creek agent. For example, in 1823, when Chief William McIntosh appropriated $8,000 from the tribal annuity payment, new agent John Crowell ordered McIntosh's brother-in-law and business associate, George Stinson, arrested for selling goods in the nation without a license. During Stinson's trial in federal court, former agent Mitchell and Chief McIntosh were the main defense witnesses, and their testimony led to Stinson's acquittal.[55]

Mitchell's effort to clear his name failed; he ended up running a tavern in Milledgeville until his appointment as a judge of the inferior court of Baldwin County in 1828, a post he held until his death in 1837. William Crawford believed Mitchell's struggle for vindication had strained their relationship. He claimed that Mitchell's quest for vindication was doomed from the start because he had put too much emphasis on the reputation he had earned before charges were brought against him by John Clark. Crawford's main concern after Clark's pamphlet was published was to refute anything that might harm his chances to succeed Monroe in the presidency. While gathering these defensive certificates, Crawford ignored Clark's effort to link him to Mitchell and the smuggled Africans, arguing that no one would take such a fantastic allegation seriously.[56]

One of Crawford's relatives believed Mitchell had been the victim of "a dirty conspiracy at Washington [,] the grand purpose of which is to defeat the views of Mr. Crawford to the Presidency." Nevertheless, he contended, Mitchell had doomed his own cause by agreeing to guidelines set by Attorney General Wirt for the investigation: "The boldness of the man evinces his innocence, but his, like the temerity of others [,] has been fatal."[57]

While sympathizing with Mitchell's plight, Crawford also attempted to distance himself from the agent, arguing that Mitchell had not been appointed Creek agent until after Crawford had moved from the War Department to the Treasury Department.[58] Crawford's explanation was more than a little disingenuous: although Mitchell did not *accept* the appointment until March 1817, he had been *appointed* in the autumn of 1816, at Crawford's urging. Moreover, it was Crawford who acted as middle man in convincing Mitchell to take the appointment.

* * * * *

Even as Mitchell, Clark, and their allies were going through a polemic ritual with roots in the 1780s, if not earlier, the political world in Georgia was changing. Next to the publications from Mitchell and Clark in the Milledgeville papers were impassioned essays on the Panic of 1819, the Missouri question, and slavery. The spark for public discussion of slavery in Georgia was not simply Missouri. The role of the American Colonization Society became more controversial, especially as the continuing claims of William Bowen and others against the Africans remaining in state custody prevented the completion of the earlier agreement to allow the society to transport them back to Africa.

At its 1820 session, the Georgia House of Representatives reiterated its support for colonizing smuggled Africans remaining in state custody, once their case had been cleared by the United States Circuit Court and they had been declared the property of the state of Georgia. The same resolution provided that, if the American Colonization Society were unable or unwilling to do so, the Africans would be sold by the state. By the following autumn, another snag had arisen—a new claimant had stepped forth, John Madrazo, who sought recovery of the slaves not yet sold and the proceeds from those already disposed of. Governor John Clark informed the legislature that he hoped for a decision from the court shortly, but "from the invention of those claiming to be interested, it may be protracted still longer."[59]

Moreover, William Bowen continued to press his claim to the Africans, and a legislative committee sympathized with his plea. In his petition, Bowen maintained that he had been moving the slaves from East to West Florida when they were arrested en route, outside Georgia in Alabama Territory, and eventually sold. Once the court condemned the Africans, the governor agreed to deliver them to the Colonization Society. The committee contended that Governor Rabun, in ordering the sale of some of the Africans, "misconceived the true spirit and intent of the act of 1818." Surely the legislature in 1818 had not meant for the governor to order a sale without a trial of the right of property or a court decision ruling that property liable to seizure, the committee argued. Thus, Rabun's interpretation of the 1818 law placed "the right of our citizens to this species of property in a most precarious situation." Because it was too late in the session to repeal the section of the 1818 act authorizing the sale, the committee recommended that the governor hold the Africans that had not yet been disposed of until the district court ruled, because acting on Bowen's petition before then would be "inexpedient"; the full house agreed.[60]

The situation had not been clarified by the time Governor Clark delivered his annual message in the fall of 1822. The case of the Africans was still pending in the district court, and two additional suits had been lodged in Baldwin County, one by Bowen's creditors and one by Bowen himself. Two weeks later, the *Georgia Journal* reported that the courts had declared a nonsuit Bowen's case against former state agent Charles Williamson regarding the fifty-nine Africans sold at Milledgeville in 1818. Toward the end of the year, a correspondent sent editor Frederick Fell of the *Savannah Republican* a copy of Mitchell's pamphlet on the African business and asserted that Mitchell had "completely refuted the charges advanced by General Clark against him, and proves that he has been a persecuted man, and badly treated by one or two officials who fill high stations in the administration of our country."[61]

A year later, the *Georgia Journal* published a report from the managers of the Putnam Auxiliary Society for colonizing free blacks. They tacitly admitted that the Missouri crisis and financial embarrassments accompanying the Panic of 1819 had led to a drop in support for their activities. They also mentioned that, if the state won custody of "certain

Africans" in the case still wending its way through the courts, the American Colonization Society would transport them back to their homeland, after reimbursing the state for any expenses, and the managers doubted that any such reimbursement would be required.[62]

In February 1824, the *Georgia Journal* noted that the federal court in Savannah had supported John Madrazo's claim and ordered the state to turn over the forty-nine remaining Africans to him, but the governor planned to appeal. Meanwhile, William Bowen continued to push *his* claim to the Africans in state court. The editors commented that, prior to 1824, the Africans had been rented out in return for "food, clothing and humane treatment," but, for the current year, the state agent had hired them out for about $1,200.[63]

The following autumn, Governor George Troup told the legislature that William Bowen had run out of patience waiting for the courts to settle his claim and had tried to carry off some of the slaves. Apprehended, Bowen admitted his guilt, but local magistrates freed him, contending that his "pretended claim" to the Africans has not yet been legally resolved. Emboldened by the ruling and by his release, Bowen then threatened to carry off by force as many of the slaves as he could, so Governor Troup ordered them to be housed in the state penitentiary. Meanwhile, the tenacious Bowen continued to pursue his claim through the courts. On another front, Governor Troup informed the General Assembly that the federal circuit court had found for Madrazo, ruling that his vessel had been engaged in traffic legally recognized by his native country, Spain, when "pirates" seized the ship and its cargo of Africans and that he had appealed the decision.[64]

About six weeks later, the legislature's joint judiciary committee reported that they believed the Africans belonged neither to the state nor William Bowen but to Madrazo, in accordance with the recent ruling by the Sixth US Circuit Court. The committee expressed bafflement that Troup was appealing the decision and offered a resolution authorizing him to withdraw the state's appeal if Madrazo would take the remaining Africans and any unexpended proceeds from the previous sales and remove the slaves from the United States. The resolution was tabled until the next day, and, after further debate, the state senate approved a different resolution, declaring that, because the dispute between Madrazo and Bowen was currently before the Supreme Court, they "thought [it] expedient that the claim of the state should be withdrawn upon certain conditions": the governor should deliver the remaining Africans and any unexpended funds to Bowen; in return, Bowen must give up his own claims and procure a statement from Madrazo releasing Georgia from any liability.[65]

The issue apparently was finally resolved in 1826. At first, the state senate recognized that the resolution passed at the previous session, authorizing the governor to deliver the Africans still in state custody to William Bowen, along with the balance of unexpended proceeds from previous sales, had not been complied with. Therefore, the senate tried again, offering virtually the same resolution, and, after considerable debate, both houses concurred in returning the remaining Africans to Bowen.[66]

*****

It is certainly possible that further snags in the court system either delayed or aborted the legislature's effort to return the remaining Africans to William Bowen, the man who had brought them into Georgia in the first place seven years earlier and had been a prime mover in events leading to the disgrace of David Mitchell. In a sense, whether there was more to the saga was irrelevant to the course of Georgia politics, though certainly not to the ultimate fate of the Africans, which remained in abeyance for a variety of reasons. While the wheels of justice ground slowly, events outside Georgia were altering the context within which the case evolved. The crisis over the future of slavery in Missouri, though "settled" by the Missouri Compromise, created ill feelings throughout the South and, in Georgia, directly affected the final decision on the fate of the Africans.

Southerners regarded the Missouri crisis as a direct attack by the rest of the country on the "peculiar institution" of the South. As the case of the Africans crept through the Georgia judicial system, legislators became much more sensitive to what they perceived as a threat to slavery. Consequently, William Bowen was transformed by successive sessions of the legislature from a heartless importer of smuggled slaves into a beleaguered "owner" of the South's distinctive form of "property." To deprive him of his "right" to that property could set a bad precedent for other southern slaveholders, so in 1826, the legislature ordered the Africans returned to Bowen.

David Mitchell's part in the melodrama seemed to be forgotten. No one besides Mitchell himself took any steps to try to repair his reputation, and the former agent's exertions got him nowhere. Yet, if President Monroe believed that Mitchell's dismissal would end the controversy, he was mistaken.

In 1824, three years after Mitchell's ouster, in the context of the maneuvering to succeed Monroe in the White House, William Harris Crawford was accused of financial irregularities while secretary of the Treasury. A congressional committee appointed to look into the accusation broadened the scope of the inquiry and asked Monroe to explain what he knew about Crawford's knowledge of Creek agent Mitchell's activities in 1817. The president naturally turned to members of his cabinet for help in drafting a response. Secretary of State John Quincy Adams claimed that Monroe's reply to the committee omitted any reference to letters between Crawford and Mitchell, because a couple of key ones had been "misplaced" by the Treasury secretary. Another issue was why a second letter from Governor Clark to Secretary Adams, enclosing documents allegedly incriminating Mitchell in the smuggling charge, had not been communicated to Congress. The administration's line on this was that the governor's letter had not arrived until after Mitchell's dismissal, so there was no reason to pass it on to the committee.[67]

In a sense, the outcome of Mitchell's battle to clear his name was rendered irrelevant by the course of Georgia politics following his dismissal. In 1823, the year after Mitchell published his pamphlet, George Troup defeated a Clarkite, Matthew Talbot, for governor by two votes in the legislature, and in 1825, eked out a narrow victory over John Clark himself in the state's first popular gubernatorial election, winning by less than seven hundred votes out of forty thousand cast. Moreover, in 1827, Clark left the state to take up a federal appointment in Florida. With Troup in firm command of Georgia's Republican Party and Clark no longer a force in state politics, the party system in Georgia had lurched, however slightly, toward replicating the national one, claiming David Brydie Mitchell as a victim in the process.

13

The News from Indian Country: Elias Boudinot, Cherokee Editor, 1828–1839

[**NOTE:** By the early 2000s, I had for nearly a decade been researching the sequel to my book, *Politics on the Periphery*. The project proved both more interesting and more challenging than I had originally anticipated, with controversial—and convoluted—issues like slavery, abolition, and Nullification playing key roles in the state's history during the later period. But, for me, the most difficult issue was Indian removal. I did not look forward to the task of grappling with it, so I kept postponing consideration of it—until the 2005/06 academic year, that is.

A few years earlier, my school had launched an interdisciplinary program called Explore to expose our students, from elementary through high school, to a different culture each year. When I learned that the next topic was to be Native Americans, I began to think that, if I took the bull by the horns, I might finally be able to enter the scholarly thicket I had thus far pretty much avoided—relations between Georgia and the native peoples within her borders. Given the nature of the Explore program, my school's location in Georgia, and the fact that my potential audience would be composed of high school students and faculty, I decided that something on the Cherokee removal crisis might work, provided I could come up with an approach to engage my listeners.

I eventually settled on the *Cherokee Phoenix*, the tribal newspaper, as the vehicle. The *Phoenix* was available online, but I had not yet worked my way through it, so a talk on the newspaper would force me to read it and take notes. My first effort, designed for a faculty workshop to provide teachers with background information on that year's Explore topic, was entitled "The *Cherokee Phoenix*, 1828–1834: Voice of a People?" While this approach seemed to suffice for the adult audience, it seemed rather dry (even to me) and, thus, perhaps not suitable for teenagers. So I revised it, focusing more on the paper's editor, Elias Boudinot, and carrying his story through his death in 1839. It was this version that I presented to my student audiences in the spring of 2006, and, with further revisions, to my Advanced Placement American History classes almost annually thereafter until I retired.

What I did *not* do was revise the piece for publication, largely because, although I had used the *Phoenix* as a primary source, the talk seemed more a synthesis of secondary works on the Cherokees, their newspaper, its editor, and the removal crisis than a piece of original scholarship. Yet the exercise allowed me to mine the columns of the *Phoenix* for items that, when combined with editorials and letters found in the Georgia press, could flesh out secondary sources and also add to the primary material I could work into the larger research project.

This time through the material, I have added notes to indicate where I found information that was most useful in shaping my interpretation of the place of the *Cherokee Phoenix* and its editor in the tribe's history and culture in general, and, specifically, in the removal crisis.]

*****

In 1802, the state of Georgia ceded its western land claims, comprising the present-day states of Alabama and Mississippi, to the federal government for $1.25 million and, more importantly to Georgia, for the government's promise to extinguish remaining Indian land claims within the state as soon as it could be done on "reasonable and peaceful" terms. This agreement became known as the Compact of 1802.[1]

The federal government did its best to fulfill the terms of this agreement. Between 1802 and 1819, Indian treaties with the southern tribes "transferred 20 million acres of land to white settlers, a greater expansion of territory open to slaveholding than the Missouri Compromise had provided."[2] Yet these cessions were neither frequent enough nor large enough for land-hungry Georgians, and when complaints to federal officials proved unavailing, Georgia struck off on its own. In 1825, at Indian Springs, the state arranged a treaty with the Creeks that secured all their remaining lands within the borders of Georgia. That the treaty had been negotiated with and signed by a minority of Creek chiefs led by

William McIntosh—a cousin of Georgia governor George Troup—and greased by corruption made no difference to Georgia.[3]

However, when President John Quincy Adams's administration got wind of the corruption accompanying the Treaty of Indian Springs, the agreement was annulled. Screams of outrage from Governor Troup, along with his threat that Georgia would proceed against the Creeks as if the treaty were still in effect, even if that meant armed clashes between the state and the national government, led Adams to back down. The administration negotiated new agreements with the Creeks that secured essentially the same territory included in the discredited Treaty of Indian Springs. By 1826, then, using a combination of corruption, state rights rhetoric, and the threat of civil war, Georgia officials had secured the ouster of the Creeks from the state.[4]

When it became clear that Georgia had won the tussle over Creek lands, the editor of a Milledgeville newspaper crowed that the time of the Cherokees had come. The Cherokees had made several land cessions to the federal government since 1802. By 1819, they had about five million acres left and refused to cede additional lands, so Georgia authorities called upon the federal government to remove them by force.[5]

* * * * *

Ever since the creation of a new, stronger American government under the Constitution of 1787, the general approach of the United States toward Indians had been to encourage "civilization"—that is, to convince Native American tribes to emulate the culture of the whites. The theory was that, if the "red men" became white men in all but skin color, then they could be assimilated within the larger national population over time. Of the native tribes remaining east of the Mississippi River, the Cherokees took this "civilization" policy most seriously, abandoning hunting for farming, and some even began to produce crops for the market instead of just for subsistence. In the early 1820s, they adopted the syllabary created by Sequoyah (George Guist), thereby laying the basis for a written language and laws and, eventually, for a tribal newspaper. In 1827, a convention created—and the Cherokees adopted—a written republican constitution modeled on that of the United States.[6]

So, the Cherokee Nation did what the federal government expected of them: they became "civilized," even to the point that the largest Cherokee planters aped neighboring white planters by becoming slaveowners. This policy of "civilizing" the "savage" tribes was grounded in the Enlightenment notion of the perfectibility of man. The differences between Indians and whites were *cultural*, in other words, and could be eliminated if the Native Americans tried hard to adapt to the "superior" white civilization. Unfortunately for the Cherokees, by the 1820s, that theory had changed, at least in the South. Southerners had begun to see differences between Indians and whites as *racial*, not cultural, which meant that they could not be eliminated.

Moreover, the creation of a Cherokee republican government in 1827 outraged Georgians, who saw it as an attempt to create a state within a state and therefore as an unacceptable attack on Georgia's sovereignty, or state rights. To whites, the imperative duty of the federal government was to fulfill the Compact of 1802, securing Cherokee lands for Georgia, or the state would be forced to act unilaterally as it had against the Creeks. Georgia would win this campaign as well, but it would do so in the glare of a spotlight shone on its actions by a Native American newspaper, the *Cherokee Phoenix*.[7]

* * * * *

In 1828, several developments once more brought into the open the question of Indian removal.[8] One was the discovery of gold within the Cherokee Nation. Another was the election to the presidency of Andrew Jackson, who was known to sympathize with Georgia's policy toward the Cherokees. Following Jackson's election, Georgia decided to extend its sovereignty over all Cherokee lands within the state. As one scholar put it, "Georgia's legislature added, by fiat, Cherokee lands to the northwestern counties of Georgia, forbade Cherokee gold mining, nullified all Cherokee laws, and prohibited Indians from testifying against whites in court."[9]

The Cherokees protested Georgia's actions to the federal Indian agent, who procured a force of US troops to police the Nation. Moreover, in 1829, the Cherokee National Council passed a law making any further cessions of tribal land without council permission a capital offense. In December 1829, Georgia reasserted its sovereignty over Cherokee territory: annexing it; extending Georgia laws over the area; prohibiting the National Council from meeting within the boundaries of Georgia (except to cede lands); forbidding Indians from mining gold found on tribal lands; and requiring an oath of allegiance to Georgia from all whites living in the Cherokee

Nation in an effort to weaken the influence of Christian missionaries there. All these provisions were to go into effect in June 1830.[10]

It was against this background of increasing tension between the Cherokees and their white Georgia neighbors that, on February 21, 1828, the first issue of the *Cherokee Phoenix* appeared. Elias Boudinot, the founding editor, could have served as the poster child for the "civilization" policy. He had attended a missionary-run boarding school in Connecticut; converted to Christianity; and, in 1826, married a white woman, Harriet Gold.[11]

In the fall of 1825, the Cherokee National Council authorized Boudinot to embark on a tour to raise funds to establish a Cherokee newspaper. In the speech he delivered at each stop on this tour, Boudinot sketched a glowing vision of what an Indian newspaper could be:

> Such a paper, comprising a summary of religious and political events, &c. on the one hand; and on the other, exhibiting the feelings, disposition, improvements, and prospects of the Indians; their traditions, their true character, as it once was and as it now is; the ways and means most likely to throw the mantle of civilization over all tribes; and such other matter as will tend to diffuse proper and correct impressions in regard to their condition—such a paper could not fail to create much interest in the American community, favourable to the aborigines, and to have a powerful influence on the advancement of the Indians themselves.

In that same speech, Boudinot also hinted at an appropriate name for the paper. If the national government continued to protect Native Americans, he said, and if that policy had the support of the American people, then "the Indian must rise like the Phoenix after having wallowed for ages in ignorance and barbarity."[12]

* * * * *

In an editorial in his inaugural issue, Elias Boudinot set forth several principles to which he would adhere during his four years as editor.[13] First, the purpose of the *Phoenix* was to inform the Cherokees of their national laws and other public documents, which, the editor promised, would be published in English *and* Cherokee. Boudinot vowed to conduct the paper with civility, though he admitted that the controversy with Georgia would "frequently make our situation trying." He also insisted that a large majority of his people opposed removal to the West, and so would the *Phoenix*. Boudinot asserted that Indians could be "reclaimed from a savage state," *and* in the area where they were presently located. Finally, the fledgling editor pleaded with the white "friends of the Cherokees," whose financial assistance had helped establish the paper, to subscribe to it so that it could thrive and, along with it, the Cherokee cause.

On his money-raising foray in 1826, Boudinot found that his audiences responded well to specific evidence that Cherokees had indeed made "progress" on the road to "civilization." He repeated this tactic in the early issues of the *Phoenix*, deluging his readers with statistics showing the increase since 1810 in the Cherokee Nation of livestock, spinning wheels and looms, plows, saw mills and grist mills, blacksmith shops, cotton gins, schools, and other accoutrements of "civilized" life.[14] He also printed, in English and Cherokee, the Cherokee constitution and laws, as well as correspondence and treaties between tribal leaders and federal officials going back forty years. Clearly, Boudinot hoped to demonstrate both Cherokee "progress" and the support offered by the US government since the administration of George Washington.

*****

As Georgia began tightening the screws on the Cherokees, Elias Boudinot put his faith in the willingness of the national government to defend Cherokee rights. If the federal administration would not protect the tribe's title to lands guaranteed them by past treaties, the editor warned, then Cherokees could not trust any promises made in future treaties. When eager Georgians began moving into Cherokee territory and the Jackson administration did nothing to stop them, an angry Boudinot asked editorially whether white Georgians actually believed it was "agreeable to [the Cherokees'] nature to have their rights trampled upon by a horde of robbers and vagabonds (we mean our intruders) and to have every avenue of justice closed against them?"[15]

In an editorial in July 1829, Boudinot took issue with a Georgia editor who predicted that, once the state acquired the Cherokee lands, its population would double in ten years and triple in twenty. According to Boudinot, however, the Cherokee territory was not large enough to sustain such growth, since only about one-sixth of it was fit for cultivation. Moreover, he added, there was another major obstacle Georgia would have to overcome to develop into a great state, and that was slavery. What

Boudinot did *not* mention was that "the Cherokees also owned slaves, and their legislature passed laws to protect and regulate the institution of slavery."[16]

By the middle of 1829, thanks largely to material published in the *Cherokee Phoenix*, public opinion *outside* the South had turned strongly against Georgia's heavy-handed Indian policy and President Jackson's willingness to support it. This gave Boudinot plenty of fresh ammunition for his columns—accounts of meetings in northern cities protesting Georgia's treatment of the Cherokees; congressional records highlighting angry debate over the Indian Removal Bill and the outraged responses of Georgia congressmen to pro-Cherokee petitions; and the long-running "William Penn" essays, written by Jeremiah Evarts, chief administrator of the American Board of Commissioners of Foreign Missions, arguing that "tribal sovereignty was superior to the claims of the states."[17]

Once Congress, at the urging of President Jackson, passed the Indian Removal Act in May 1830, aligning two branches of the national government with Georgia against the Cherokees, the tribe's last chance seemed to lie with the judiciary. That hope soon died, however, because Georgia's governor refused to recognize the Supreme Court's jurisdiction in the matter and ignored the court's decisions. And, when the Marshall court sided with the Cherokees in *Worcester v. Georgia* (1832), President Jackson himself refused to enforce it.[18]

The movement of those Boudinot called "white intruders" into the Cherokee Nation kept increasing, especially after June 1830, when Georgia's laws were officially extended over the territory. At the same time, President Jackson ordered US troops withdrawn, leaving to the newly created Georgia Guard the task of keeping order in the Cherokee Nation. The state legislature also approved a lottery to distribute Cherokee lands to fortunate whites. All this proved too much for the *Phoenix*'s editor, who angrily informed readers that Georgia had taken away their "rights as freemen" and replaced them with "Christian laws, placed before you in a language you cannot understand, and which withhold from you the last particle of right."[19]

The Georgia Guard harassed the missionaries working in the Cherokee Nation, because they refused to take an oath of loyalty to Georgia as required by a recently passed law. Boudinot gave the Guard's antimissionary campaign, and the brutal treatment accompanying it, prominent play in the columns of the *Phoenix*. Naturally, this brought upon his head the wrath of the guard's commander, Colonel Charles Nelson, who threatened to shut down the paper and to chastise Boudinot physically.[20]

More significant than Nelson's bluster was the president's order that the Cherokees' annuity be paid to individuals instead of in a lump sum to the tribal treasury. This move both crippled the tribe's efforts to mount a legal defense of their claims and threatened the future of the *Phoenix*. So, in December 1831, Elias Boudinot set off on another fund-raising tour and was absent from his editorial labors for more than six months. (His brother Stand Watie had charge of the paper in his absence.) Boudinot was joined on this trip by his cousin John Ridge, who served on the delegation lobbying on behalf of the Cherokees in Washington.[21]

In recent months, John Ridge had heard from Cherokee supporters in the nation's capital, including one Supreme Court justice, that there was no longer any hope the tribe could stave off emigration; he also had seen editorials in northern newspapers that had formerly defended Cherokees, conceding the time had come to give up their fight. President Jackson himself had told Ridge that, while the Cherokees were certainly free to try to remain in the east, the national government could do nothing to aid them. As a result, John Ridge finally had concluded that removal to the west was inevitable, so the tribe must arrange for a treaty on the best possible terms.[22]

The cousins surely discussed these developments between speaking engagements, and, by the time Elias Boudinot returned to Georgia in June of 1832, he had become a convert to the cause of Indian removal. The editor naturally wished to defend the need for a removal treaty in the columns of the *Phoenix*, but Principal Chief John Ross would have no defeatist talk in the Nation's newspaper, so Boudinot resigned in August. He was replaced by Ross's brother-in-law, Elijah Hicks.[23]

* * * * *

Elijah Hicks was loyal to Ross, so during his tenure, the *Phoenix* demanded a united front against emigration in the face of continuing white pressure. At the same time, the new editor publicly criticized John Ridge; Ridge's father, Major Ridge; Elias Boudinot; and other leaders of the so-called Treaty Party as traitors to their people. The *Phoenix* also became more overtly political after Hicks's arrival, reprinting a raft of anti-Jackson material from the papers of the opposition Whig Party. Only by defeating Andrew Jackson's bid for reelection and choosing Henry

Clay could the Cherokees be saved, the new editor contended. Hicks also echoed charges of hypocrisy aimed at President Jackson by southern papers supporting state rights, because Jackson opposed South Carolina's effort to nullify the federal tariff law while supporting Georgia's move to "nullify" a Supreme Court decision.[24]

John Ross and the National Council continued to reject all suggestions of removing to the west, even after Jackson was triumphantly reelected in November, but the handwriting was clearly on the wall, especially once the formation of the Treaty Party gave the administration a group to work with who supported emigration. Late in 1832, editor Hicks actually published pieces on both sides of the question, but this did not mean that he was ready to concede. He claimed that last-minute intervention, either by Congress or, failing that, by God Himself, would sustain the Cherokees' rights.[25]

Georgia's campaign of harassment against the *Phoenix* continued unabated. By early 1834, the paper's white printer had been ordered by Georgia authorities to leave the Cherokee Nation; mail service was frequently disrupted; Hicks was being sued for libel by a local white sheriff; and the paper was once more in perilous financial straits. On May 17, 1834, the print shop in the all-but-deserted Cherokee capital of New Echota published what would turn out to be the last issue of the *Cherokee Phoenix.*[26]

A year later, when it appeared that the Treaty Party would sign a removal treaty, Principal Chief John Ross decided to revive the *Cherokee Phoenix* in order to continue his fight against emigration. The Georgia Guard heard rumors of Ross's plan and, aided by Elias Boudinot's brother Stand Watie went to New Echota and raided the newspaper office, scattering the type, removing the press, and burning the building. The final act of the Cherokee removal tragedy would play out with no further commentary from a tribal newspaper.[27]

In December 1835, the Treaty Party signed the Treaty of New Echota, exchanging Cherokee lands in Georgia for new lands west of the Mississippi River. Even though the leaders of the Treaty Party represented a minority of the Cherokee people, both the Jackson administration and the government of Georgia accepted the New Echota agreement as legitimate. Principal Chief John Ross worked strenuously to abort the new treaty, or at least secure better terms, enlisting sympathetic whites to defend the Cherokee case in print and even writing two pamphlets himself.[28]

Elias Boudinot answered these efforts with a pamphlet of his own, *Letters and Other Papers Relating to Cherokee Affairs: Being a Reply to Sundry Publications Authorized by John Ross*, published in 1837, in which he both defended the Treaty of New Echota and offered a scathing critique of John Ross's leadership. Boudinot's bitter attack on Ross furnished additional ammunition to white Georgians and other defenders of Jackson's Indian policy, especially after congressional leaders made the pamphlet part of the public record, publishing it as *Senate Document 121, 25th Congress, 2nd Session.*[29]

The end of the Indian removal crisis finally came in the winter of 1838/39. Most remaining eastern Cherokees moved west along the infamous "Trail of Tears," during which an estimated four thousand to five thousand of them died. And, as a bloody epilogue to the removal drama, on June 22, 1839, several groups of Cherokees, loyal to John Ross but purportedly acting without his knowledge, executed Major Ridge, John Ridge, and Elias Boudinot for their part in arranging the Treaty of New Echota.[30]

*****

In significant ways, the *Cherokee Phoenix* resembled the newspapers published by and for white Georgians. Those journals, at least since the 1790s, had been vigorously—and sometimes viciously—partisan. By the early nineteenth century, Georgia newspaper editors were no longer simply "ink-stained wretches" skilled only at setting type. Increasingly, they were educated, articulate professionals, frequently lawyers, adept at interpreting current events through the prism of a particular political party. Letters, essays, and editorials were printed only if they supported the principles of the political party controlling the paper.

The same was true of the *Cherokee Phoenix*. It was launched in 1828 to spread the views of the Cherokee National Council, usually as the tribe's principal chief, John Ross, articulated those views. Ross was reputedly one-eighth Cherokee and fluent in English but not in the Cherokee tongue, yet he served for forty years as the chief defender of the tribe and its traditions. From its inception, the *Phoenix* opposed Cherokee removal to the West, and when founding editor, Elias Boudinot, decided in 1832 that emigration was the only way to preserve the Cherokees and their culture, he was forced to resign his post.

At its peak, the *Cherokee Phoenix* had a circulation of perhaps two hundred copies a week. Many copies were sent out of state, either to individual subscribers or to editors who sent copies of their papers in exchange. Boudinot regularly translated New Testament passages and Christian hymns into Cherokee and published them in the *Phoenix*, along with other items of a religious nature. Apparently, he did so to further the work of Christian missionaries living among the Cherokees. Boudinot was a very devout Christian (only health problems derailed his plan to study for the Christian ministry and serve as a missionary to the Cherokees), but his approach was misleading, to say the least: between 1826 and 1835, the percentage of Cherokees who converted to Christianity only rose from less than 5 percent to about 9 percent. Likewise, perhaps recognizing the antislavery sensibilities of his northern and midwestern readers, Boudinot recorded but did not comment on the number of Negro slaves in the Cherokee Nation (1,217 amid a reported Cherokee population of 13,563 in the east in 1825). And while the regular appearance of columns in Cherokee reinforced the notion of Cherokee "progress," in 1835, the tribal census revealed that almost 40 percent of the households in the Cherokee Nation included *no* literate members.[31]

In essence, then, perhaps the *Cherokee Phoenix* was no more the voice of the Cherokee people than the Milledgeville *Georgia Journal* or *Southern Recorder* were the voices of the state capital's white state rights supporters or the same town's *Federal Union* was the voice of those who defended the idea of the Union during the Nullification Crisis. Instead, Georgia's newspapers, including the *Cherokee Phoenix*, informed their readers what they *should* believe. Whether those readers actually accepted the "party line" or the extent to which they did so must remain an historical conundrum.

Thus, it is possible to see *Phoenix* editor Elias Boudinot as a Cherokee propagandist, trying to put the best face possible on the tribe's "progress" in order to win white support for Cherokee efforts to hold on to their lands in Georgia. His vision of a new, improved Cherokee Nation proved so alluring to Boudinot that he was unable to accept the much less glamorous reality. As one critical biographer wrote, while "Boudinot hoped to save a Nation,"

> his "Nation" of literate industrious farmers, nuclear family homesteads, English schools, Christian churches, and a republican government that would reach all levels of society had little basis in

> reality. It was a vision, a fantasy, a dream few of his people shared. Elias Boudinot was a tragic figure not just because he made a serious error in judgment or because he paid the ultimate price but because he could not accept his people, his heritage, or himself.[32]

And yet there is another way to see the man—like his cousin John Ridge, Elias Boudinot became convinced that, in the face of Georgia's intransigence and the unwillingness of President Andrew Jackson to help the Cherokees, the only realistic chance to preserve the tribe and its traditions lay in moving beyond the Mississippi. Boudinot and other leaders of the Treaty Party signed the Treaty of New Echota knowing full well that, in doing so, they were also signing their own death warrants because of the 1829 Cherokee law making any cessions of tribal land without council permission a capital offense.

Whichever view of Boudinot one takes, what can be said with certainty about him and the *Cherokee Phoenix* is that, over the four years of his editorship, the newspaper spoke its version of truth to the power brought against the Cherokees by Georgia and, increasingly, by the federal government. It was a valiant effort in a noble cause and deserved a better fate.

14

Antebellum Georgia's Dueling Memoirists: George R. Gilmer, Wilson Lumpkin, and the Cherokees

[NOTE: I had first encountered both Wilson Lumpkin's and George Gilmer's memoirs during my original dissertation research. I looked into both, trying to see what they could tell me about the factions and parties of James Jackson's era, but I found very little. Yet, when I began to explore the later period, I knew that I'd have to pay more attention to their accounts of party development after Jackson's death. Moreover, each had served as governor of Georgia during the Cherokee removal business. Consequently, I made substantial use of their memoirs in the second project in an effort to understand Cherokee removal, which occupied a substantial portion of the manuscript.

When I retired from The Westminster Schools at the end of May 2010, one of the first things I did was to launch a blog, *Retired But Not Shy*. During my years as head of the History Department, I had edited an online departmental newsletter and really enjoyed the experience. In a sense, the blog replaced the newsletter as a way for me to spend time creatively and, I hoped, constructively, after retirement. Its subtitle, *Doing History after Leaving the Classroom*, gave me freedom in choosing a topic for each month's post. One such running topic was, not surprisingly, Georgia history.

By the autumn of 2011, I was ready to tackle Lumpkin, Gilmer, and their memoirs over three blog posts. I treated each man and his autobiography separately and then, in the third segment, tried to compare and contrast them, their recollections of Cherokee removal, and their comments on the state's political culture. It was an interesting exercise, as I hope the following essay shows. I have reorganized the three posts into a more straightforward exposition. Unlike other chapters in this volume, this one lacks scholarly apparatus, because it basically combines reviews of two books, with a section of comparisons and contrasts of the two authors thrown in for good measure.]

*****

Almost four decades ago, while looking for useful contemporary descriptions of Georgia politics in the first decade of the nineteenth century, I stumbled upon former governor Wilson Lumpkin's ponderous two-volume autobiography, *The Removal of the Cherokee Indians from Georgia*, which is available online through Google Books. I found a couple of apt quotations early in volume 1 and immediately stopped looking for anything else. After all, Lumpkin's claim to fame, his role in helping to oust the Cherokees from Georgia, fell well outside the chronological boundaries of the dissertation I was then completing. Like Lumpkin, Georgia governor George R. Gilmer produced a memoir, *Sketches of the First Settlers of Upper Georgia, of the Cherokees, and the Author* (1855), defending *his* role in the Indian removal controversy of the 1830s but shedding no light on the earlier period in the state's political history in which I was interested. Nevertheless, a quarter of a century later, when I decided to begin research on a sequel to that first study, I had to revisit the autobiographies of both Gilmer and Lumpkin in an effort to understand their roles in bringing about the "Trail of Tears."

*****

George Gilmer opens his book with warm, fuzzy sketches of some of the early settlers of Georgia's Broad River valley, who, along with Gilmer's own family, had come from Virginia after the American Revolution. Next, he offers portraits of several prominent emigrants from North Carolina who settled in Wilkes County, Georgia; Gilmer looks down his "aristocratic" Virginia nose at this group, picturing their way of life in unflattering terms. Not surprisingly, the Virginia clique eventually produced members of the Crawford/Troup party, to which Gilmer himself belonged, while the descendants of the scruffy North Carolinians dominated the political opposition, headed by General (and, later, Governor) John Clark and, eventually, by Wilson Lumpkin. The last half of Gilmer's *Sketches* focuses on his own life and political career, especially his part in bringing about the removal of the Cherokees from Georgia.

Born in Georgia in 1790, George Gilmer studied at Moses Waddel's famous academy in Willington, South Carolina, leaving at age eighteen to teach school for a year before reading law under Stephen Upson in Lexington, Georgia. He took a break from his legal studies to serve as a militia officer engaged against the Creeks during the War of 1812 and then returned to Lexington to practice law. That same year, the young attorney was elected to the legislature from Oglethorpe County, launching a career in politics that would span more than two decades. Though he professed to have a low opinion of Georgia's political factions, Gilmer did admit he was a "friend" of William Crawford—and, the way politics worked in the state at the time, that made him an "enemy" of John Clark. Over the next several years, Gilmer alternated between serving Georgia in Congress and representing Oglethorpe County in the state legislature. He was reelected to Congress in 1828, but his seat was declared vacant on a technicality by Crawford party governor John Forsyth. Following a debate in the state press between Gilmer and Forsyth, couched in the highfalutin language of "Southern honor," Gilmer "retired to private life," but that proved short-lived.

At the annual epicenter of Georgia politics, the college commencement in Athens in 1829, Gilmer was asked by his "friends" to run for governor, despite the fact that another member of the Crawford party, Joel Crawford, had already announced for the office. Because Gilmer and his "friends" believed Joel Crawford's candidacy had been engineered by outgoing governor John Forsyth, the man who had declared Gilmer ineligible to hold the congressional seat to which they believed he had been elected in 1828, Gilmer entered the gubernatorial race. In a very confusing campaign, even by Georgia standards, Gilmer and Joel Crawford both ran as members of the Crawford party, much to the chagrin of party leaders, while the Clark party supported Gilmer rather than run a candidate of their own. Gilmer was elected.

On the morning of his inauguration, Gilmer wrote, a Clark party editor demanded that he split state patronage between the Crawford and Clark forces as a reward for Clark party votes during the gubernatorial campaign, but he refused. This meant that he entered the governorship having earned the enmity of *both* factions, Clark supporters because of his refusal to offer them patronage and the Crawford party because he had defied party leaders and opposed Joel Crawford for governor. As Gilmer ruefully summarized his situation, "I soon found that to be chief magistrate of the State, when party politics are violent, without party support, is to run barefooted over a thorny way." (Gilmer, 245)

In his memoir, Gilmer made two things clear: he had a very low opinion of the state's Native American population; and, with Andrew Jackson now in the White House, he believed that the new president would be on Georgia's side on the Indian removal question. Gilmer had been in office only a few months when he received a letter from former US attorney general William Wirt, informing him that the Cherokees had retained Wirt to push their suit against Georgia before the US Supreme Court (Gilmer, 270–272).

Gilmer was livid, answering Wirt's mild missive with biting sarcasm and white-hot, state-rights-fueled anger. When Wirt praised the "civilized and well-informed men" on the Cherokee delegation in Washington, for example, the governor responded that they were "not Indians ..., but the children of white men" who lived among the Cherokees. "The real aborigines" (i.e., those without "white blood"), he continued, had "become spiritless, dependent, and depraved, as the whites [among them] and their children have become wealthy, intelligent, and powerful." These mixed-blood leaders, the governor thundered, had "destroyed the ancient laws, customs, and authority of the tribe, and subjected the natives to that most oppressive of governments, an oligarchy." And that development, in turn, "rendered it obligatory upon the State of Georgia to vindicate her rights of sovereignty, by abolishing all Cherokee government within its limits." Finally, the governor maintained, for Georgia willingly to participate in settling the controversy before the Supreme Court would endanger the efforts of "the friends of liberty and the rights of the people [who were] endeavoring to sustain the sovereignty of the States." George Gilmer was consistent in his attitude toward the Supreme Court, refusing to recognize its authority in two important cases involving the Cherokees, *Cherokee Nation v. Georgia* (1831) and *Worcester v. Georgia* (1832). (Gilmer, 273–275)

Once a law extending Georgia's control over the Cherokee territory took effect on June 1, 1830, Governor Gilmer was concerned with enforcing that authority. The Cherokees and the gold in their territory both needed to be protected from greedy whites, the governor believed, but the only force authorized to keep the peace there was the United States Army, which aroused Gilmer's state rights scruples. Consequently, he secured the withdrawal of federal troops and the creation by the legislature of a forty-man unit, the Georgia Guard, to police the area. This group of "patriotic" good old boys soon earned a reputation for harassing and intimidating residents of the Cherokee territory. They especially enjoyed rousting white missionaries who refused to take an oath of loyalty to Georgia as required by state law, arresting them and dragging them in chains to the state penitentiary. In the face of angry criticism of the Georgia Guard's conduct from outside the state, Governor Gilmer defended their actions in letters to religious leaders, but he also warned the unit's commander to avoid excessive brutality.

* * * * *

Wilson Lumpkin was a polarizing figure in Georgia politics. Yet the idea of moving Georgia's Native American inhabitants west of the Mississippi River, which Lumpkin considered his "particular mission," was not that controversial among white Georgians at the time. There were occasional spats about means, but the end to be achieved, Indian removal, had broad support across party lines. So, why was Wilson Lumpkin such a controversial politician?

To his foes, Lumpkin was an opportunist, a perpetual candidate who wouldn't have known a principle if it bit him on the leg. While "patriotic" Georgians were fighting and bleeding during the War of 1812, his critics charged, Lumpkin stayed home and nursed his political fortunes. In the eyes of those opponents, Lumpkin's early support of Andrew Jackson for president in 1824 was disloyal to Georgian William Crawford, the leader of the state party Lumpkin belonged to, who was angling for the nomination himself. Moreover, critics asserted, when, as governor, he pardoned two missionaries to the Cherokees, imprisoned for refusing to take a loyalty oath to Georgia, Lumpkin betrayed the concept of "state rights" developed by one of his gubernatorial predecessors, George Troup. According to the political opposition, Lumpkin also was all over the map on the doctrine of Nullification, *posing* as an opponent of John C. Calhoun's theory but *practicing* Nullification by ignoring John Marshall's pro-Cherokee ruling in *Worcester v. Georgia* (1832). Finally, despite the popularity of Indian removal in Georgia and much of the South, observers outside the region took frequent editorial potshots at Governor Lumpkin, refusing to credit his sincerity in claiming to "protect" the Cherokees and their culture while at the same time forcing them beyond the Mississippi.

Lumpkin's autobiography suggests that he never forgot an insult or a criticism. For example, in dealing with the charge that he had no political principles, Lumpkin argued that, when his public career began, the motive force in Georgia politics "turned more upon popular leaders [William H. Crawford and John Clark]–more on men than on measures" (Lumpkin, vol. 1, 14). He also claimed that he "imbibed a disrelish [*sic*] to becoming a partizan [*sic*] to either of the factions" (Lumpkin, vol. 1, 15–17). When his memoir reached the War of 1812, Wilson Lumpkin dealt forthrightly with another sore point, harsh criticism of his decision not to join the fight against Great Britain on the battlefield, asserting that he "never had a taste for human slaughter, and therefore did not seek the glory of military fame" (Lumpkin, vol. 1, 20).

After the War of 1812, Lumpkin counted himself among those Republicans who, though originally committed to strict construction of the Constitution, had come to believe that changes ushered in by the war made it necessary for the national government to establish a new Bank of the United States; enact a protective tariff in order to encourage manufactures; and aid in the construction of internal improvements (e.g., roads and canals) to help tie the nation's regions together. Yet, he continued, as he gained more knowledge and experience over the course of his public career, he eventually repudiated those "liberal and latitudinarian measures," deciding instead that "the consolidating tendency of the Federal [Government] is the great rock upon which our glorious union of states will be sundered to fragments" (Lumpkin, vol. 1, 21–25).

As for refusing to support fellow Georgian William Crawford for President in 1824, Lumpkin averred that he knew Crawford's health was too precarious for him to discharge the duties of the presidency (he'd had a stroke, the severity of which was kept from the public). Lumpkin ran as a Jackson elector in 1824, and, though he lost, the experience brought him closer to the pro-Jackson party, whose head, General John Clark, had no love for William Crawford, the titular leader of the state's other party. When Andrew Jackson finally was elected president in 1828, Wilson Lumpkin was a prominent Georgia supporter, while many in the opposition Crawford-Troup party ultimately moved into the camp of the anti-Jackson Whig Party, although they refused officially to adopt the Whig name as their own until after 1840.

Wilson Lumpkin penned his autobiography in the early 1850s, but he remained sensitive to criticism of the Indian removal policy that he and other white Georgians had championed in the 1820s and 1830s. He claimed that his interest in the Indian question had developed when he accompanied Georgia's chief engineer on a tour to prepare a list of necessary internal improvement projects. This junket took him into the Cherokee section of Georgia, where he met several tribal leaders and tried to persuade them to support removal to the west. That experience, according to Lumpkin, had convinced him that "it was my particular mission, to do something to relieve Georgia from the incumbrance [*sic*] of her Indian population, and at the same time benefit the Indians" (Lumpkin, vol. 1, 40).

Winning a congressional seat in the fall of 1826, Wilson Lumpkin spent the time between his election and the start of the new congressional term studying the issue of Indian removal and preparing himself for his "particular mission." He believed that no system of internal improvements could be put in place until "Cherokee Georgia" was inhabited exclusively by white citizens, and he contended that the biggest obstacle to Indian removal was the activity of Cherokees "composed mostly of mixed breeds and white bloods" (Lumpkin, vol. 1, 42). Lumpkin and others in the removal camp, including future president Andrew Jackson, were constantly frustrated that the Cherokees could not understand how removing west of the Mississippi River would preserve their tribal culture by separating them from whites and putting them under the benevolent control of the federal government.

When Wilson Lumpkin finally took his seat in Congress, he wangled an appointment to the House Committee on Indian Affairs and, in December 1827, introduced an Indian removal resolution. Adoption of that resolution won him support in Georgia and in other states with Indian "problems," but it also stirred up, according to Lumpkin, "Northern fanatics, male and female," who launched a petitioning movement to block Indian removal, maligning Georgia in general and Congressman Lumpkin in particular (Lumpkin, vol. 1, 47). Still, convinced that Andrew Jackson would be the next president, Lumpkin waited patiently.

Following reelection to Congress, Lumpkin spent additional time boning up on the removal issue, convinced that he was "laboring in the cause of humanity, and to promote the best interest of the Indian, as well as the white race" (Lumpkin, vol. 1, 49). This time, the Indian Affairs committee submitted both an elaborate report and an Indian removal bill, a measure Lumpkin championed in debate, warning that, if Congress did not pass the bill, Georgia was prepared to go it alone, as she had five years earlier in dealing with the Creeks. Congress narrowly approved the Indian removal bill in the spring of 1830, and President Jackson signed it into law on May 28.

Wilson Lumpkin found himself on the horns of a dilemma following his next reelection to Congress in 1830: while he hoped to continue his "particular mission" as a member of Congress, his "friends" in Georgia pressed him to resign and run for governor, arguing that he would be more effective on Indian removal in that office than in Congress. After performing a highly publicized Hamlet act ("To be governor of Georgia, or not to be"), Lumpkin gave in to his supporters' pressure, entered the governor's race, and was elected over George Gilmer by 1,500 votes out of 51,000 cast in a nasty campaign highlighted by debate over Gilmer's "aristocratic" ways, the continuing schism in the ranks of the Crawford Party and Gilmer's Indian policy (e.g., his refusal to include Cherokee gold mine properties in the lottery used to dispose of the lands).

* * * * *

When, early in Lumpkin's first term, the US Supreme Court summoned Georgia to defend its policy toward the Cherokees, the governor informed the legislature that he would disregard the court's order on state rights grounds, terming it "Federal usurpation" (Lumpkin, vol. 1, 94). And his response was no warmer several months later, when John Marshall's court handed down the *Worcester* ruling.

Knowing that President Jackson supported Georgia, Governor Lumpkin confidently ignored the Supreme Court's decision. To bolster his view of Cherokee removal, Lumpkin included in his autobiography a collection of addresses and letters from his years as governor, and he concluded the survey of his governorship with the assertion that he saw the hand of God in Cherokee removal (Lumpkin, vol. 1, 368–369).

Volume 2 of Lumpkin's memoirs picks up the story when, after retiring as governor, he was appointed a federal commissioner to implement the controversial Treaty of New Echota (1835), signed by a small minority of tribal leaders but accepting removal and therefore recognized as legitimate by both Georgia and the Jackson administration. The remainder of the second volume follows the process of Indian removal through the forced departure of the Cherokees from Georgia in 1838, during the Van Buren administration.

Lumpkin was elected by the Georgia legislature to the US Senate in late 1837 and, not surprisingly, threw himself wholeheartedly into the task of finally bringing about the removal of the Cherokees from the state. He believed that Andrew Jackson's presidential successor, Martin Van Buren, spent too much time trying to convince principal chief John Ross to drop his opposition to Cherokee removal. Angrily, Lumpkin charged that Van Buren's ham-handed policy had contributed to the deaths by assassination of Major Ridge, John Ridge, and Elias Boudinot, Cherokee leaders who had defied the Ross faction and signed the Treaty of New Echota, but nothing was ever done to punish the murderers. Lumpkin insisted that, on the question of Cherokee removal, there was only "one party" in Georgia: "The whole people anxiously desired the speedy removal of the Indians, in terms of the late Treaty [of New Echota]" (Lumpkin, vol. 2, 218).

* * * * *

In George Gilmer's second gubernatorial term (1837–1839), as the deadline approached for the Cherokees to leave the state, the situation grew quite tense. White Georgians were eager to see the Cherokees depart—the sooner the better—while the tribe's principal chief, John Ross, was in Washington trying to negotiate with the Van Buren administration an extension of the deadline for removal. To Gilmer's chagrin, Ross's stalling tactics seemed on the verge of success. Governor Gilmer refused to countenance any further delay in executing the Treaty of New Echota (1835), stubbornly insisting the Cherokees must go, and, if the federal government would not act, he vowed that Georgia would. Of course, the Cherokees did go, on the infamous "Trail of Tears," where thousands of them died, before Gilmer retired from office.

Gilmer's final assessment of his own role in Cherokee removal was that he "felt it was something to have overcome, by directness of purpose, and the means at my command, the power and subtility [*sic*] of Mr. Van Buren and John Ross, and to have secured to the State and the people the great good which has followed what was done" (Gilmer, 431).

* * * * *

George Gilmer, who valued things Virginian above all, came from a family with roots in the Old Dominion but was himself born in Georgia. Wilson Lumpkin, whom Gilmer in his memoir grouped with the lower-class North Carolinians who formed the Clark party, actually also was from a Virginia family and, unlike Gilmer, had been born there. Moreover, while Lumpkin did wind up in the Clark party, he began his political career, like Gilmer, as a member of the Crawford/Troup party. Both men's fathers served as local magistrates. Gilmer studied under Moses Waddel in South Carolina and read law under Stephen Upson in Lexington, Georgia, while Lumpkin got what education he could locally and then polished his skills by helping his father with his duties as clerk of the superior court.

In his autobiography, Lumpkin remarked, "Political parties fifty years ago in Georgia, and indeed long since, turned more upon popular leaders–more on men than on measures." William Crawford and John Clark were "personal enemies," Lumpkin conceded, and each controlled a "considerable portion" of both houses of the legislature, "while perhaps a majority of the members, *like myself*, desired to keep aloof from the personalities of these gentlemen" (Lumpkin, vol. 1, 14). Lumpkin wrote that Crawford and his supporters referred to the Clark party as "*the Federal party*," because some had held office under John Adams, and he also charged that some members of the Clark party had participated in the Yazoo land fraud (1794-1795). Yet, Lumpkin asserted, "Clark and most of his leading friends of that day professed to be, and in many respects sustained well, the character of real Democrats, if not *Red Republicans*" (Lumpkin, vol. 1, 14).

George Gilmer also claimed to have a low opinion of political factions, but, as a "friend" of William Crawford, he also was an "enemy" of John Clark. Moreover, during his initial campaign for the state legislature, Gilmer had to fight off charges of "Federalism" aimed at him by the Clark party. (Gilmer, 201–202).

Wilson Lumpkin worked to secure removal of the Cherokees from Georgia because he believed that was his "particular mission," while Gilmer did so because he saw Indian removal as in the best interests of (white) Georgians and because dealing with that issue was part of serving in the state legislature, in Congress, and, eventually, as governor.

Both men also "bucked the system" when it was in their political interests to do so. Lumpkin throughout his career was portrayed by his enemies as without firm political principles, largely because he had abandoned the

Crawford/Troup party for the Clark party, and had supported Andrew Jackson for president in 1824, when the leader of the faction to which Lumpkin belonged at the time, William Crawford, wanted the presidential nomination for himself but was disqualified by illness.

Gilmer, in his turn, successfully challenged Joel Crawford for the Crawford/Troup party gubernatorial nomination in 1829, despite the fact that Crawford had announced for the nomination first, which, under the party's usual practice, should have made him the nominee. When Gilmer won the election, supported by some members of the Crawford party *and* by the Clark party, he pledged to govern in the interests of all the people, not those of one party. Yet, because he successfully challenged Joel Crawford and refused to offer patronage appointments to the Clark party in return for their support during the campaign, Gilmer was beset on all sides during his term in the governor's chair by angry members of *both* parties.

Wilson Lumpkin comes across in his memoirs as a "democrat," a believer in the power of "the people" to act in their own best interests, if given the necessary information. For instance, when Congress in 1816 passed the Compensation Act, changing pay for congressmen from a per diem basis to a salary, the popular uproar was tremendous. Even those who, like Lumpkin and his fellow Georgia congressmen, had voted against the bill were sent packing. Looking back on the furor a generation later, Lumpkin claimed it proved to him that, while "the people" might err, they could nevertheless be counted upon to regain their equilibrium eventually (Lumpkin, vol. 1, 30). His memoirs make Lumpkin seem humorless, though that might be because his modern editor shaped the manuscript autobiography to focus on Lumpkin's political career.

In his memoir, George Gilmer seems a self-styled "aristocrat," quite capable of peering archly at "the people" or their self-appointed champions (i.e., Lumpkin and other members of the Clark Party) when he thought they were wrong, which, evidently, was quite often. In contrast to Lumpkin, Gilmer possessed a sharp sense of humor, though one heavily conditioned by a sardonic feeling of noblesse oblige. Thus, his story about how John Clark, drunk and on his way to Milledgeville to chastise Governor David Mitchell for a perceived insult, was found "asleep upon a log which projected over a precipice, where a turn the wrong way would have precipitated him below, and probably killed him—the recklessness of his temper and his desire to fight Mitchel [*sic*] having put him into the humor to hunt for danger" (Gilmer, 159).

Following his defeat by Lumpkin for reelection, Gilmer found himself at a public dinner arranged for him by his party, where he "was called upon to say how, and why, I had contrived to deprive those by whom I was surrounded of the public offices to which they considered themselves entitled" (Gilmer, 359). In his speech, Gilmer claimed that his most unpopular decision, refusing to order an immediate survey and distribution of the Cherokee lands, had been made for two reasons: "what I considered justice to our Indian population"; and a belief that, given President Jackson's support for the state's Cherokee policy, Georgia should not aid Old Hickory's political enemies by doing anything to put Georgia on a collision course with the federal government when the president was already dealing with the Nullification issue in South Carolina (Gilmer, 360).

* * * * *

George Gilmer *published* his memoirs in 1855. Wilson Lumpkin *wrote* his in the early 1850s, but the volume was not published during his lifetime, which was to Lumpkin's advantage: he was able to "correct the record" in his manuscript whenever something was said or printed about him with which he disagreed (i.e., he was, in a sense, a "blogger" before blogging was cool). Lumpkin did this, for example, after Gilmer's book appeared and after George White issued a new edition of *Statistics of Georgia*, because both works included interpretations of Lumpkin's Indian policy that he believed wrongheaded. In criticizing Gilmer's book, Lumpkin got off a zinger that applied just as well to *his own* memoirs: "[Gilmer] can neither speak nor write of those with whom he differs, without manifesting a superlative degree of prejudice" (Lumpkin, vol. 2, 300).

The dueling memoirists also furnish insights into Georgia's political culture in the early antebellum period. About his initial nomination for the state legislature, Gilmer modestly noted that, "Whilst I was temporarily absent from Lexington [his home town],… it was determined by some of the leading politicians of the county that I should be a candidate" (Gilmer, 201). Gilmer also recounted an episode revealing the bitterness of the rivalry between the Crawford and Clark parties. An ardent Crawford supporter, Baptist preacher Jesse Mercer, delivered a sermon at the funeral of Governor William Rabun, a member of the Crawford party, with newly elected Governor John Clark in attendance. According to Gilmer, Mercer "enforced the doctrine with great zeal, that when the Lord taketh away a good and righteous man [Rabun], he does it on account of the sins of the people, and will punish them by putting wicked rulers [e.g., Clark] over them, and [he] ended by saying Georgia had reason to tremble" (Gilmer, 214). Gilmer also denied that his decision to challenge Joel Crawford for governor was motivated by personal ambition, claiming instead that his "friends" had convinced him he was the better candidate.

Wilson Lumpkin, too, commented on the power of political "friendship," asserting that, while he preferred to remain in Congress, his "friends" in Georgia pressed him to run for governor against Gilmer in 1831, arguing that, if he won, he could work more effectively on behalf of his "particular mission," Cherokee removal (Lumpkin, vol. 1, 90). Lumpkin knew that his candidacy would anger Gilmer's supporters, and he was not sure he could defeat the incumbent. But he was "forced to become a candidate," he wrote, "because nothing else would satisfy my beloved friends and constituents who had stood by me through evil and good reports, for upwards of thirty years" (Lumpkin, vol. 1, 91; vol. 2, 302–03). And, reminding us that being a "good loser" was no more popular in antebellum Georgia than it is today, Lumpkin told how, after his inaugural address, Gilmer escorted him to the governor's office, but then he and all but one of his staff left the new governor to find his own way—and to locate papers called for by the legislature (Lumpkin, vol. 1, 92).

By 1826, public opinion in Georgia had embraced Andrew Jackson as a presidential candidate for 1828, but, according to Wilson Lumpkin, some members of the Crawford/Troup party were too pushy in jumping on the general's bandwagon, alienating members of "the old original panel of the Jackson party," by which he meant members of the Clark party like himself. (Lumpkin, vol. 1, 41). In *his* memoir, George Gilmer remarked that "all in Georgia were Jackson men whilst Gen. [*sic*] Jackson was in office, the Clark party from choice, the Crawford party from necessity, so that the old factions began to lose their lines of demarcation, and new parties to be formed upon the general principles which divided the people of the United States" (Gilmer, 438). The Crawford/Troup / State Rights Party—of which Gilmer had been a member—eventually became the Whigs shortly after he retired from public life, while the Clark/Union

Party to which Lumpkin belonged morphed into the Democrats, with Lumpkin himself playing a key role in making that happen.

Wilson Lumpkin, derided by his political foes for his lack of consistency, always had an answer. After admitting that he had supported the broader vision of the federal government's role in guiding the nation's destiny that emerged after the War of 1812, he added that he had "long since repudiated these votes" and was "firmly resolved that no necessity whatever should ever induce me to contribute my mite to the enlargement of the powers of the Federal Government one hair's breadth beyond the limits of the Constitution." Lumpkin even claimed (in 1852) that he had "long believed … that the consolidating tendency of the Federal Government is the great rock upon which our glorious union of states will be sundered to fragments" (Lumpkin, vol. 1, 24–25).

George Gilmer also was quite capable of boxing the political compass without a blush. For instance, in 1832, responding to voters interested in his stand on the Nullification Crisis, Gilmer wrote that he did not believe a state could nullify an act of Congress, but also disagreed with the group's opinion that the recently passed tariff was an improvement over previous ones. Moreover, Gilmer informed his constituents, he rejected their statement "that the evils of the tariff have been greatly exaggerated," and disagreed that the tariff question should be left to the state legislature, preferring that the issue be decided by a popularly elected state convention; yet he also asserted that any recommendations by such a convention could not be binding until approved by a popular referendum (Gilmer, 361–62). How about an "a-men!" for Gilmer's effort at political obfuscation?

Becoming reacquainted with Wilson Lumpkin was definitely an acquired taste. Evidently, he was sincere in his view of the Cherokees, as well as in his statement that he worked hard to familiarize himself with the issue of Indian removal, but clearly he had made his mind up on the question long before his election to Congress. By his own admission, he was already convinced that the Cherokees must leave Georgia when he visited tribal leaders in 1825, and he pushed that view unwaveringly over the next fifteen years, until his "particular mission" became a reality. So give Lumpkin an A for consistency. It is important to remember, though, that his view of the Cherokees was shared by many whites, including President Andrew Jackson, which both bolstered Governor Lumpkin's confidence and doomed the Cherokees.

Like Wilson Lumpkin, George Gilmer's perspective on Indian removal was heavily tinged with racism. He believed that all the "advances" made by the Cherokees were attributable to members of the tribe who had "white blood"; yet that very taint supposedly led those modernizers to oppose removal. According to both Gilmer and Lumpkin, Cherokee opponents of removal did not represent the views of "the real aborigines" (Gilmer's phrase). In fact, Gilmer believed, again like Lumpkin, that John Ross and his allies were only interested in money and did not care what happened to the majority of the tribe. Ironically, their dismissive view of Cherokee leaders opposed to removal could also fit members of the so-called Treaty Party like Major Ridge, John Ridge, and Elias Boudinot, who signed the New Echota agreement and eventually forfeited their lives for doing so.

The Treaty Party represented the views of only a small minority of the Cherokees, but President Jackson and the State of Georgia nevertheless regarded the treaty as valid, and it was ratified narrowly by the United States Senate. This blatant hypocrisy made it easier for men like Gilmer and Lumpkin to congratulate themselves on their roles in driving the Cherokees west of the Mississippi, where, they professed to believe, the "aborigines" would be "protected" from whites and allowed to preserve their tribal way of life in an Edenic setting, in perpetuity. As Gilmer wrote, the time had come for whites to celebrate "the great good which has followed what was done," and, after the Trail of Tears, there was no need to invite the Cherokees to the party.

* * * * *

The insistence of Georgia whites that Native Americans must be forced out of the state had many causes. The main one was the so-called Compact of 1802, whereby the state sold the "Yazoo lands" (roughly, modern-day Alabama and Mississippi) to the national government in return for a pledge that Washington would eliminate tribal land claims in Georgia when that could be done peacefully. Numerous treaties were concluded with the Creeks and Cherokees after 1802, but this piecemeal process was too slow for land-hungry Georgians caught up in the burgeoning cotton economy's demands for fresh fields to be exploited. The discovery of gold in the Cherokee region of North Georgia was simply the last straw.

Ironically, had it not been for the controversy stirred by the removal of the Cherokees, it is unlikely that either Gilmer or Lumpkin would have written a memoir. Both attempted to place their actions in a historical context that made them appear founts of wisdom and restraint in dealing with the "backward" Cherokees, their irrational northern supporters, and feckless administrations in Washington. Establishing that context led both men to consider their broader political careers. For anyone trying to understand the political culture of antebellum Georgia, the dueling memoirs of George Gilmer and Wilson Lumpkin are more useful than either man probably intended.

While it is certainly not necessary for historians to *accept* the worldview of white Georgians in the early nineteenth century regarding Native Americans, it is crucial that they *understand* it and take it seriously. Only then can the broader context be established for the decades-long drive to oust the Creeks and the Cherokees from the state. Among the richest sources for viewing antebellum Georgia through the eyes of an intelligent, articulate, and politically significant figure are Wilson Lumpkin's *The Removal of the Cherokee Indians from Georgia* and George R. Gilmer's *Sketches of the First Settlers of Upper Georgia, of the Cherokees, and the Author.*

Epilogue

Howell Cobb and the Union, 1850–1854

[NOTE: The first two years of grad school were incredibly busy: I was expected to take three classes each quarter; read widely in preparation for comprehensive exams, a prerequisite for moving on to the dissertation stage; and, oh yes, look around for a dissertation topic.

My favorite Emory professor, Dr. James Rabun, offered a graduate course on "The Old South," which I took during the 1969/70 school year. Dr. Rabun required a seminar paper in the spring quarter, and, still looking for a topic in Georgia history, I decided to examine the pre–Civil War career of Howell Cobb, especially his crucial role as Speaker of the US House of Representatives during the crisis over the Compromise of 1850. The result was an essay of almost ninety pages, "The Limitations of Principle: Howell Cobb, 1849–1854." My findings seemed to strike a chord with Dr. Rabun, who had spent years on a combined biography of Cobb, Alexander Stephens, and Robert Toombs, three of antebellum Georgia's most significant political figures. Perhaps a biography of Cobb would be an acceptable dissertation topic, I thought, but I shortly learned that a grad student at the University of Georgia, repository for most of Cobb's papers, was engaged on just such a project, so obviously that topic was closed to me.

So, I returned to Georgia politics during the generation after the American Revolution but held on to the Cobb paper, pack rat that I had become. Imagine my surprise when, four decades later, I realized that my research project on Georgia political factions and parties, 1807–1845, would come perilously close to the parameters of the Cobb piece. I dragged the paper out of my files and began hacking, pruning, reorganizing, trying to see how—or whether—I could use it in the book. Eventually, though,

I decided to include only a brief reference to the events depicted in the Cobb essay.

Still, I really like the shortened treatment of Cobb and the Crisis of the Union, so I thought I would include it here.]

*****

On September 8, 1850, the exuberant Speaker of the United States House of Representatives, Howell Cobb of Georgia, writing to his wife during the session that produced the Compromise of 1850, informed her that the final measures had been passed on the preceding day:

> Peace and harmony will now I trust, be restored to the country & that miserable faction in Georgia who have been warring on me for years will be reduced to their proper level. I have no doubt that people throughout the country will approve and sanction the action of Congress.[1]

The situation in Georgia belied such easy optimism, however. Following passage of the California statehood bill, Governor George Towns had called for a convention to meet in Milledgeville in December 1850. Pursuant to a series of resolutions passed by the legislature in February 1850, that convention would decide upon the state's future course with regard to the most recent acts of Congress. Excitement mounted as the date for electing delegates approached. Newspapers usually considered organs of the Georgia Democracy vied with one another in denouncing the compromise and calling for secession.[2]

Georgia's acceptance of the compromise measures hinged upon the election of a preponderance of "conservative" delegates to the Milledgeville convention. To secure this end, Democrat Howell Cobb and Whigs Alexander Stephens and Robert Toombs decided to return to Georgia from Washington and travel throughout the state speaking on behalf of the compromise. The exertions of Toombs, Stephens, and Cobb had the desired effect, with Unionists winning an overwhelming victory, 46,000–24,000.[3] The December convention, dominated by those favoring acceptance of the compromise, adopted the so-called Georgia Platform, stating that, while not satisfied with parts of the congressional settlement, the state would accept it as the final resolution of the slavery controversy. However, the platform also contained a warning: if, at some future date,

Congress reneged on any of the measures promised in the compromise, Georgia would resist, even to the point of breaking up the Union.[4]

What had taken place in Georgia between August and December 1850 was yet another political reorganization. The emotion engendered in the state as a result of the passage of the compromise, Governor Towns's call for a convention, the ensuing campaign to elect delegates, and the adoption of the "Georgia Platform," had shattered the Whig and Democratic parties that had emerged in the early 1840s. Out of the rubble two new political entities arose, each with a specific mission for the present but an uncertain future.

* * * * *

The ominously named "*Southern* Rights Party" (as opposed to Georgia's "*State* Rights Party" of the 1830s), created in August 1850, was composed of the overwhelming majority of Georgia Democrats and a few Whigs. These "fire-eaters" argued that the compromise represented a violation of the constitutional rights of the South and ought to be repudiated.[5] The bulk of the state's Whig Party had combined with Democrats who eschewed the secessionist doctrine of their Southern Rights brethren to form the Constitutional-Union Party. Significantly, Democratic support for the Constitutional-Union Party initially emanated from Howell Cobb's political fiefdom, the northwest, or Cherokee, section of the state. While unhappy with some parts of the compromise, Georgia Unionists pinned their hopes on the measure's faithful execution. They believed that, if the nation accepted the compromise as the final solution of the slavery question, then divisive agitation would cease, and the manifold blessings of the Union would be preserved.[6]

In Congress, Howell Cobb had supported the national Democratic Party as the political organization most capable of securing the rights of the South. He had stumped his state, along with Whig Congressmen Stephens and Toombs, as part of a bipartisan task force to gain approval of the Compromise, the most consistent congressional supporters of which had been Democrats.[7] A fervent adherent of the Democratic Party, Cobb had contended strongly for the preservation of the Union. Since the Democratic and Whig labels had been subsumed in his native state by the formation of new parties, continued defense of the Union seemed possible to Cobb, on the state level, only through the medium of the Constitutional-Union Party.

In essence, the situation in mid-December 1850 was one in which Cobb could have his cake and eat it too. There was little risk in lending moral support to Georgia's Constitutional-Union Party while Cobb was firmly ensconced in the Speaker's chair in Washington. Late in December, however, he received a report on the Milledgeville convention that provided abundant food for thought. According to a correspondent, the question of who would be the next governor of Georgia had engaged the attention "of the Union men and I but repeat what you will learn from all quarters that for that high office you were & are the general favorite[.]"[8]

Even after Cobb reluctantly agreed to accept the Constitutional-Union Party's gubernatorial nomination, there was no semblance of unanimity on that party's future course. Whig members continued to support the formation of a national Union party, an idea that many Union Democrats, including Cobb, already had abandoned as chimerical.[9]

Union Democrats, on the other hand, tended to agree with Cobb that a sizable portion of the national Democratic Party had been, and would continue to be, "sound" on the slavery question. Accepting this basic premise, they felt that Georgia's Constitutional-Union Party must look to the national Democracy for succor. Yet they also perceived trouble ahead, unless southern Whigs could be persuaded to abandon their old party label and, armed with their Unionist principles, march into battle under the Democratic banner. For example, William Hope Hull, a personal friend and political ally from Athens, confided to Cobb in February 1851 that

> if the Southern Whigs can be got to attach themselves to the Democratic Party *eo nomine* then it will all be well—I have no belief whatsoever that they will do so. Names are everything in politics, and though they would without difficulty have taken up Democratic doctrines if you call them Union doctrines and they would gladly be called Union men—yet they will never consent to be called Democrats.[10]

Three months later, another correspondent asserted that there was no reason for Union Whigs like Toombs and Stephens to object to cooperating with the national Democratic Party, because the Democrats were bound to nominate a "conservative" candidate for the presidency in 1852. Indeed, this writer even declared that, when he looked at the stands taken by Union

Whigs on the issues of the day, he was unable to "see what they lack now of being Democrats."[11]

The organization of the Constitutional-Union Party proceeded apace, despite the fact that most Southern Rights men claimed to agree with the tenets of the Georgia Platform. This led Southern Rights Democrats "to convert the local Democratic organizations they still controlled into a Southern Rights party to save their own careers from the Unionist onslaught." Veteran State Rights / Whig politician Charles Dougherty contended angrily, in a letter to John Berrien, that there was no reason for Georgia's parties to divide over the Compromise of 1850, because secession was out of the question. The real reason for all the agitation, Dougherty believed, was desire for office, and he predicted that the Constitutional-Union Party could not endure, because the South had accepted the compromise, and "parties cannot be maintained on past questions." According to a modern historian of the Whig Party, Dougherty "could not know it, but he had written an apt epitaph not only for Georgia's Union party, but also for the national Whig party."[12]

Constitutional-Union gubernatorial candidate Howell Cobb was expected to carry the party's standard in a campaign emphasizing the finality of the Compromise of 1850, while his Southern Rights opponent, former two-term Union/Democratic governor Charles J. McDonald, stood upon a platform supporting the abstract right of secession, the assertion that, even if never exercised, each state had "the right, in virtue of its independence and sovereignty, of *seceding* from the Union whenever the people thereof, in their sovereign capacity, shall determine such a step to be necessary."[13] Realizing that the emotional impact of the secession question would probably not allow him to ignore it, and fully aware that Whigs and Democrats arrayed under the Constitutional-Union banner held very different views on the issue, Cobb offered his opinion in a letter circulated among leaders of the new party.

One of them, Union Whig Robert Toombs, noted pointedly that the convention committee of which he had been chairman had already dealt with the issue, arguing that "the whole doctrine of secession was an open question & any member of the party had a right to hold what opinions he pleased upon it without giving cause of complaint to any one [*sic*] & that whatever might be your opinion it would in no wise affect their support of you." Toombs's view influenced Cobb to withhold his letter from general circulation, at least temporarily.[14]

Another important issue growing out of the campaign was the question of the future course of the Constitutional-Union Party. One week after receiving his party's gubernatorial nomination, Cobb outlined his conception of the role the party would play in a letter to Pennsylvanian James Buchanan, whom he hoped to see as the Democratic presidential candidate in 1852:

> We stand pledged to support the candidate and cooperate with the party who maintain the principles of the Georgia platform—We know that the northern Whigs will present no such candidate and therefore regard ourselves as virtually pledged to the support of the nominee of the national democratic [*sic*] convention.[15]

In other words, if the national Democratic Party vindicated his faith in its rectitude, then Cobb saw no reason he could not lead Georgia's Constitutional-Union Party into the ranks of the Democracy en masse. Obviously, Cobb continued to believe that his political future, like his past, was inextricably bound to the national Democratic Party.

Realizing the fragility of the organization he represented, Cobb accepted the Constitutional-Union gubernatorial nomination in a letter fraught with ambiguity. Defending the wisdom of the people of Georgia in accepting the Georgia Platform, and warning against dangers posed to that settlement by southern fire-eaters in general and Georgia's Southern Rights Party in particular, Cobb nevertheless felt compelled to inject a note of truculence, quoting from the Georgia Platform and vowing that

> should however the time ever arrive when the conditions of [Georgia's] remaining in the confederacy are *degradation* and *inequality*, I shall be prepared with her 'to resist, with all the means which a favoring Providence may place at her disposal,' even (*as a last resort*) 'to a disruption of every tie which binds her to the Union,' any and every power that seeks to put her upon such debasing terms. Nor am I particular by what name this resistance may be characterized—whether secession, revolution, or anything else; … [S]hould this fearful collision ever come, the issue will be decided only by the arbitrament [*sic*] of the sword.[16]

In the ensuing campaign, both candidates visited nearly every corner of the state. Between train rides, barbecues, and handshakes, Howell Cobb engaged in spirited debates or solo harangues, delivering a thinly disguised version of his letter of acceptance. Meanwhile, clad in the armor of righteousness, opposing newspaper editors exchanged insults, confident that their readers would vindicate them at the polls.

As the campaign progressed, the so-called abstract right of secession came to overshadow other issues. Almost from the first, the Southern Rights press had demanded that Cobb reveal the contents of his earlier letter on that question which, they charged, had been "suppressed" by leaders of his party. When he finally deigned to respond, Cobb's letter was a masterpiece of political obfuscation.[17]

He began by asserting that, in claiming the right to secede at pleasure, those who championed the "abstract right of secession" were arguing that "the framers of the constitution did that which was never done by any other people possessed of their good sense and intelligence—that is to provide in the very organization of the government for its own dissolution." Citing James Madison, Cobb countered that the framers had intended the Union to be perpetual, not temporary or conditional. Yet, while denying a state's right to secede at pleasure, the would-be governor also opposed the use of military force to bring a wayward state back into the Union, assuring Georgians that "only a short absence [would] teach the wanderer the benefits and advantages from which she had voluntarily exiled herself."

On the other hand, Cobb contended that military power would not suffice to maintain the Union if the government alienated popular support. In that case, he argued, the people would prove "as true to the principles of liberty and equal rights as our honored and venerated fathers; nor will we stop to look at the provisions of a violated constitution for the mode or measure for the redress of our grievances." Although denying the "abstract right of secession," Cobb emphasized that he was prepared to recognize a more practical right, "the right of a State to secede in case of oppression or 'a gross and palpable violation' of her constitutional rights ..." Finally, he promised that, in the unlikely event Congress empowered the president to use force to coerce a recalcitrant state back into the Union, he would ask for a state convention to determine the will of the people, and "as Georgia spoke, so would I endeavor, if her Executive, to give power and effect to her voice," Cobb pontificated.

In October, Howell Cobb defeated Charles McDonald, 57,397–38,824, while his new party gained control of both houses of the state legislature and sent several members to Congress. Recalling the tension that had surrounded the convention of 1850 and the state legislature's adoption of the Georgia Platform, a majority of voters seemed to view the struggle as an extension of the earlier one and acted to secure the "finality" of the compromise. Principle and expediency had blurred into a contest between good and evil, union and disunion, and Cobb and the Union had emerged victorious.[18]

And yet, even as the Whigs and Democrats comprising the Constitutional-Union Party fretted about their future, the defeated Southern Rights Party executed a stunning maneuver that completely altered the political situation in Georgia. After the legislature convened in Milledgeville, Southern Rights legislators resolved themselves into "a portion of the Democratic Party of Georgia" and adopted a report asserting that, in the late election, the people had acquiesced in the compromise. Therefore, they contended, the need for a strictly southern party had passed. Southerners of every political stripe should ally themselves with the national Democratic Party, the only national party that had demonstrated a willingness "to consider the compromise, as a *permanent and final settlement of the slavery controversy, to enforce the faithful execution of the Fugitive Slave Law, and to oppose its repeal or material modification.*" The paramount consideration now, according to the report, was to ensure a unified delegation to the Democratic National Convention so that "if Georgia shall not be represented as a unit in the Baltimore Convention, *it shall not be our fault.*"[19]

Early in 1852, while on his way to New York City to oversee preparations for a state bond issue, Governor Cobb spent a couple of days in Washington, where, he informed his wife, he had "seen enough to satisfy me that things will probably work well for the good and faithful followers of true democracy." He remarked that he had "put out a few feelers and already see their workings," and planned to stop in Washington again on his way home from New York.[20] Even before leaving for New York, Cobb saw one feeler come to fruition. He had written to the newly elected congressman from Georgia's Fifth District, Elijah Chastain, who had yet to make his maiden speech, expressing the wish that he could "be a member of Congress one hour just to make a speech upon the position of parties." In reply, Chastain asked for Cobb's "views at length upon the subject … and if you have no objections I would like to be the organ through whom those views may be communicated to the country." The governor did as the new congressman asked, and Chastain, concurring "in full" with Cobb's ideas, vowed that he would deliver them on the floor of Congress and give them "extensive circulation."[21]

When Governor Cobb reached New York City, he was invited to address local Democrats at Tammany Hall. The speech he delivered was almost a carbon copy of the address given in Congress by Elijah Chastain on his behalf. Cobb added an explicit defense of his conduct in choosing to head the Constitutional-Union ticket in 1851, declaring that, while his foes had charged him with abandoning the principles of the Democracy for those of the opposition, "If the course that I have pursued assigns me a position outside the Democratic party, nine-tenths of the democratic [*sic*] party must go outside with me." The governor also insisted that the approaching Democratic national convention in Baltimore must "affirm the finality and faithful enforcement of the Compromise, illustrative as it is of those democratic principles so often proclaimed by the democracy."[22]

On his return trip, Cobb stopped in Washington again, visiting the gallery of the House of Representatives, where he heard Junius Hillyer, his successor in the state's Sixth District seat, deliver yet another version of Elijah Chastain's speech. As a hostile observer described the scene, "Mr. Cobb sat blandly listening, while his disciple expounded the text, and nasally enunciated the doctrine of the democratic perfectability [*sic*] of [the Cobb] party." Hillyer placed even greater emphasis than Chastain had on the wisdom of the Constitutional-Union Party being represented in Baltimore, and he insisted there were no real ideological differences between Union Whigs and Union Democrats.[23]

The problem, insoluble as it turned out, was that, while Cobb saw no reason Union Whigs should object to marching arm in arm with Union Democrats into the ranks of the national Democratic Party, Union Whig members were not willing to go along, even after the national Whig Party nominated for president General Winfield Scott, who was supposedly under the influence of the notorious antislavery New Yorker William H. Seward. While Alexander Stephens and Robert Toombs, Georgia's most prominent Union Whigs, asserted that they opposed Scott's nomination and were determined to abide by the Constitutional-Union Party's decision at their upcoming convention, Toombs informed Cobb privately that "I will in no event do either of two things *vote for Scott* or the *fire-eating* [Democratic] *ticket.*"[24]

Meanwhile, Southern Rights Democrats had selected electors committed to Franklin Pierce and William R. King, and, since they claimed to be *the* Democratic Party of Georgia, they naturally referred to their slate as the "official" Democratic ticket. Even if Cobb's Union

Democrats succeeded in having the Constitutional-Union convention approve the Pierce-King ticket, how were they to deal with this so-called official slate of Democratic electors? Moreover, Alexander Stephens, who had promised to abide by the outcome of the July 15 convention, appealed for the nomination by that gathering of a *third* presidential candidate, and this letter was published by the Union Whig press early in July.[25]

On the eve of the Constitutional-Union convention in Savannah, Governor Cobb huddled long into the night with leading Union Democrats, mapping strategy. They could not support the Southern Rights Democrats' Pierce-King electoral slate, because, to do so "would be self-degradation." Instead, they must nominate their own electors pledged to Pierce and King and work strenuously on their behalf during the state Democratic convention. But, according to a Cobb ally, although Union Whigs might support Union Democratic nominees, they would *not* do so *as Democrats*, and Cobb's "interest and principles and those of the Union democracy that you represent requires [*sic*] that we should not be outside the National Democratic organization."[26]

Cobb's defense of and identification with the principle of Union had put him in an extremely awkward position. Already an outcast from the reconstituted Georgia Democracy, Cobb realized that, if the Constitutional-Union Party disintegrated, he would be deprived of his last bargaining chip in the vicious war of patronage and political influence he was waging against the Southern Rights forces. Stripped of its rhetoric, Cobb's course had brought him face-to-face with a painful political truism: political parties merely gave lip service to principle; with votes, an unprincipled politico could go far; without them, a man of principle could go nowhere.

By mid-September, the Constitutional-Union Party had dissolved, and many of its former members were trying to scramble back into the state Democratic Party. Overtures for the creation of a compromise ticket, with electors from among Constitutional-Union and Southern Rights Democrats, got nowhere, as the fire-eaters now controlling the Georgia Democracy, willing to readmit penitent former Union Democrats, were not about to reward them for their obstinacy.[27] Governor Cobb, who attended the Democratic convention in person, claimed he had opposed the withdrawal of the Union Democrats' Pierce-King ticket but had agreed reluctantly to support the decision:

> We have now to contend with our enemies *in* the organization of the democratic party [*sic*] instead of *out* of it. Time alone can tell what is

> to be the result. At present we are certainly under a cloud; but with proper energy and spirit we shall have a brighter day to dawn upon us, and *we must bide our time.* There will be an exhibition of much bad feeling in our own small column, though I think it will die away.[28]

In fact, some Union Democrats denounced the majority's decision to withdraw their electoral ticket, declaring that "the principles of that Southern Rights organization and of the men who compose it are at war with the principles of the National Democratic party [*sic*], and are sectional and revolutionary in their tendency."[29] These so-called Tugalo Democrats nominated their own slate of Pierce-King electors, arguing tenaciously that their course was the only one consistent with true Democratic principles. One Tugalo newspaper, the Marietta *Union*, informed its readers that

> rumor lays the conception of the infamous plot at the door of Gov. Cobb and his Savannah friends. Whether he has forsaken principles and *bartered* his soul for a mess of pottage, or whether he has been but a passive victim among unprincipled friends and bitter enemies, we know not. This much is at least certain, that the Delegation from Chatham county, representing what they were pleased to designate the *re-united* Democracy, controlled the action of the Convention against the united voice of the whole delegation present from Cherokee Georgia.[30]

The national campaign of 1852 must have been confusing for Georgia voters, because a plethora of presidential candidates confronted them: two slates of electors pledged to Pierce and King; one slate for the regular Whig nominee Winfield Scott; a Daniel Webster–Charles J. Jenkins ticket backed by Whig Unionists Alexander Stephens and Robert Toombs; and an extreme Southern Rights ticket headed by John Quitman of Mississippi. The picture was further complicated when Webster died in October, at which point at least one Georgia paper added an "independent" Millard Fillmore–John Crittenden slate to its masthead. Moreover, Democratic voters who attended public meetings must have been disconcerted by the plethora of "leaders" who addressed them. For instance, a Democratic gathering in Rome was scheduled to include speeches by Howell Cobb and his fellow Union Democrat Henry R. Jackson; the conciliatory Southern Rights Democrat Herschel V. Johnson; and two dyed-in-the-wool fire-eaters—Walter Colquitt and Cobb's former gubernatorial foe, Charles McDonald.[31]

In the aftermath of Democrat Franklin Pierce's victory in the 1852 presidential election, all Democratic eyes turned toward Washington. The battle over the Compromise of 1850 had split the party not only in Georgia but throughout the South. Although candidate Pierce had accepted the finality of the compromise and called for healing breaches in the ranks of his southern colleagues, the sincerity of his protestations would be demonstrated by the composition of his cabinet, especially his choices of southern members for that body. Would he include a representative from both the Union and fire-eating camps or exclude one group entirely? Only rumors found their way south from the nation's capital.

Howell Cobb's fate became symbolic: his appointment to a cabinet position would be seen as vindication of the tortuous peregrinations that had led him from the Georgia Democracy to the Constitutional-Union Party, then, after the death of that party, to the Union Democracy, and, most recently, back once more to the fire-eater-dominated Georgia Democracy. Both Union and Southern Rights Democrats understood this, and they planned accordingly, with Cobb's friends doing everything in their power to ensure his appointment and his enemies striving to prevent it. By mid-January 1853, it was clear to Cobb that President Pierce would select his Cabinet from the free-soiler and secessionist wings of the Democracy, while "national men" like Cobb himself were to be ostracized, "a fatal blunder [that] will prostrate the democratic party [*sic*]," he asserted.[32]

With Cobb's once impregnable political power base crumbling beneath him, the time had arrived to mend fences in the Georgia Democratic Party. While Southern Rights Democrats had welcomed the dissolution of the Constitutional-Union Party, they had been less than effusive about Cobb's role in that action. Moreover, the governor had been criticized for taking an inactive part in the presidential campaign and for quietly backing the Tugalo Democratic ticket. Southern Rights editors generally opposed his appointment to the cabinet. Preaching the virtues of Democratic harmony, Cobb, his eyes already on the upcoming Democratic nomination for US senator from Georgia, did whatever the party's leaders asked him, including backing Democratic gubernatorial nominee Herschel V. Johnson in Cherokee Georgia. When Johnson defeated the Whig candidate, Charles Jenkins, by a miniscule margin of five hundred votes, Cobb's efforts on his behalf appeared to have been crucial, and some prominent Democrats gratefully supported him for the Senate seat.[33]

And yet Cobb had lost his usual optimism. As he explained to his wife on the eve of his last day as governor, "My friends are in good spirits, but I understand these things better than they do, and my honest opinion is that I shall be beat—and am prepared for it."[34] When the Democratic caucus met in mid-November, they awarded their senatorial nomination to Charles J. McDonald, whom Cobb had defeated decisively for Governor in 1851. Cobb's personal friend, but political foe, Alexander Stephens, informed his brother in the wake of Cobb's defeat for the Senate, "How foolish is a man puffed up with the inflation of vain glory—Cobb had done his friends & allies of 1850 & 1851 infinite mischief—But I am sorry for him—His course I believe was the result rather of a blunder of the head than an error of the heart."[35]

Cobb had not yet experienced his full measure of humiliation. No sooner had he returned to his Athens home than he received an invitation to travel back to Milledgeville and address the assembled Democrats on the topic of party unity. Cobb did as he was bid, and his speech was, by all accounts, effective. In light of his experience at the hands of his Democratic brethren, Cobb's pleas that former Union Whigs would be welcomed into the ranks of the Democracy bore more than a trace of irony: "Repentance first then confession of faith was all that any man had a right to ask," he claimed. "To exclude converts was the policy of revengeful men—not that of statesmen or patriots."[36]

There was a coda of sorts to Cobb's failure to obtain his party's senatorial nomination in November 1853. The legislature adjourned for the traditional Christmas holiday, to reconvene in January. In the interim, rumors circulated that Charles McDonald, who coveted a position in Pierce's cabinet, would resign the Democratic senatorial nomination at the next session of the legislature.[37] By mid-January 1854, this report had been further embellished: McDonald would resign the Georgia senate seat; Jefferson Davis of Mississippi would surrender his post as Pierce's secretary of war; McDonald would replace Davis in the Cabinet; and the Mississippi legislature would send Davis to the Senate. Perhaps Cobb could reach the US Senate, after all.[38]

Any hope Cobb entertained of retrieving the lost prize of a US Senate seat was smashed when the Democratic caucus next met. Although McDonald did surrender the senatorial nomination, the party conferred the Senate seat upon another fire-eater, Alfred Iverson of Columbus.

Cobb's enforced retirement would be relatively brief. His old Sixth District returned him to Congress in 1855, and in 1857, he entered the cabinet as secretary of the Treasury under his old friend James Buchanan, a post he held until after the election of Abraham Lincoln in 1860, when he resigned and returned to Georgia to follow the fortunes of his state and region.

*****

Howell Cobb, a veteran Jacksonian Democrat, was the point man for the Constitutional-Union movement and, elected governor in 1851, tried to drag his state party into the national Democratic Party. He failed, because Union Whigs like Alexander Stephens and Robert Toombs, willing to collaborate with Cobb and the Union Democrats against the threat of disunion, were averse to joining the Democracy; and the state rights Democrats dominating the Southern Rights Party were loath to readmit Cobb to their ranks, let alone endorse his national ambitions.

What Cobb must have viewed, at least at first, as a repetition of Georgia's State Rights versus Union split in the 1830s, which had ended the hoary division between the Troup and Clark parties and helped lead to the formation of the Whig and Democratic parties in the state, turned out very differently than he expected. This misjudgment cost Cobb a national political future. The reorganization of parties ushered in by the Compromise of 1850 disrupted Georgia's versions of *national* parties, not, as had been the case during the Nullification Crisis of the 1830s, parties that were *peculiar to* Georgia, which proved ominous for the future. Georgia had at long last reached the stage in party development where the frequently bruited phrase "Principles, Not Men" had some significance—but how much? After all, as the history of Georgia's factions and parties from the era of the American Revolution through the mid-nineteenth century showed, politicians died but ideas lived on, though sometimes in exaggerated or truncated form.

Once again, "principles" seemed to trump "men," but there remained a potentially serious problem: the dominant party in Georgia, the Democrats, had clung to power by falling back on the doctrines of "state rights" and "secession," both of which had been anathema to their Union/Democratic forebears in the 1830s. Meanwhile, Georgia's Whigs, who had evolved from the state rights-oriented Troup party of the 1820s and the State Rights Party of the 1830s, wound up defending the policies of, first,

Henry Clay and, then, William Henry Harrison. Once more, politics in Georgia baffled outsiders.

By the mid-1850s, in other words, political developments in Georgia had produced a situation where principles seemed to matter more than men. Yet if the principles to which the state was dedicated included the legitimacy of state rights and secession, and if the national government refused to accept those concepts, then the only way to defend these principles might be to sacrifice large numbers of men, in civil conflict. If that possibility arose, would Georgia meet the challenge? In 1854, to anyone cognizant of the political evolution of Georgia since 1807, the prospects were far from heartening.

Notes—1

[NOTE: This essay originally appeared in a different form as part of Chapter 1 in my doctoral dissertation, "Politics on the Periphery: Factions and Parties in Georgia, 1776–1806" (Emory University, 1973).]

1 "The Letters of Honorable James Habersham, 1756–1775," *Collections* of the Georgia Historical Society, VI (Savannah, 1904): 238. This series cited hereafter as GHS *Collections*, with appropriate volume numbers.

2 William W. Abbot, *The Royal Governors of Georgia, 1754–1775* (Chapel Hill, N.C., 1959) treats the nature of politics in the colony during the periods of royal rule and revolutionary ferment. The first four chapters in Kenneth Coleman, *The American Revolution in Georgia, 1763–1789* (Athens, Ga., 1958), concentrate on disputes after 1763.

3 This process is described in detail in Abbot, *Royal Governors*, Chapter 8, and Coleman, *Revolution in Georgia*, Chapter 4.

4 James Habersham to Joseph Habersham, October 13, 1770, "Letters of Habersham," GHS *Collections* VI: 89.

5 In February 1779, the colony's exiled Royal Governor, Sir James Wright, compiled "A List of the Officers of His Majesty's Province of Georgia and Their Present Places of Residence." Of the more than forty placemen listed, only four were believed by Wright to have become "rebels." See "Letters from Governor Sir James Wright to the Earl of Dartmouth and Lord George Germain, Secretaries of State

for America, from August 24, 1774, to February 16, 1782," GHS *Collections*, III (Savannah, 1873): 251–253.

6 Charles F. Jenkins, *Button Gwinnett: Signer of the Declaration of Independence* (Garden City, N.Y., 1926), chapters 1-7, treat the radical leader's early career. For his questionable business dealings see Stephen Drayton to John Houstoun, March 20, 1773, *ibid.*, pp.51–53, and Alexander A. Lawrence, "General Lachlan McIntosh and His Suspension from Command During the Revolution," *Georgia Historical Quarterly* (*GHQ*) 38 (1954): footnote 38, pp.115–116. On McIntosh's pre-Revolutionary career, see Lawrence, pp.104–108, and Harvey H. Jackson, *Lachlan McIntosh and the Politics of Revolutionary Georgia* (Athens, Ga., 1979), chapters 1–3.

7 Coleman, *Revolution in Georgia*, p.75.

8 Hall to Roger Sherman, May 16, 1777, printed in Jenkins, *Button Gwinnett*, p. 228. For the most part, references to the Liberty Society (or Liberty Club) are scattered and appear almost exclusively in the writings of conservative Whigs. The following account of the Society's activities draws heavily upon a tract in Volume XXXIX of the *Hazard Pamphlets*, Rare Book Room, Library of Congress (LC), *Remarks on a Pamphlet, Entitled, "Strictures on a Pamphlet, entitled the Case of George McIntosh, …" To Which is Added, A concise account of the Justice of the Executive and Legislative bodies of the State of Georgia: Together with Some Account of the Lives and upright Principles of the Leaders of the Nocturnal Junto* (n.p., 1777). Hereafter cited as *Remarks.* This work apparently was the parting shot in a controversy over the conduct of George McIntosh (to be discussed below), a topic dealt with at length by every major chronicler of events in Georgia between 1776 and 1783. Nevertheless, even the most careful of these writers, Kenneth Coleman, omits this pamphlet from his bibliography, while listing the other three polemics on the George McIntosh affair bound with it in the *Hazard Pamphlets, XXXIX.*

9 *Remarks*, p.15.

10 Lilla M. Hawes, ed., "The Papers of Lachlan McIntosh, 1774–1799," GHS *Collections*, XII (Savannah, 1957): 159–160.

11 *Remarks*, p.15.

12 The only explicit reference to vocal opposition to Gwinnett's continuing as colonel is in *Remarks*, p.15, but there is evidence to support the pamphleteer's assertion that Gwinnett initially won the command, resigned it, and was appointed to the Continental Congress as part of a compromise. See Joseph Habersham to William Henry Drayton [*circa* February 1776], in R.W. Gibbes, ed., *Documentary History of the American Revolution … Chiefly in South Carolina …* (New York, 1855) II: 259; George Walton to Lachlan McIntosh, May 1, 1777, Peter Force Georgia Transcripts, LC, Microfilm, GHS; Petition of Ann Gwinnett to the Continental

Congress, August 1 [1777], in Jenkins, *Button Gwinnett*, p.238; and Joseph Clay to Henry Laurens, October 16, 1777, "Letters of Joseph Clay, Merchant of Savannah, 1776–1793," GHS *Collections*, VIII (Savannah, 1913): 50. Cited hereafter as "Letters of Clay."

13 Jenkins, *Button Gwinnett*, p.71.

14 "Proceedings of the Georgia Provincial Congress, July 4–8, 1775"; "Proceedings of the Georgia Council of Safety, 3rd November, 1775, to 17th February, 1777; Account of the Siege of Savannah, from a British Source," GHS *Collections*, V, Part 1 (Savannah, 1901): 104–104.

15 George Walton to Lachlan McIntosh, April 18, 1777, in Jenkins, *Button Gwinnett*, p.225; Elbert to McIntosh, September 23, 1776, Dreer Collection, Historical Society of Pennsylvania.

16 Historians of Georgia are virtually unanimous in agreeing that Gwinnett sought the generalship. See, for example, Jenkins, *Button Gwinnett*, p.94; Charles C. Jones, Jr., *The History of Georgia* (Boston, 1883), II: 264; E. Merton Coulter, *A Short History of Georgia* (Chapel Hill, N.C., 1933), p.140; Coleman, *Revolution in Georgia*, p.87. For contemporary comments on the choice of brigadier general and its aftermath, see Walton to McIntosh, April 18, 1777, cited in n.15, above, and McIntosh to Henry Laurens, July 30, 1777, in Jenkins, *Button Gwinnett*, p. 254. Fine studies of the Gwinnett-McIntosh rivalry and its tragic consequences are Alexander A. Lawrence, "General Lachlan McIntosh and His Suspension from Continental Command During the Revolution," *GHQ* 38 (1954): 101–141; Harvey H. Jackson, "Consensus and Conflict: Factional Politics in Revolutionary Georgia, 1775–1777," *ibid.* 59 (Winter 1975): 388–401.

17 Lachlan McIntosh to William McIntosh, November 25, 1776, Hawes, ed., "Papers of McIntosh," p.20; same to same, January 8, 1777, *ibid.*, p.34; John Wereat to George Walton, August 30, 1777, *ibid.*, p.67.

18 *Ibid.*, p.23. For a defense of William McIntosh's conduct as commander of the Georgia Light Horse, see Peter Force Georgia Transcripts, LC.

19 Surviving evidence regarding the George McIntosh affair is contradictory, as are the interpretations of the incident offered by historians. Relevant documents may be found in *The Case of George McIntosh, Esquire, A Member of the late Council and Convention of the State of Georgia; With the Proceedings thereon in the Hon. The Assembly and Council of the State* (n.p., 1777). Lengthy extracts from this pamphlet appear in Edith Duncan Johnston, *The Houstouns of Georgia* (Athens, Ga., 1950), pp.348–365, a pro-McIntosh account. John Wereat and General Lachlan McIntosh published over their signatures *An Addition to the Case of George McIntosh, Esquire, Earnestly recommended to the serious Attention of every Reader, particularly those of the State of Georgia* (n.p., 1777). Anti-McIntosh forces

replied to the first of these tracts in *Strictures on a Pamphlet, entitled, The Case of George McIntosh, Esq., Published by Order of the Liberty Society* (Savannah, 1777). In response to this Liberty Society effort, someone, presumably Wereat and General McIntosh, published *Remarks*, already referred to in connection with the origins of the Liberty Society. All four tracts are in the *Hazard Pamphlets, XXXIX*, Rare Book Room, LC. Charles F. Jenkins offers Gwinnett's side in *Button Gwinnett*, pp.135–172 and 215–221. Charles C. Jones, Jr., also treats the affair in his *History of Georgia, II*: 278–280, as do Kenneth Coleman, *Revolution in Georgia*, pp.88–89, and Jackson, *Lachlan McIntosh*, pp.68–70.

20 On January 8, 1776, the Georgia Council of Safety had refused Panton's request to be allowed to carry gunpowder and foodstuffs to East Florida (Allen D. Candler, comp., *The Revolutionary Records of Georgia* [Atlanta, 1908], I: 90). In the same month that George McIntosh and his original partners decided to allow Panton to join their venture, the Council of Safety, with McIntosh absent, drew up a list of those persons "whose going at large is dangerous to the liberties of America"—one of those named was William Panton (*ibid.*, 146). For other comments on Houstoun, Baillie, and Panton, see Georgia Governor John Adam Treutlen to John Hancock, June 19, 1777, Jenkins, *Button Gwinnett*, p.244; *ibid.*, p.138; Johnston, *Houstouns of Georgia*, p.120; and "Resolve of the St. Andrews Parochial Committee 10th Sept. 1776, with List of Torys," in Hawes, ed., "Papers of McIntosh," pp.56–57.

21 Quoted in Johnston, *Houstouns of Georgia*, p.351.

22 *Ibid.*, p.352.

23 *Ibid.*, pp.352–353; Laurens to Lachlan McIntosh, September 1, 1777, Letterbook, January 24, 1776–March 5, 1778, p.146, Henry Laurens Papers, South Carolina Historical Society [Microfilm edition, reel 6].

24 Treutlen to Hancock, June 19 and August 6, 1777, in Jenkins, *Button Gwinnett*, pp.243–250; "Part of G McIntosh's journal," in Lilla M. Hawes, ed., "Lachlan McIntosh Papers in the University of Georgia Libraries," *University of Georgia Miscellanea Publications Number 7* (Athens, Ga., 1968), pp.94–95; Lachlan McIntosh to George Walton, July 14, 1777, in Jenkins, *Button Gwinnett*, pp.256–262.

25 A copy of the Chatham County petition is in the Force Georgia Transcripts, LC. A slightly different version appears in Jenkins, *Button Gwinnett*, pp.266–271. The circular letter and the tale of the travelling agitators are in John Wereat to George Walton, August 20, 1777, Hawes, ed., "Papers of McIntosh," pp.66–74.

26 Force Georgia Transcripts, LC.

27 The tenor of Wereat's letter to Henry Laurens, August 4, 1777, which apparently has not survived, is evident from Laurens's reply, August 30, 1777, Laurens Papers,

SCHS, Letterbook, January 24, 1776–March 5, 1778, pp.142–144 [Microfilm edition, reel 6]. See also Wereat to Walton, August 30, 1777, cited in note 25, above.

28 Laurens to McIntosh, August 11, 1777, Laurens Papers, SCHS, Letterbook, January 24, 1776–March 5, 1778, p.117 [Microfilm edition, reel 6]; McIntosh to Walton, July 14, 1777, in Jenkins, *Button Gwinnett*, pp.256, 261; Lawrence, "General Lachlan McIntosh," p.118.

29 Clay to Henry Laurens, October 16, 1777, "Letters of Clay," p.50.

30 This discussion of McIntosh's suspension from Continental command relies upon Lawrence, "General Lachlan McIntosh," pp.101–104, 121–141. See also, William Bacon Stevens, *A History of Georgia ...* (Philadelphia, 1859), II: 290–331; Jones, *History of Georgia*, II: 364–374; Coleman, *Revolution in Georgia*, pp.147–167; and Edward J. Cashin, "'The Famous Colonel Wells': Factionalism in Revolutionary Georgia," *GHQ* 58 (1974): 137–156.

31 Coleman, *Revolution in Georgia*, p.157.

32 Quoted in Jones, *History of Georgia*, II: 428.

33 On McIntosh's struggle for vindication, see Jackson, *Lachlan McIntosh*, chs. 11–12; Lawrence, "General Lachlan McIntosh," pp.125–141.

34 Alexander A. Lawrence, in his fine piece on McIntosh's suspension from command, tends to downgrade the significance of the fact that Walton's effort to discredit Wereat and the Supreme Executive Council began *before* his attack on McIntosh, but close enough in time to support the contention that one evolved from the other.

35 Testimony of George Walton, *Proceedings of a General Court Martial ... For the Trial of Major General Howe* (Philadelphia, 1782), reprinted in *Collections of the New York Historical Society for the Year 1879* (New York, 1880), pp.245–246. On McIntosh's part in the siege of Savannah, see Lawrence, "General Lachlan McIntosh," pp.122–123; Jackson, *Lachlan McIntosh*, pp.98–101. For Wereat, see Major General Augustine Prevost to Lord George Germain, November 1, 1779, in Benjamin F. Stevens, *Facsimiles of Manuscripts in European Archives* Relating to America, 1776–1783 (London, 1895), XXIII: Number 2020.

36 McIntosh espoused neutrality, but not very convincingly, in a letter to General Benjamin Lincoln, December 11, 1779, Lachlan McIntosh Papers, GHS (photocopy of manuscript in the Duke University Library). *Cf.* the comments of James Jackson, writing some years after the Revolution, in Lilla M. Hawes, ed., "The Papers of James Jackson, 1781–1798," GHS *Collections*, XI (Savannah, 1955): 14–15.

Notes—2

[**NOTE:** This is a revised version of an article originally published in *Richmond County* (Ga.) *History* 5 (Winter, 1973): 40–46.]

1 For the concept of "versatile Georgians," see George R. Lamplugh, *Politics on the Periphery: Factions and Parties in Georgia, 1783–1806* (Newark, Delaware, 1986), pp.22–26.

2 According to a 1784 law, there was to be but a single polling place in each county, located at the county courthouse. (Allen D. Candler, comp., *The Colonial Records of the State of Georgia, XIX, Part 2* [Atlanta, 1911]: 160–162. Cited hereafter as *CRG.*) The record of Few's attendance in the Continental Congress may be found in Edmund Cody Burnett, ed., *Letters of Members of the Continental Congress* (Washington, D.C., 1921–1936), VI: xliv; VII: lxvi.

3 Allen D. Candler, comp., *The Revolutionary Records of the State of Georgia* (Atlanta, 1908), III: 23. Hereafter cited as *RRG.*

4 Edward J. Cashin, *The Story of Augusta* (Augusta, Ga., 1980), p.21. In the [Savannah] *Georgia Gazette*, August 4, 1785, Richard Call advertised 200 acres of land for sale on Germany's Creek, several miles east of Wrightsborough, "20 miles from Augusta and 6 from Brownsborough." On December 5, 1798, James Few signed an affidavit regarding an altercation he had witnessed at "Brownsborough, in Columbia County." (Mrs. F.F. Baker, comp., *Columbia County, Georgia, Early Court Records* [Albany, Ga., n.d.], p.8.)

5 William Few, Sr., patriarch of the clan, was appointed by the Council of Safety as a justice of the peace for the Kiokee District on June 20, 1776 (*RRG*, I: 143).

6 *RRG*, III: 292; *CRG*, XIX, Pt. 2: 132–133; *RRG*, II: 287.

7 *RRG*, III: 234.

8 *RRG*, III: 240, 256, 262.

9 *RRG*, III: 292–294.

10 James Jackson to ______________, March 22, 1783, James Jackson Papers, Duke University. Few had studied law on his own while living in North Carolina and may have begun to practice informally in Richmond County, but he was not formally admitted to the Georgia bar until August 1, 1783. (*RRG*, III: 417)

11 *RRG*, III: 422–423.

12 The Augusta election returns are in [Savannah] *Georgia Gazette*, December 11, 1783; the list of those seated on January 8, 1784, in *RRG*, III: 423–425. It should be noted that the Assembly Minutes list only those on the compromise delegation who actually were in attendance on the day the compromise solution was adopted.

Of those eight men, only one, William Glascock, appeared on the Augusta tally. He later was joined on the Richmond delegation by two others elected in Augusta, Charles Crawford and James McNeil. (*Ibid.*, 447, 456)

13 This paragraph and the next are based on the legislative history of the bill "for fixing and Establishing Court Houses & Jails and Regulating Elections in the different Counties," *RRG*, III: 434, 442, 444, 454, 456, 463, and 565–568. The measure in its final form is in *CRG*, XIX, Pt. 2: 360–362.

14 [Savannah] *Georgia Gazette*, April 15, 1784.

15 [Augusta] *Georgia State Gazette*, October 3, 1789; Cashin, *Story of Augusta*, p.48.

Notes—3

1 A summary of the major problems facing Georgia at the end of the War for Independence may be found in George R. Lamplugh, "Farewell to the Revolution: Georgia in 1785," *GHQ* 56 (Fall, 1972): 387–402; for a more detailed treatment, see Lamplugh, *Politics on the Periphery: Factions and Parties in Georgia, 1783–1806* (Newark, Del., 1986), chapter 1. For an assessment of local problems on the postwar career of another prominent upcountry man, see "William Few's Brownsborough Plan," above.

2 For contrasting views of Walton's conduct toward General McIntosh during the Revolution, compare Lamplugh, "'To Check & Discourage the Wicked & Designing': John Wereat and the Revolution in Georgia," *GHQ* 61 (Winter 1977): 295–307; Edward J. Cashin, "George Walton and the Forged Letter," *ibid.*, 62 (1978): 133–145; and Harvey H. Jackson, *Lachlan McIntosh and the Politics of Revolutionary Georgia* (Athens, Ga., 1979), chapter 11.

3 Lilla M. Hawes, ed., "The Papers of Lachlan McIntosh, 1774–1799," *Collections* of the Georgia Historical Society, 12 (Savannah, 1957): 117–118; *Georgia Gazette* (hereafter cited as *GG*), February 6, 1783.

4 The notice of intent and the "Defence of Capt. William McIntosh—before a General Court Martial—1783" for horsewhipping Walton are in Lilla M. Hawes, ed., "Lachlan McIntosh Papers in the University of Georgia Libraries," *University of Georgia Miscellanea Publications Number 7* (Athens, Ga., 1968), pp.58–63.

5 "A Citizen," *GG*, February 6, 1783; "Hercules Wormwood" to Gen. Lachlan McIntosh, March 3, 1783, in Hawes, ed., "Papers of McIntosh," *Collections* of the GHS, 12: 120; "Scourge," *GG*, February 27; March 13, 27, 1783.

6 These presentments, as well as a second set dealing with the usual array of local complaints, are in *GG*, March 13, 1783.

7 Allen D. Candler, comp., *The Revolutionary Records of the State of Georgia*, 3 vols. (Atlanta, 1908) 2: 471–472.

8 Charge and Presentments at Chatham, *GG*, March 11, 1784; for responses in other counties, see *ibid.*, April 8, 15, 22; May 20, 1784.

9 Charge at Wilkes, *ibid.*, November 18, 1784; at Liberty, *ibid.*, April 22, 1784.

10 "A Citizen," *Cursory Remarks on Men and Measures in Georgia* (n.p., 1784); "The Modern Brutus sends greetings to all who are capable of feeling for the Distresses of an Unfortunate Man," a broadside (probably by William McIntosh), bound after *GG*, September 2, 1784, in the microfilm edition of that newspaper; and "Philo Brutus," *ibid.*, October 7, 1784. *Cursory Remarks*, p.5, mentions a coauthor; that Richard Howley, Walton's ally in 1779–1780, was the person referred is evident from the caustic description of Walton's supposed collaborator. On the wartime alliance between Walton and Howley, directed against John Wereat and the Supreme Executive Council, see sources cited in chapter 2, above.

11 "Brutus," *GG*, July 15, 1784. On the amercement policy, which removed certain "tories" from the May 1782 confiscation and banishment act in return for payment of a heavy fine, see Lamplugh, *Politics on the Periphery*, pp.45–49.

12 "Brutus," *GG*, July 22, 1784.

13 For comments on the method used to distribute the pamphlet, see *GG*, December 30, 1784; January 6, 1785. Quotations are from *Cursory Remarks*, pp. 4, 2.

14 *Cursory Remarks*, pp. 3–7, *passim*. A list of purchasers of confiscated property and the extent of their indebtedness was published in the [Augusta] *Georgia State Gazette or Independent Register*, July 28; August 4, 11, 1787. The information contained therein seems to bolster the contention of "A Citizen" in 1784 (*Cursory Remarks*, p. 8) that Walton was "himself among the deepest in the publick books." As of January 1, 1787, Walton still owed more than *L*5000 for confiscated property, and he was almost *L*900 in arrears on interest payments.

15 Walton's charge at Liberty County, *GG*, November 25, 1784; "Brutus, No. 8," *ibid.*, September 9, 1784. For the response of the Governor and Council to the opinion delivered by Walton in Liberty County, and a rebuttal by the chief justice, see *ibid.*, December 2, 9, 1784.

16 William Samuel Johnson to Roger Sherman, April 30, 1785, in Edmund C. Burnett, ed., *Letters of Members of the Continental Congress*, 8 vols. (Washington, 1921–1936) 8: 101; see also letters from Nathan Dane--to Nathaniel Phillips, January 20, 1786, and to John Choate, January 31, 1786, *ibid.*, 287–288, 293.

17 Walton was elected to the Continental Congress and the Philadelphia Convention early in 1787, but he attended neither. For an account, probably apocryphal, of Walton's "campaign" for governor in 1789, see Abiel Holmes to Jedediah

Morse, February 12, 1789, American Prose Collection, Historical Society of Pennsylvania, Philadelphia.

Notes—4

1 Allan Johnson and Dumas Malone, eds., *Dictionary of American Biography* (20 vols.; New York, 1928–1936), VII: 243. The present author's sketch of Gibbons's life was published in Kenneth Coleman and Charles Stephen Gurr, eds., *Dictionary of Georgia Biography* (2 vols.; Athens, Ga., 1983), I: 343–345.

2 Affidavit of Thomas Mills, [Augusta] *Georgia State Gazette or Independent Register* (hereafter *GSGIR*), September 6, 1788.

3 Allen D. Candler, comp., *The Revolutionary Records of the State of Georgia* (3 vols.; Atlanta, 1908) [cited hereafter as *RRG*], I: 376; II: 389; III: 217. Gibbons' copy of an order from the Executive Council permitting him to travel to South Carolina and an order from the Chatham County Sheriff requiring him to return to Savannah by January 1, 1783, were in the possession of a private collector, Mr. Robert W. Carver of Chatham, New Jersey, who kindly shared them with me.

4 *RRG*, III: 365. For more on the Assembly's dispute with Governor Hall, see George R. Lamplugh, *Politics on the Periphery: Factions and Parties in Georgia, 1783–1806* (Newark, Del., 1986), 45–47.

5 This paragraph and the next are based on Assembly Minutes, February 21, 1785, typescript, Georgia Archives, Morrow, Ga. (hereafter, Ga Arch)

6 On this point, see Robert S. Lambert, "The Repossession of Georgia, 1782–1784," *Proceedings* of the South Carolina Historical Association (1957), pp. 23–24.

7 Assembly Minutes, August 2, 1786, typescript, Ga Arch.

8 [Savannah] *Georgia Gazette* (cited hereafter as *GG*), September 14, 21, 1786.

9 The following discussion of the Gibbons-Jackson imbroglio is based upon documents published by Gibbons, *ibid.*, September 28; Jackson's rebuttal, *ibid.*, October 5; and the statement of Benjamin Fishbourn, *ibid.*, October 12, 1786.

10 The various blows to low country pride are treated in more detail in Lamplugh, *Politics on the Periphery*, pp. 49–56.

11 The act restoring to the nine former loyalists "all the rights and privileges of free citizens of this state, any law to the contrary notwithstanding," is in *RRG*, I: 616–617.

12 *GSGIR*, August 9, September 6, 1788.

13 *GG*, September 17, 1789.

14 Richard Wayne to Anthony Wayne, September 30, 1789, Anthony Wayne Papers, Historical Society of Pennsylvania, Philadelphia; "Extract of a letter from a

gentleman in Savannah to his friend in Augusta, dated July 27 [1789]," *Augusta Chronicle and Gazette of the State*, August 8, 1789.

15 *GG*, October 1, 1789. Of the fourteen men who represented Chatham in the legislature during 1789, eight were serving their first terms. Another, Jacob Waldburger, who had entered the Assembly in 1788, also was attacked by name by "A Planter." If to these nine is added the name of the principal object of that writer's wrath, Thomas Gibbons, then the resulting total of ten is approximately "Two thirds of our Members last year ..."

16 The broadsides by Gibbons, Montfort, and "A Planter" are bound between issues on *GG* for October 1 and October 8, 1789 in the microfilm edition of that paper.

17 For the list of winners, see *ibid.*, October 8, 1789.

18 For an analysis of the Georgia style of politics prior to 1789, see Lamplugh, *Politics on the Periphery*, chapter 2.

Notes—5

1 For the texts of these various laws, consult Allen D. Candler, comp., *The Colonial Records of the State of Georgia*, XIX, Part 2 (Atlanta, 1911): 142–362. Hereafter cited as *C.R.G.*

2 Chatham County Grand Jury Presentments (hereafter cited as GJP.), *Georgia Gazette*, March 10, 1785 (cited hereafter as *GG*); Typescript Minutes of the Georgia House of Assembly, January 17; February 14, 16, 1785 (hereafter, Assembly Minutes), Georgia Archives, Morrow, Georgia (hereafter, GaArch).

3 Assembly Minutes, January 17, 1785; Effingham and Richmond G.J.P., *GG*, March 24 and April 14, 1785.

4 William B. Stevens, *A History of Georgia,* II (Philadelphia, 1859): 414–417; Assembly Minutes, January 22; February 14, 17, 1785.

5 Manuscript Executive Council Minutes, June 14, 1785 (hereafter cited as E.C. Minutes), GaArch; Governor Samuel Elbert to Chesley Bostick, July 19, 1785, in "Letter Book of Governor Samuel Elbert, from January, 1785, to November, 1785," Georgia Historical Society *Collections*, V, Part 2 (Savannah, 1902) [cited hereafter as *Elbert Letters*, by date only]; *GG*, August 25, 1785.

6 *C.R.G.*, XIX, Part 2: 419–433.

7 *Elbert Letters*, September 14, 1785; *C.R.G.*, XIX, Part 2: 380.

8 Letter from Chief Justice George Walton, *GG*, December 22, 1785; *C.R.G.*, XIX, Part 2: 476; E.C. Minutes, April 26, 1785.

9 "A Citizen," *GG*, January 20, 1785; Richmond County GJP, *ibid.*, April 14, 1785; for the 1786 Tariff law, see *C.R.G.*, XIX, Part 2: 514–515.

[10] Assembly Minutes, January 19, 26, 27; February 1, 1785; letter from "T.G.," *GG*, October 13, 1785.

[11] *C.R.G.*, XIX, Part 2: 363–371.

[12] *Ibid.*, 395–398. According to Reba C. Strickland, *Religion and the State in Georgia in the Eighteenth Century* (New York, 1939), p.167, this measure apparently never went into effect, and it was subsequently invalidated by the new state Constitution of 1798.

[13] *C.R.G.*, XIX, Part 2: 455–458.

[14] E.C. Minutes, June 3, 1785; "A Philanthropist," *GG*, November 10; "Benevolus," *ibid.*, December 1, 1785.

[15] State Treasurer's list of licensed tavern keepers, *GG*, December 29, 1785; Burt and Stebbins's advertisement, *ibid.*, November 17, 1785.

[16] Randolph C. Downes, "Creek-American Relations, 1782–1790," *Georgia Historical Quality*, XXI (1937): 142–144.

[17] For the best account of McGillivray's career, see John W. Caughey, *McGillivray of the Creeks* (Norman, Okla., 1938).

[18] *C.R.G.*, XIX, Part 2: 440.

[19] The "talks" accompanied a letter to George Walton, in *Elbert Letters*, March 10, 1785; Elbert to William Clark, *ibid.*, May 20, 1785.

[20] Houstoun to Elbert, April 2, 1785, in Edmund C. Burnett, ed., *Letters of Members of the Continental Congress*, VIII (Washington, 1936): 81–83; E.C. Minutes, June 9, 1785; Elbert to Elijah Clarke, *Elbert Letters*, June 9, 1785.

[21] Elbert to Georgia congressional delegation, *Elbert Letters*, June 21, 1785; Elbert to Hawkins, Pickens, and Martin, July 20, 1785, *ibid.*; E.C. Minutes, August 31, 1785.

[22] Walter Lowrie and Matthew St. C. Clarke, comps., *American State Papers, Indian Affairs*, I (Washington, 1832): 15*ff*; Merritt B. Pound, *Benjamin Hawkins—Indian Agent* (Athens, Ga., 1951), p.45.

[23] *American State Papers, Indian Affairs*, I: 17.

[24] *C.R.G.*, XIX, Part 2: 371–375; D.C. Corbitt, ed., "Some Papers Relating to Bourbon County, Georgia," *GHQ*, XIX (1935): 255.

[25] Governor Elbert to Colonel John Baker of the Liberty County militia, *Elbert Letters*, May 16, 1785; Pengree to Elbert, September 4, 1785, Joseph B. Lockey, ed., *East Florida, 1783–1785* (Berkeley and Los Angeles, 1949), pp. 717–718; Liberty County GJP, *GG*, November 24, 1785.

[26] Lockey, ed., *East Florida*, pp.459–460; O'Neill, Semple, and Zespedes correspondence, *ibid.*, pp.542–548.

[27] Assembly Minutes, February 11, 19, 1785.

28 In addition to Houstoun, the Assembly elected John Habersham, Edward Telfair, William Gibbons, Sr., and Abraham Baldwin (Assembly Minutes, January 19, 1785). By May 30, Habersham and Baldwin had arrived in New York City to take their seats (Burnett, ed., *Letters of Members of the Continental Congress*, VIII: lxxxv–lxxxvi).

29 See, for example, Walton's charge to the Liberty County Grand Jury, *GG*, April 21, 1785. For a more detailed account of Chief Justice Walton's efforts on this and other questions, see "George Walton, Chief Justice of Georgia, 1783–1785," in the present volume.

30 "A Gentleman in Spain to His Friend," *GG*, March 17; for activities of American merchants, see news items, *ibid.*, May 26; June 9; July 7, 14, 21. On the debate over strengthening Congress, see, in *GG*, "O.F.H.," April 21; "Agricola," September 29; "T.G.," October 13; "A Citizen," November 24; and "An Old Georgian," December 15. At least two public meetings in Savannah considered the wisdom of granting the impost power to Congress: see *GG*, September 1, and "Agricola," *ibid.*, September 29, 1785.

31 Elbert to Houstoun, Habersham, and Baldwin, *Elbert Letters*, September 14, 1785; *C.R.G.*, XIX, Part 2: 492–498; Abraham Baldwin to Charles Thomson, February 14, 1786, "Papers of Charles Thomson, Secretary of the Continental Congress," New York Historical Society *Collections*, XI (New York, 1879): 202–204.

32 John C. Fitzpatrick, ed., *Journals of the Continental Congress, 1774–1789*, XXIX (Washington, 1933): 450, 556. For more on John Wereat's accomplishments as state Auditor, see "John Wereat and Georgia," below.

33 *C.R.G.*, XIX, Part 2: 416; 443–447.

34 Seth John Cuthbert, Treasurer of Georgia, to Governor Elbert, July 9, 17, 1785, in Cuyler Collection, University of Georgia; *GG*, June 2, 1785; Joseph Clay to Edward Telfair, April 15, 16; July 27, 1785, Telfair Family Papers, Georgia Historical Society, Savannah.

35 Houstoun's letter, April 2, 1785, and Habersham's letter, June 24, 1785, are in Burnett, ed., *Letters of Members of the Continental Congress*, VIII: 82; 150–151.

Notes—6

1 Harvey H. Jackson, "The Road to the Constitution: Georgia's First Secession," *Atlanta Historical Bulletin*, XX (1976): 43.

2 On the background of the adoption by Georgia of the Federal Constitution, see Kenneth Coleman, *The American Revolution in Georgia, 1763–1789* (Athens, Ga., 1958), chapter 17; John P. Kaminski, "Controversy Amid Consensus: The

Adoption of the Federal Constitution in Georgia," *Georgia Historical Quarterly* [*GHQ*], LVIII (1974): 244–261.

3 For the attendance of the Georgia delegates, see Max Farrand, *The Records of the Federal Convention of 1787* (4 v.; paperback reprint; New Haven and London, 1974).

4 William Pierce to St. George Tucker, September 27, 1787, *Georgia Gazette*, March 20, 1788, reprinted in *American Historical Review*, XIII [1897–1898]: 313–317.

5 "A Georgian," *GG*, November 15; "Demosthenes Minor," *ibid.*

6 Quote from "A Farmer," *ibid.*, November 29; see also, "Demosthenes Minor," November 22, December 6; "A Citizen," and "A Georgian," *ibid.*, December 6, 1787.

7 McIntosh to Wereat, December 17, 1787, Lilla M. Hawes, ed., "The Papers of Lachlan McIntosh, 1774–1799," *Collections* of the Georgia Historical Society, XII (Savannah, Ga., 1957): 144–146.

8 For the ratification of the Federal Constitution in Georgia, see E. Merton Coulter, ed., "Minutes of the Georgia Convention Ratifying the Federal Constitution," *GHQ*, X (1926): 223–237.

9 Joseph Habersham to Mrs. Habersham, December 30, 1787, U.B. Phillips, ed. "Some Letters of Joseph Habersham," *GHQ*, X (1926): 157.

10 Harvey H. Jackson, *Lachlan McIntosh and the Politics of Revolutionary Georgia* (Athens, Ga., 1979), p.144.

11 Clay, Telfair, & Co. to [A.F. Delaville?], June 20, 1788, Clay, Telfair, & Co. Letterbooks, III: 1787–1795, Georgia Historical Society, Savannah.

12 Reprinted in *Georgia Gazette*, June 12, 1788, where it was attributed to "W.O____n."

Notes—7

1 My treatment of the life and times of John Wereat was published as: "'To Check and Discourage the Wicked and Designing': John Wereat and the Revolution in Georgia," *Georgia Historical Quarterly* (*GHQ*) 61 (Winter 1977): 295–307; "'The Duty of Every Good Citizen': John Wereat and Georgia, 1782–1793," *Atlanta Historical Journal* 27 (Spring 1983): 87–94; and "John Wereat and Yazoo, 1794–1799," *GHQ* 72 (Fall 1988) 502–517.

2 Obituary of John Wereat, *Georgia Gazette*, January 31, 1799 (cited hereafter as *GG*); will of John Collier, July 8, 1780, Plaintiff's Exhibit "D," *Isaacs v. Wereat*, Circuit Court Records, A/24, National Archives at Atlanta, Morrow, Ga.; Miscellaneous Bonds, Book J, 1755–1762, pp.470–476, Georgia Archives,

Morrow, Ga. (hereafter cited as Ga. Arch.); obituary of Hannah Wereat, *GG*, January 28, 1790; Allen D. Candler, comp., *The Colonial Records of the State of Georgia* (Atlanta, 1904–1916) 8: 526 (cited hereafter as *CRG).*

3 Conveyances, Books C1–C2, 1750–1776, pp.521, 547, 985, Book S, 1766–1769, pp.166, 368, Books X1–X2, 1771–1774, p.394, Book V, 1769–1771, p.144; Miscellaneous Bonds, Book R, 1765–1772, pp.321–324, Book J, 1755–1762, pp.470–476; Mortgages, Book Q, 1762–1770, pp.166–167, all at Ga. Arch.; *GG*, October 17, 1763, November 1, 1764; *John Nutt v. Exrs. Of John Wereat*, Circuit Court Records A/18, National Archives at Atlanta, Morrow, Ga.; William Knox to James Habersham, April 4, May 14, 1770, James Habersham Papers, Georgia Historical Society, Savannah (hereafter, GHS).

4 Mortgages, Book P, 1762–1770, pp.86–87, 166–167, 176–178; Book Q, 1762–1770, pp.56–57, 109–111, both at Ga. Arch.

5 Allen D. Candler, comp., *The Revolutionary Records of the State of Georgia* (Atlanta, 1908) 1: 48 (cited hereafter as *RRG*; Lilla M. Hawes, ed., "The Papers of Lachlan McIntosh, 1774–1799," *Collections* of the Georgia Historical Society 12 (Savannah, 1957): 51 (hereafter cited as Hawes, ed., "Papers of McIntosh"); *GG*, January 17, 1776.

6 Allen D. Candler, comp., "The Colonial Records of the State of Georgia" (unpublished typescript, Ga. Arch.) 38, Pt.2, 110; "Proceedings of the Georgia Council of Safety, 1775 to 1777," *Collections* of the Georgia Historical Society, 5, Pt.1 (Savannah, 1901): 43–78, *passim*; Lachlan McIntosh to George Walton, July 11, 1776, Hawes, ed., "Papers of McIntosh," 8; Kenneth Coleman, *The American Revolution in Georgia, 1763–1789* (Athens, Ga. 1958), p.112.

7 On factional maneuvering before 1776, see Harvey H. Jackson, "Consensus and Conflict: Factional Politics in Revolutionary Georgia, 1774–1777," *GHQ* 59 (1975): 388–395; on the Liberty Society, see [John Wereat and Lachlan McIntosh], *Remarks on a Pamphlet, Entitled, "Strictures on a Pamphlet, entitled the Case of George McIntosh, ..." To Which is Added, A concise account of the Justice of the Executive and Legislative Bodies of the State of Georgia: Together With Some Account of the Lives and Upright Principles of the Leaders of the Nocturnal Junto* (n.p., 1777), and chapter 1 in the present work.

8 Detailed accounts of the development of the Gwinnett-McIntosh rivalry and its ramifications include Lamplugh, "Whigs Divided," ch. 1 of this work; Jackson, "Factionalism Personified: The McIntosh-Gwinnett Affair," paper presented at the Georgia Studies Symposium, Georgia Department of Archives and History, February 7, 1976; Alexander A. Lawrence, "General Lachlan McIntosh and His Suspension from Continental Command During the Revolution," *GHQ*

38 (1954): 101–141; and Charles F. Jenkins, *Button Gwinnett: Signer of the Declaration of Independence* (Garden City, N.Y., 1926).

9 Three pro-McIntosh pamphlets have survived: *The Case of George McIntosh, Esquire, A Member of the late Council and Convention of the State of Georgia; With the Proceedings thereon in the Hon. the Assembly and Council of that State* (n.p., 1777); *An Addition to the Case of George McIntosh, Esquire, Earnestly recommended to the serious Attention of every Reader, particularly those of the State of Georgia* (n.p., 1777); and *Remarks ...*, cited above. Wereat and McIntosh published *An Addition ...* over their own signatures; internal evidence suggests that Wereat also collaborated with the General on the others. For an anti-McIntosh view, see [Edward Langworthy], *Strictures on a Pamphlet, entitled, The Case of George McIntosh, Esq., Published by Order of the Liberty Society* (Savannah, 1777).

10 Wereat to George Walton, August 30, 1777, Hawes, ed., "Papers of McIntosh," 66–74. A letter from Wereat to Henry Laurens, August 4, 1777, which apparently has not survived, must have contained similar sentiments (see Laurens's reply, August 30, 1777, Letterbook, January 24, 1776–March 5, 1778, Laurens Papers, South Carolina Historical Society).

11 Wereat revealed his plan to George Walton in the letter cited in note 143, above. Extracts of the Chatham Grand Jury Presentments are in the Peter Force Georgia Transcripts, Library of Congress (microfilm, GHS).

12 Wereat to Lachlan McIntosh, March 13, 1778, Lachlan McIntosh Papers, Duke University. *Cf.* "An Act for the Expulsion of the Internal Enemies of this State," September 16, 1777, *GHQ* 55 (1971): 274–282 (edited by Heard Robertson).

13 Hawes, ed., "Papers of McIntosh," 86; William Glascock to the President of Congress, July 10, 1779, Papers of the Continental Congress (hereafter PCC), No.73, pp.240–244, National Archives; *RRG*, 2: 146.

14 *RRG*, 2: 147–148; "Affidavit of Wm. Glascock," Hawes, ed., "Papers of McIntosh," p.123; Wereat to Lachlan McIntosh, January 19, 1780, Force Georgia Transcripts.

15 *RRG*, 2: 146, 154, 170.

16 *Ibid.*, 160–176, *passim*. *Cf.* Edward J. Cashin, "'The Famous Colonel Wells': Factionalism in Revolutionary Georgia," *GHQ* 58 (1974): 145–147.

17 *RRG*, II: 151–152, 165; Joseph Clay and Benjamin Lincoln to John Wereat, November 2, 1779, "Letters of Joseph Clay, Merchant of Savannah, 1776–1793," *Collections* of the GHS 8 (Savannah, 1913): 160–161.

18 Major General Augustine Prevost to Lord George Germain, November 1, 1779, in Benjamin F. Stevens, *Facsimiles of Manuscripts in European Archives Relating to America, 1776–1783* (London, 1895) 24: no. 2020[3].

19 Charles C. Jones, Jr., *The History of Georgia* (Boston, 1883) 2: 428; Edward J. Cashin, "Augusta's Revolution of 1779," *Richmond County History* 7 (1975): 13, note 21.

20 A letter, dated October 17, 1779, from General Benjamin Lincoln to George Walton in the Letterbooks of Benjamin Lincoln, Boston Public Library, does, however, help to explain why Walton arrived in Augusta when he did and throws some light on how he was able to organize a government so quickly. My thanks to Dr. Edwin Bridges for information on this point.

21 Wereat to Lachlan McIntosh, January 19, 1780, Force Georgia Transcripts.

22 Jackson, "General Lachlan McIntosh," p.196; Wereat to McIntosh, January 19, 1780, Force Georgia Transcripts. For Wereat's low opinion of Richard Howley, see the undated fragment in his hand, *circa* January 1780, Keith Read Collection, University of Georgia.

23 Wereat to McIntosh, January 19, 1780, Force Georgia Transcripts.

24 Richmond County Grand Jury Presentments, Hawes, ed., "Papers of McIntosh," 86–89; Wereat to [Benjamin Weld?], June 1, 1780, Sol Feinstone Collection of the American Revolution, Boston Public Library; William Glascock to President of Congress, May 12, 1780, Hawes, ed., "Papers of McIntosh," 91–92.

25 Heard Robertson, "The Second British Occupation of Augusta, 1780–1781," *GHQ* 58 (1974): 422–436, *passim.*

26 Wereat to McIntosh, February 26, 1781, Peter Force Papers, Series 9, Box 29, Library of Congress.

27 Wereat to Thomas McKean, President of Congress, October 17, 1781, Papers of the Continental Congress, No.778, 24: 343; "An Account of the losses sustained by John Wereat in consequence of the present War," n.d. (but *circa* 1782), Miscellaneous Manuscripts, GaArch; Wereat to James Jackson, April 8, 1782, Lilla M. Hawes, ed., "The Papers of James Jackson, 1781–1798," *Collections* of the GHS 11 (Savannah, 1955): 5–6; Wereat to Jackson, April 17, 1782, James Jackson Papers, Duke University.

28 Wereat to ______________, September 22, 1782, in Stan V. Henkels, comp., *Revolutionary Manuscripts and Portraits* [Catalogue No. 683] (Philadelphia, 1892), p.68; Wereat's petition on behalf of Thomas Young, n.d. (but *circa* 1783), Keith Read Collection, University of Georgia, cited in Robert S. Lambert, "The Confiscation of Loyalist Property in Georgia, 1782–1786," *William & Mary Quarterly, Third Series* 20 (1963): 89–90.

29 John Wereat to James Edward Powell, August 6, 1783, Georgia Loyalist Claims, A.O.13, P.R.O. (Microfilm, GaArch).

30 Cashin, "'The Famous Colonel Wells'," 152–153; John Wereat to James Jackson, February 12, 1782, Society Collection, Historical Society of Pennsylvania, Philadelphia.

31 Candler, comp., *RRG*, 3: 89–90, 93–94, 118, 122–125, 166.

32 Wereat to Jackson, April 8, 1782, in Hawes, ed., "Papers of Jackson, 6; Cashin, "'The Famous Colonel Wells'," 151.

33 Jackson to Wereat, November 31, 1782, Hawes, ed., "Papers of McIntosh," 104–105; Wereat to Jackson, December 2, 1782, *ibid.*, 105–106. On Walton's career as Chief Justice of Georgia, see "George Walton, Chief Justice of Georgia, 1783–1785," chapter 3, above.

34 Wereat to Jackson, March 20, 1782, Keith Read Collection, UGa; Wereat to General Anthony Wayne, March 20, 1782, Wayne Papers, Historical Society of Pennsylvania.

35 Candler, comp., *RRG*, 2: 355–356; Governor Tonyn to Governor Martin, August 22, 1782, Hawes, ed., "Papers of McIntosh," 101–103; William McIntosh, Samuel Stirk, and John Wereat to Governor Martin, December 5, 1782, Miscellaneous Manuscripts, Ga. Arch.; Wereat to James Edward Powell, September 2, 1782, Georgia Loyalist Claims, A.O., 13, 36a, P.R.O. (microfilm, Ga. Arch.).

36 Candler, comp., *CRG*, 19, Part 2: 183–200, 442–443; Wereat's instructions as auditor are in Candler, comp., *RRG*, 2: 286–291.

37 Lambert, "Confiscation of Loyalist Property in Georgia," 89–90; Wereat to James Edward Powell, August 6, 1783, Georgia Loyalist Claims, A.O. 13, 36a, P.R.O. (microfilm, Ga. Arch.).

38 E. James Ferguson, *The Power of The Purse: A History of American Public Finance, 1776–1790* (Chapel Hill, 1961), ch. 9; Wereat to Lachlan McIntosh, July 30, 1784, Peter Force Papers, Series 7E, Box 3, Mss. Div., LC.

39 Wereat to Houstoun, November 8, 1784, Telamon Cuyler Collection, UGa; see also Wereat to Governor Edward Telfair, March 13, 1786, *ibid.*

40 [E. Merton Coulter, ed.,] "Minutes of the Georgia Convention Ratifying the Federal Constitution," *GHQ* 10 (1926): 223–237.

41 Ms. Senate Minutes, November 16, December 1, 1790, Ga. Arch.

42 Wereat to Telfair, May 10, 1791, Cuyler Collection, UGa.

43 Wereat to Telfair, June 14, 16, 1791, *ibid.*; Wereat to Lachlan McIntosh, July 11, 1791, Hawes, ed., "Papers of McIntosh," 152.

44 Lachlan McIntosh to Wereat, June 23, 1791; Wereat to McIntosh, July 11, 1791; McIntosh to Wereat, August 13, 1791, in Hawes, ed., "Papers of McIntosh," 150–153. Wereat to Mordecai Sheftall, July 16, 1791; Sheftall Sheftall to Mordecai Sheftall, July 8, 1792, both in Sheftall Family Letters and Papers, Library of the American Jewish Historical Society.

45 Ms. Senate Minutes, December 9, 1791, Ga. Arch.; Bond of John Wereat, April 20, 1792, Miscellaneous Bonds, Book DDD, 1783–1813, Ga. Arch.; Mordecai Sheftall to Sheftall Sheftall, April 25, 1792, Sheftall Family Letters and Papers, Library of the American Jewish Historical Society.

46 Wereat to Telfair, January 4, 1790, Executive Department Minutes, November 12, 1789–May 8, 1790, Ga. Arch.; same to same, January 17, 1791, Cuyler Collection, UGa; Executive Department Minutes, May 31, 1792, Ga. Arch.; Telfair to Wereat, July 17, 1792, *ibid.*

47 Wereat to Telfair, August 10, 1792, Edward Telfair Papers, Duke University.

48 Wereat to Telfair, November 30, 1792, Cuyler Collection, UGa.; same to same, January 2, 1793, Miscellaneous Manuscripts, Ga. Arch.

49 Thomas McKean to Edward Telfair, August 2, 1793, Telfair Papers, Duke University; Dwight F. Henderson, ed., "Georgia's Federal Grand Jury Presentments, 1791–1796," *GHQ* 55 (1971): 286, 290–291.

50 "An Augustian," [Augusta] *Southern Centinel* [hereafter cited as *SC*], November 14, 1793.

51 "A.B.," *ibid.*, November 21, 1793.

52 *Ibid.*, December 26, 1793; Wereat to Edward Telfair, August 25, 1794, Telfair Papers, Duke University.

53 For a more detailed treatment of land and politics in the 1780s, see Kenneth Coleman, *The American Revolution in Georgia, 1763–1789* (Athens, Ga., 1958), 260–265; George R. Lamplugh, *Politics on the Periphery: Factions and Parties in Georgia, 1783–1806* (Newark, Del., 1986), 31–37.

54 On the Yazoo sale of 1789, see Thomas Perkins Abernethy, *The South in the New Nation, 1789–1819* (Baton Rouge, La., 1961), 74–101; Lamplugh, *Politics on the Periphery*, 66–72.

55 Wereat to William Bingham, July 9, 1782, Gratz Collection, Historical Society of Pennsylvania, Philadelphia; Will of John Wereat, April 8, 1798, Chatham County Ordinary; Wereat to Lachlan McIntosh, July 30, 1784, Peter Force Papers, Ms. Div., LC.

56 Wereat to Ingersoll and Dallas, December 15, 1794, John Wereat Papers, Duke University. For comments on his straitened financial circumstances, see Wereat to President of Congress Thomas McKean, October 17, 1781, Papers of the Continental Congress, No.778, XXIV, 343, National Archives; "An Account of the losses sustained by John Wereat in consequence of the present War," n.d. (but *circa* 1783), Miscellaneous Manuscripts, Ga. Arch.; Wereat to Governor John Houstoun, November 8, 1784, and Wereat to Governor Edward Telfair, March 13, 1786, both in Telamon Cuyler Collection, UGa.

57 Nathaniel Pendleton to editors, *Columbian Museum & Savannah Advertiser*, April 12, 1796 (hereinafter cited as *CMSA*). General treatments of the Yazoo sale of 1795 include Abernethy, *South in the New Nation*, 136–168; Lamplugh, *Politics on the Periphery*, 104–119; C. Peter Magrath, *Yazoo: Law and Politics in the New Republic—The Case of Fletcher vs. Peck* (Providence, R.I., 1966); and Lisle A. Rose, *Prologue to Democracy: The Federalists in the South, 1789–1800* (Lexington, Ky., 1968), 85–98.

58 Thomas P. Carnes to Seaborn Jones, George Walker, and Peter Carnes, January 20, 1794, Seaborn Jones Papers, Duke University; Wade Hampton's statement, January 27, 1804, Walter Lowrie and Matthew St. Clair Clarke, comps., *American State Papers: Public Lands* (Washington, D.C., 1832) 1: 197–198 (hereinafter cited as *ASP: PL*); David Ross to John B. Scott, November 14, 1794, *ibid.*, 199.

59 Pendleton to editors, *CMSA*, April 12, 1796.

60 John Wereat to Edward Telfair, August 25, 1794, Edward Telfair Papers, Duke University.

61 Unless otherwise noted, the sequence of events present in this and the following paragraphs is that outlined in *State of Facts, Showing the Right of Certain Companies to the Lands Lately Purchased by them from the State of Georgia* (Boston, 1795), 30–31, a pro-Yazoo pamphlet, but the chronology presented therein is supported by extracts of official documents, including the journals of the Georgia legislature, the originals of which are no longer extant.

62 On Cox's bid, see Abernethy, *South in the New Nation*, 142.

63 On January 1, 1795, following the veto of the Yazoo Act and the passage of the new version, the Supplementary Act (see below), John B. Scott withdrew the offer of the Virginia Company, claiming that the stipulations in the Supplementary Act would be unacceptable to his backers. He thereupon formed a new organization, the Upper Mississippi Company, in partnership with John C. Nightingale and Wade Hampton, and had the name of the new company inserted in the Supplementary Act (*ASP: PL* 1: 201).

64 Wereat, *et al.*, to the legislature, December 11, 15, 20, 1794; January 1, 1795, Yazoo Manuscripts, Georgia Surveyor General Department, Ga. Arch.; "Copy Letter to A.J. Dallas," in Wereat's hand, January 5, 1795, Edward Telfair Papers; Raymond Walters, Jr., *Alexander James Dallas: Lawyer—Politician—Financier* (Philadelphia, 1943), 117.

65 Georgia Union Company to Mathews, December 22, 1794 (copy), Edward Telfair Papers; James Gunn, *et al.*, to Mathews, December 25, 1794, Yazoo Manuscripts, Georgia Surveyor General Department, Ga. Arch.

66 *ASP: PL* 1: 156–157.

67 The Supplementary Act is reprinted in *ASP: PL* 1: 152–155.

68 Wereat to Mathews, January 3, 1795, Edward Telfair Papers.

69 Wereat to Dallas, January 5, 1795, Edward Telfair Papers.

70 *State of Facts*, 33; "Expono," *SC*, January 15, 1795; Robert Watkins to editor, *ibid.*, January 29, 1795; "Pliny," [Savannah] *Georgia Gazette*, April 7, 1796 (hereafter, *GG*).

71 Affidavits of Henry Mitchell, Peter Van Allen, Clement Lanier, and James Lucas, *ASP: PL* 1: 145–148, *passim*. On this phase of the Yazoo sale, see Lamplugh, *Politics on the Periphery*, 107–110.

72 Few debated Yazoo defender Robert Watkins in *SC*, February 19, 26; March 12, 26; April 9, 16, 1795. Twiggs and Telfair were attacked for their supposed roles in rallying anti-Yazoo forces during the fall election campaign. See Twiggs's announcement of his candidacy for a seat in the legislature and "One of the People," probably by Telfair, both in the *Augusta Chronicle and Gazette of the State*, October 10 (hereafter *ACGS*); "Another of the People," *ACGS*, October 17; "A Voter," *SC*, October 15; "An Elector," *SC*, October 29, 1795. For the attack on Wereat and Telfair, see "A Traveller," *SC*, October 29, 1795; the anonymous reply was published in *SC*, November 12, 1795.

73 *Journal of the Convention of the State of Georgia Convened at Louisville, on Monday, May 3rd, 1795* (Augusta, 1795); proposed amendments were published in *GG*, May 21; extracts of convention proceedings, *GG*, May 14, and *SC*, May 25, June 4, 11, 18, 1795.

74 For a detailed account of this campaign, see Lamplugh, *Politics on the Periphery*, 128–132.

75 House Journal, January 14, 15, 1796, Ga. Arch.

76 The work of Jackson's committee and the progress of the Rescinding Act through the lower house (the Senate journal is no longer extant) may be followed in House Journal, January 14, 15, 18, 22, 25–29; February 1, 4, 9, 13, 1796, Ga. Arch. The report of Jackson's committee and the affidavits upon which it was based have been published in *ASP: PL* 1: 144–149; the Rescinding Act is reprinted *ibid.*, 156–158.

77 Clayton's affidavit, as reported by Jackson's committee, is in *ASP: PL* 1: 146. For charges that Jackson had "suppressed" Clayton's testimony about Wereat's alleged statement, see "An extract of a letter from a gentleman in Georgia, to his friend in [Philadelphia]," *Federal Gazette & Baltimore Daily Advertiser*, March 5, 1796; James Gunn to editor, *Gazette of the United States*, March 15, 1796, reprinted in *Federal Gazette & Baltimore Daily Advertiser*, April 6, 1796; "Zeno," *SC*, April 7, 1796; "Quarko," *CMSA*, June 21, 1796. Wereat refuted Clayton's allegation in an affidavit dated April 21, 1796, enclosed in a letter to the editor of *CMSA*, published on April 26. This letter was not Wereat's final word on Yazoo. One year

later, he served as foreman on Bryan County's first grand jury when that body denounced the Supplementary Act (*CMSA*, June 6, 1797).

78 *CMSA*, January 9, 1798.

79 *Ibid.*, January 23; *SC*, February 8, 1798.

80 *SC*, March 1, 1798.

81 John Wereat Estate Records, Chatham County Ordinary.

82 *Isaacs v. Wereat*, Circuit Court Records, A/24, The National Archives at Atlanta, Morrow, Ga.

83 *GG*, January 31, 1799.

84 John Wereat to James Jackson, February 12, 1782, Society Collection, Historical Society of Pennsylvania, Philadelphia.

Notes--8

1 On these aspects of Georgia politics in the Early Republic, see George R. Lamplugh, *Politics on the Periphery: Factions and Parties in Georgia, 1783–1806* (Newark, Del., 1986), chapters 3–4.

2 For Thomas Carr's activities prior to 1793, consult *ibid.*, pp. 69, 72–75.

3 A detailed account of the 1790 congressional campaign and its aftermath may be found *ibid.*, 92–95.

4 Savannah *Georgia Gazette*, July 9, 16, 1789; October 21, 1790; October 13, 1791 (hereafter cited as *GG*); Executive Department Minutes, December 14, 1790, microfilm, Georgia Archives, Morrow, Georgia (hereafter cited as Ga Arch).

5 Manuscript Senate Journal, December 16, 19, 1791, Ga Arch.

6 Executive Department Minutes, December 24, 1791, Ga Arch. Named to the inferior court bench along with Williams were John King and Abner Hammond; the other justices of the peace were John King and Hugh Brown.

7 The account in this and the following paragraph is based on "Extracts from the Journal of the Georgia Senate," November 22–27, 1792, Thomas Carr Collection, Special Collections, University of Georgia Libraries; and Manuscript Senate Journal, November 17, 26, 27, 29, 1792, Ga Arch. The extracts in the Carr Collection include a copy of the petition submitted by Carr, Williams, and Dillingham; the Senate Journal does not.

8 Carr to Telfair, January 5, 1793, Miscellaneous Manuscripts, Ga Arch. Governor Telfair's decision to divide Camden into four company districts was probably influenced by this letter. At the ensuing election for field officers, the votes of company officers, from a district a critic claimed was virtually uninhabited,

proved decisive in procuring for Carr the position of commandant. On this point, see "A Querist," *GG*, October 31, 1793.

9 Jackson to Telfair, March 31, 1793, in Lilla M. Hawes, ed., "The Papers of James Jackson, 1781–1798," *Collections* of the Georgia Historical Society, 11 (Savannah, 1955): 48 (cited hereafter as "Papers of Jackson").

10 Jackson to Telfair, April 8, *ibid.*, p.53; Petition of Sundry Inhabitants of Camden County to Governor Telfair [n.d., but *c.* April 1], Telamon Cuyler Collection, Special Collections, University of Georgia Libraries; Jackson to James Seagrove, May 8, 9, 1793, "Papers of Jackson," pp.60–61.

11 The account of the shooting of Abner Williams and its aftermath in this and the following paragraph has been pieced together from the warrant for the arrests of John and Thomas King, July 12, and the statement by constable John Hardie on their refusal to surrender, October 19 (on the reverse of the warrant), Thomas Carr Collection; Carr to Telfair, July 20, *ibid.*; Augusta *Southern Centinel*, August 1; *GG*, August 8, 1793.

12 Executive Council Minutes, July 22, 23, 29 (typescript), Ga Arch; "A Querist," *GG*, October 31, 1793.

13 Carr's regimental order, September 2; Randolph McGillis to Carr, September 4; Hammond to Carr, September 3, 1793, all in Carr Collection.

14 Carr to Telfair, September 10, 1793, *ibid.*

15 Jackson to Telfair, July 29, "Papers of Jackson," p. 81; Hugh Brown to Carr, September 14, in Louise F. Hays, comp., "Georgia Military Affairs" (typescript), 1: 452, Ga Arch; Abner Hammond to Carr, September 14, Carr Collection; Jackson to Telfair, September 30, 1793, James Jackson Papers, William L. Perkins Library, Duke University.

16 Hammond to Carr, September 14; Randolph McGillis and others to Carr, September 20, 1793, both in Carr Collection.

17 Gunn to Carr, September 15; Carr to Telfair, September 22; Jackson to Carr, September 28, all *ibid.*

18 Carr to Joseph Miller, September 22; Henry Wright to Carr, September 26, 28, 1793, all *ibid.*

19 William Dawson to Carr, September 27; Henry Wright to Carr, September 28, 1793, both *ibid.*

20 Henry Wright to Carr, September 29; William Norris to Carr, September 29; John F. Randolph to Carr, October 4, 1793.

21 Jackson to Telfair, October 14, 1793, Miscellaneous Manuscripts, Ga Arch.

22 Carr to Telfair, October 15, 1793, Carr Collection.

23 Carr to Telfair, October 16; Daniel Miller to Carr, __October 1793, both *ibid.*

24 Governor George Mathews to Lieutenant-Colonel Daniel Stewart, January 3, 1794, Governor's Letterbook, November 28, 1793–March 27, 1794 (typescript), Ga Arch; Lieutenant-Colonel Stewart to Adjutant General Elholm, March 16, 1794, in Hays, comp., "Georgia Military Affairs," vol. 2, pt. 1: 124.

25 Thomas King and others to [Adjutant General Elholm], February 24, 1794, Hays, comp., "Georgia Military Affairs," vol. 2, pt. 1:121; Governor Mathews to John King and others, April 24, 1794, Governor's Letterbook, November 18, 1793–October 14, 1794 (typescript), Ga Arch.

Notes—9

1 William Omer Foster, Sr., *James Jackson: Duelist and Militant Statesman, 1757–1806* (Athens, Ga.).

2 John Wereat to [the Rev. John Collier], September 7, 1772, Dreer Collection, Historical Society of Pennsylvania, Philadelphia; "Character of J J Drawn By Himself," in Lilla M. Hawes, ed., "The Papers of James Jackson, 1781–1798," *Collections of the Georgia Historical Society*, 11 (Savannah, Ga., 1955): 37; Foster, *James Jackson*, ch. 1.

3 On the nature of Georgia politics in the 1780s, see George R. Lamplugh, *Politics on the Periphery: Factions and Parties in Georgia, 1783–1806* (Newark, Del., 1986), chs. 1–2.

4 Lamplugh, *Politics on the Periphery*, ch.4, treats Jackson's political career in the 1780s, including the origins of his rivalries with Gunn and Gibbons.

5 T. Lowther to James Iredell, May 9, 1789, in Griffith J. McRee, *Life and Correspondence of James Iredell* (1857; reprint, 2 vols. In 1, New York, 1949), 2: 258; Lance Banning, *The Jeffersonian Persuasion: Evolution of a Party Ideology* (Ithaca, N.Y., 1978), pp.123, 142–144; Foster, *James Jackson*, pp.73, 79, 85.

6 Foster, *James Jackson*, ch.5; Dwight F. Henderson, ed., "Georgia Federal Grand Jury Presentments, 1791–1796," *Georgia Historical Quarterly*, 55 (Summer 1971): 282–292; Kenneth Coleman, *The American Revolution in Georgia, 1763–1789* (Athens, Ga., 1958), chs. 16–17.

7 *Georgia Gazette* (cited hereafter as *GG*), July 28; August 4, 11; October 13; November 24; December 8, 1791. Letter from John Burrowes, *ibid.*, October 27, 1791; ___________ Keen to Robert Hobart, October 6, 1791, Georgia Miscellaneous Papers, State, 1782–1805 (Duke University, Durham, N.C.); Georgia Senate Journal, December 16–21, 1791, Georgia Archives, Morrow, Ga. (cited hereafter as Ga. Arch.)

8 *Proceedings in the House of Representatives ... Respecting the Contested Election for the Eastern District of Georgia* (Philadelphia, 1792); James Gunn to Anthony Wayne, January 31, 1793, Wayne Papers, Historical Society of Pennsylvania, Philadelphia.

9 Lamplugh, *Politics on the Periphery*, pp. 31–37, 66–77.

10 On the passage of the Yazoo Act, see Thomas P. Abernethy, *The South in the New Nation, 1789–1819* (Baton Rouge, 1961), pp. 136–147; Lisle A. Rose, *Prologue to Democracy: The Federalists in the South, 1789–1800* (Lexington, Ky., 1968), pp. 85–92; and Lamplugh, *Politics on the Periphery*, pp. 104–119.

11 Jackson to Madison, November 17, 1795, Madison Papers (Library of Congress); James Jackson, *Letters of Sicilius . . .* (1795), pp.21–22.

12 According to Jackson's own tally of the results, anti-Yazooists would outnumber supporters of the sale 14–6 in the state senate, 30–17 in the house. Hawes, ed., "Papers of Jackson," p.101.

13 House Journal, January 14–15,18, 22, 25–29, 1796 (Ga. Arch.). The report of Jackson's committee and the affidavits upon which it was based have been published in *American State Papers: Public Lands* (Washington, D.C., 1834), 1: 124–129.

14 House Journal, February 12, 20, 1796; "Pliny," *GG*, April 28, 1796; "Benedict," [Augusta] *Southern Centinel*, March 17, 1796.

15 "An extract of a letter from a gentleman in Georgia, to his friend in [Philadelphia]," January 29, 1796, *Federal Gazette & Baltimore Daily Advertiser*, March 5, 1796.

16 Lamplugh, *Politics on the Periphery*, pp. 84–85, 94; "Extract from a letter from Augusta (Georgia) [February 26, 1796]," *Federal Gazette & Baltimore Daily Advertiser*, March 19, 1796; Jackson to John Milledge, March 8, 1796, in Harriet Milledge Salley, ed., *Correspondence of John Milledge* (Columbia, S.C., 1949), pp. 38–41; "Extract of a letter from Augusta, dated May 13," *Gazette of the United States* (hereafter cited as *GUS*), June 6, 1796; Jackson to Milledge, May 14, 1796, in Salley, ed., *Milledge Correspondence*, p. 45; Foster, *James Jackson*, p. 127.

17 *Annals of Congress*, 4th Cong., 1st Sess., 402–403, 786–798; Jackson to Milledge, April 11, 1796, in Salley, ed., *Milledge Correspondence*, pp. 42–44.

18 "A and Z," *Columbian Museum & Savannah Advertiser* (hereafter cited as *CMSA*), September 11, 1801; "Q," *ibid.*, September 18, 1801; George Troup and Thomas Charlton to editor, *ibid.*, September 22, 1801; editorial, *ibid.*, September 25, 1801.

19 "Sketch of the Yazoo Speculation, in Jackson's Hand," in Hawes, ed., "Papers of Jackson," p. 36; Jackson to Madison, November 17, 1795, Madison Papers; "A Mechanic," *GG*, September 10, 1795.

20 Jackson inserted the excerpt of Baldwin's letter in the *CMSA* for June 26, 1798. The development of the anti-Baldwin campaign can be traced in the following

pieces, all published in the same newspaper: "A Citizen of Georgia," July 3; "Americus," September 7; "Another Subscriber," September 28; "An Elector of Chatham County" and "An Elector," October 12; "Another Elector," October 19, November 2; and "A Christian," November 2, 1798.

21 See Jackson to Milledge, March 13, 1799, Salley, ed., *Milledge Correspondence*, pp.60–61. Perhaps as a reward for acquiescing in the political necessities on 1799, Tattnall was elected governor in November 1801. *GG*, November 12, 1801.

22 Jackson to Baldwin, November 26, 1800, Baldwin Papers (Yale University, New Haven, Conn.); House Journal, November 9, 1799, November 5, 1800. For Federalist responses to the Governor's truculent address in 1800, see Anonymous, Augusta *Herald*, November 19, 1800; "Un bon Citoyen," *CMSA*, December 2, 1800.

23 Anonymous, *Louisville Gazette & Republican Trumpet* (hereafter, *LGRT*), August 5, 1800. See also "A Jeffersonite," *ibid.*, March 4, 1800, and "A Citizen," *ibid.*, April 8, 1800.

24 "B," *Augusta Herald* (cited hereafter as *AH*), June 11, July 9, 1800; Troup and Charlton to the editors, *CMSA*, September 22, 1801; "A [Johnson]," *LGRT*, September 9, November 26, 1800.

25 Editorials, *LGRT*, June 17, July 1; "Honestus," "D," and "An Up Countryman," *ibid.*, July 1, 1800.

26 Jackson to Milledge, n.d., but *ca.* November 20, 1800, in Salley, ed., *Milledge Correspondence*, pp.110–111; Jackson to Baldwin, November 26, 1800, Baldwin Papers, Yale; Jackson to Baldwin, December 10, 1800, Abraham Baldwin Papers, University of Georgia. For an opposition view confirming use of a caucus in this election, see "An American Soldier," *CMSA*, December 5, 1800.

27 Jefferson to Jackson, May 28, 1801, Jefferson Papers, Library of Congress; Baldwin to Jefferson, May 1, 1801, Letters of Application and Recommendation During the Administration of Thomas Jefferson, 1801–1809 [hereafter, LAR: TJ], National Archives, Washington, D.C.; Jackson to Jefferson, July 18, 1801, *ibid.*; Jackson to Milledge, September 1, 1801, Salley, ed., *Milledge Correspondence*, p.75.

28 Jackson to Jefferson, July 18, 1801, LAR: TJ; Lamplugh, *Politics on the Periphery*, pp.169–172.

29 Milledge to Harris, September 8, 11, 1800, Salley, ed., *Milledge Correspondence*, pp. 66–69; *CMSA*, July 30, 1803, February 8, 1804. See also George R. Clayton to ____________, May 25, 1802, George R. Clayton Papers, Duke.

30 See Jackson to Milledge, March 16, 1803, Salley, ed., *Milledge Correspondence*, pp.99–100; editorials, *Augusta Chronicle and Gazette of the State* (hereafter cited as *ACGS*), June 18, September 3, 1803; "Telamon," *AH*, September 14, 1803; "An

Old Whig," *ACGS*, April 20, 1805; editorial, *ibid.*, August 10, 1805; letter from Josiah Meigs, *ibid.*, August 31, 1805; "Gladiator," *ibid.*, September 14, 1805.

31 Richard Dennis to Joseph Alston, April 5, 1802, enclosed in Alston to __________, May 15, 1802, LAR: TJ; "Extract of a Letter from a gentleman in Savannah, to a friend in [Washington]," *Washington Federalist*, April 30, 1802; Jefferson to Abraham Baldwin, May 1, 1802, Jefferson Papers; Jefferson to Jackson, May 1, 1802, *ibid.*

32 *CMSA*, August 31, 1802; Jackson to Jefferson, November 19, 1802, LAR: TJ.

33 "Extract of a letter from Louisville, dated February 12," Augusta *Southern Centinel*, February 16, 1797; William Cobbett, *Porcupine's Works* (12 vols., London, 1801), 10: 22–32; letter from Solicitor General Caldwell, *Southern Centinel*, October 18, 1798.

34 Cobbett, *Porcupine's Works*, 10: 9. On Jackson's refusal to pay M'Millan, see his message to the legislature, February 13, 1799, Governor's Letterbook, January 11–October 30, 1799, Ga. Arch. In December 1801, the House finally appropriated, by a slim margin of 23–21, $1,090 to compensate M'Millan for publishing the 1799 legislative journals (House Journal, December 5, 1801).

35 "Extract of a letter from Augusta, dated May 13," *GUS*, June 6, 1796. The minutes of the meeting of "a number of Citizens Electors of the County of Chatham, held in Savannah on the 2nd of May 1796" are printed as a broadside in the George Jones Papers, Georgia Historical Society, Savannah.

36 Jackson to George and James Jones, February 15, 1798, James Jackson Papers, Duke.

37 "To the Freemen of Chatham County," by "Anti Balthazar," broadside [Savannah, *ca.* October 1795], mistakenly bound following page two of the *GG*, July 23, 1793, in the microfilm edition of that paper; the mechanics' letter to Jackson and his reply were published *ibid.*, November 5, 1795; "Extract of a letter from Augusta, dated May 13," *GUS*, June 6, 1796; *CMSA*, December 21, 1798, January 2, 1801.

38 "A North-Carolinian," *ACGS*, January 16, 1796; "A Subscriber and Citizen of Columbia County," *ibid.*, July 23, 1796.

39 *CMSA*, July 6, 1803; *ACGS*, July 10, 17, 24, 31, 1802.

40 *CMSA*, March 10, 20, 1801; July 7, 1804.

41 Albert B. Saye, ed., "Journal of the Georgia Constitutional Convention of 1798," *Georgia Historical Quarterly* 36 (December 1952): 375–376.

42 Jackson to John Twiggs, March 5, 1795, James Jackson Papers; *Annals of Congress*, 3rd Cong., 2nd Sess., 1278–1279; Robert Goodloe Harper to Seaborn Jones, January 4, 1797, Seaborn Jones Papers, Duke; House Journal, February 8, 10, 1797, Ga. Arch.

43 Jackson to Gallatin, March 27, 1802, Madison Papers; Augustin Smith Clayton, comp., *A Compilation of the Laws of the State of Georgia* (Augusta, 1812), pp. 48–51.

44 Senate Journal, April 18, May 6, 1803; House Journal, May 2, 1803; James Jackson to David B. Mitchell, September 5, 1805, Keith Read Collection, University of Georgia; John Milledge to Charles Harris, June 13, 1806, Salley, ed., *Milledge Correspondenc*, p.136; "Extract of a letter, from a gentleman in Louisville (Ga.), to the Editors of this paper, dated 12th June, 1806," *CMSA*, June 18, 1806.

45 Obadiah Jones to Joseph Bryan, September 8, 1802, Arnold-Screven Papers, Series A: Bryan-Screven Papers, Southern Historical Collection, University of North Carolina, Chapel Hill); "Extract of a letter, from a Gentleman of respectability, in Savannah, to the Editors—dated September the 2d, 1802," *LGRT*, September 15, 1802; Jackson to David Mitchell, September 5, 1805, Keith Read Collection, UGa; John Milledge to Charles Harris, June 13, 1806, Salley, ed., *Milledge Correspondence*, p.136; editorial, *CMSA*, September 10, 1806; editorial, *LGRT*, October 27, 1802.

46 Jackson to Milledge, March 8, 1796, Salley, ed., *Milledge Correspondence*, p.39.

47 On the rise of John Clark, see Lamplugh, *Politics on the Periphery*, pp.190–196.

48 *CMSA*, October 29, 1803, reprinting a letter from the Fredericktown (Maryland) *Hornet*, August 29, 1803.

Notes—10

[**NOTE:** The two parts of the Gunn life originally were published as: "The Importance of Being Truculent: James Gunn, the Chatham Militia, and Georgia Politics, 1782–1789," *GHQ*, 80 (Summer 1996): 227–245; and "James Gunn: Georgia Federalist, 1789–1801," *GHQ*, 94 (Fall 2010): 313–341.]

1 James H. Broussard, "The Georgia Federalists," unpublished paper (1987), pp.1, 11, in possession of present author. See also: Broussard, *The Southern Federalists, 1800–1816* (Baton Rouge, La., 1978), 247–256; Lisle A. Rose, *Prologue to Democracy: The Federalists in the South, 1789–1800* (Lexington, Ky., 1968); and George R. Lamplugh, *Politics on the Periphery: Factions and Parties in Georgia, 1783–1806* (Newark, Del., 1986).

2 For the prewar estimate, see Evarts B. Greene and Virginia Harrington, *American Population Before the Federal Census of 1790* (New York, 1932), p.182. The 1790

figure is from *Return of the Whole Number of Persons Within the United States* (Facsimile of the 1791 edition; New York, n.d.), p.55.

3 Gordon den Boer, *et al.*, eds., *The Documentary History of the First Federal Elections, 1788–1790*, 4 vols. (Madison, Wis., 1976–1989), 2: 482 (hereafter cited as *DHFFE*).

4 George Washington Greene, *The Life of Nathanael Greene*, 3 vols. (New York, 1871), 3: 455; the report of the board of inquiry is in the Papers of the Continental Congress (microfilm edition, reel 162), item 149, pp.595–598 (cited hereafter as PCC).

5 Greene, *Life of Greene*, 3: 456.

6 For Greene's decision and Congress's response, see PCC (reel 162), item 149, p.597; Greene to General Benjamin Lincoln, June 22, 1782, *ibid.*, pp.599–601; and John C. Fitzpatrick, ed., *Journal of the Continental Congress*, 34 vols. (Washington, D.C., 1904–1937), 23: 526.

7 Allen D. Candler, comp., *The Revolutionary Records of the State of Georgia*, 3 vols. (Atlanta, Ga., 1908), 1: 454 (hereinafter cited as *RRG*); Mary Granger, ed., *Savannah River Plantations* (Savannah, Ga., 1947), pp. 203–204; *Georgia Gazette* (Savannah), April 28, 1785 (hereafter, *GG*).

8 Catherine Greene to Jeremiah Wadsworth, January 31, 1789, *DHFFE*, 2: 477. Mrs. Gunn died in May, 1797, at the age of 32, which would have made her about 17 at the time of her marriage (obituary of Mary Jane Gunn, *Columbian Museum & Savannah Advertiser*, May 16, 1797). I am indebted for additional information about Mary Jane Gunn to Mr. Farris Cadle of Garden City, Ga., a registered land surveyor and land title researcher who discovered Mrs. Gunn's grave, located next to that of her father, Joseph Wright, amid the ruins of what had once been Wright's home, Litchfield Plantation, on the Ogeechee River in Chatham County (Cadle to author, e-mail, October 18, 2010).

9 Kenneth R. Bowling and Helen E. Veit, eds., *The Diary of William Maclay and Other Notes on Senate Debates*, Vol. 9 in *Documentary History of the First Federal Congress* (Baltimore, 1988), 18n; *GG*, October 20, 1783; Executive Department Minutes, December 3, 1790, Georgia Archives, Morrow, Ga. (cited hereafter as Ga Arch).

10 *GG*, October 20, 1783. On anti-Tory activities in the low country, see Lamplugh, *Politics on the Periphery*, pp. 43–49.

11 *RRG*, 3: 560.

12 *Ibid.*, 3: 457–458. For a more detailed account of the Assembly's vendetta against Lyman Hall, see Lamplugh, *Politics on the Periphery*, pp. 46–47.

[13] Assembly Minutes, February 21, 1785, Ga Arch. For a survey of Gibbons' activities after the war, see "Waiting for the Steamboat: The Political Career of Thomas Gibbons in Georgia, 1783–1789," in the present volume.

[14] On the importance of the concept of honor in the antebellum South, see Bertram Wyatt-Brown, *Southern Honor: Ethics and Behavior in the Old South* (New York, 1982), especially "Part One: Origins and Definitions."

[15] Greene to George Washington, April 25, 1785, Washington Papers, Library of Congress (microfilm edition, reel 95); Greene, *Life of Greene*, 3: 528.

[16] Greene to Washington, April 25, 1785, Washington Papers (microfilm, reel 95); John C. Fitzpatrick, ed., *The Writings of George Washington*, 39 vols. (Washington, D.C., 1931–1944), 28: 144.

[17] For a more detailed treatment of these events, consult Lamplugh, *Politics on the Periphery*, pp. 49–56.

[18] *GG*, August 4; September 14, 21; October 19, 1786.

[19] "A Plain Militiaman," *ibid.*, September 28, 1786; Chatham Grand Jury Presentments, *ibid.*, October 19, 1786.

[20] "A Private," *ibid.*, September 28, 1786; Fishbourn to Wayne [*ca.* October 1786], Anthony Wayne Papers, Clements Library, University of Michigan.

[21] *GG*, May 10, 1787.

[22] "Cassius," "To Brigadier General Jackson, No. I," *Georgia State Gazette or Independent Register*, September 29, 1787 (cited hereafter as *GSGIR*).

[23] James Jackson to [Seaborn Jones], October 18, 1787 [fragment], Seaborn Jones Papers, Perkins Library, Duke University; Executive Council Minutes, October 15, 1787, Ga Arch; Jackson to Governor George Handley, October 3, 1788, Miscellaneous Manuscripts, Ga Arch.

[24] The treatment of the Gunn-Welscher affair in this and the next four paragraphs is based on the following items in *GG*: affidavit of Joseph Welscher, July 12; court-martial of Joseph Welscher, July 26; and James Gunn to *GG* editor James Johnston, July 25, 26, 1787. In the 1790s, both William Stephens and Joseph Welscher were stalwart supporters of James Jackson and, thus, bitter enemies of James Gunn. See Lamplugh, *Politics on the Periphery*, pp. 157, 168, 170–172 (on Stephens); 151–152 (on Welscher).

[25] *GG*, December 4, 1788.

[26] Anonymous, *GSGIR*, January 31, 1789; Job Sumner to Henry Knox, December 14, 1788, *DHFFE*, 2: 449; [Telfair] to "The Author of the piece signed 'A Planter,'" January 5, 1789, Edward Telfair Papers, Perkins Library, Duke University.

[27] Anthony Wayne to Elijah Clarke, November 1, 1788, *DHFFE*, 2: 444–445; on Wayne's travels in the 1780s, see *ibid.*, 444, headnote.

28 Anthony Wayne to George Washington, May 10, 1789, PCC (reel 179), item 161, 241; James Seagrove to Samuel Blachley Webb, February 22, 1789, *DHFFE*, 2: 478; Catherine Greene to Jeremiah Wadsworth, January 31, 1789, *ibid.*, 477.

29 During his two terms in the United States Senate (1789–1801), Gunn continued to attend most meetings of the Georgia legislature before leaving for the national capital. As a result, he almost invariably arrived late for each session of Congress (*Annals of Congress*, 1st–6th Congresses, *passim*).

30 Wayne to Elijah Clarke, November 1; Benjamin Fishbourn to Wayne, November 3; Elihu Lyman to Wayne, November 3, 1788; all in *DHFFE*, 2: 444–447, *passim*.

31 Anthony Wayne to Elijah Clarke, November 1, 1788, *ibid.*, 445; Wayne to George Mathews and Benjamin Fishbourn, November 5, 1788, *ibid.*, 447.

32 Assembly Minutes, January 18, 1789, Ga Arch.

33 *Ibid.*, January 19, 1789. The minutes do not record the number of votes received by the various senatorial candidates.

34 Benjamin Fishbourn to Anthony Wayne, November 12; George Mathews to Wayne, November 18; Job Sumner to Henry Knox, December 14, 1788; all in *DHFFE*, 2: 448–449.

35 See, for example, Cradock Burnell to The Rev. Mr. Thomas Jones, March 21, 1789, Samuel and Thomas Jones Papers, Georgia Historical Society (hereafter cited as GHS); Gunn to Mordecai Sheftall, May 18, [1789], Marion Abrams Levy Collection, microfilm, Ga Arch; James Seagrove to Samuel Blachley Webb, February 22, 1789, Worthington C. Ford, ed., *The Correspondence and Journals of Samuel Blachley Webb*, 3 vols. (New York, 1893–1894), 3: 123; James Gunn to Alexander Hamilton, November 11, 1790, Harold C. Syrett *et al.*, eds., *Papers of Alexander Hamilton*, 27 vols. (New York, 1961–1981), 8: 147–148.

36 Benjamin Fishbourn to President Washington, May 12, 1789, Washington Papers, 7: 39, microfilm, reel 120, Library of Congress, Washington, D.C.

37 For Fishbourn's disappointment at Wayne's loss in the senatorial election, see his letter to George Washington, May 17, 1789, Washington Papers, 7:39, microfilm, reel 120. On Fishbourn's rejection as naval officer, see Washington's message to the Senate, *Annals of Congress*, 1st Cong., 1st Sess., 1: 59–61; "Extract of a letter from a friend in New York to his friend [Benjamin Fishbourn] in this place, dated 10th August 1789," *GG*, August 27, 1789; Fishbourn to Washington, September 25, 1789, Papers of the Continental Congress, 78, 9: 645, microfilm, reel 95, Library of Congress; William Jackson to Benjamin Fishbourn, September 25, 1789, in Fitzpatrick, ed., *Writings of Washington*, 30: 412.

38 The Impost Bill was designed to place excise taxes on certain items in order to raise money to begin paying interest on the public debt. James Gunn to Mordecai Sheftall, June 22, 1789, Sheftall Papers, Library of the American Jewish Historical

Society, Newton Center, Massachusetts. In an earlier to Mordecai Sheftall, Gunn had expressed himself opposed to the Excise Bill. For James Jackson's early, consistent opposition to the Hamiltonian program, see "'Oh the Colossus! The Colossus!' James Jackson and the Jeffersonian Republican Party in Georgia," in the present volume.

39 William Smith to Edward Rutledge, July 5, 1789, in George C. Rogers, ed., "The Letters of William Loughton Smith to Edward Rutledge, June 6, 1789 to April 28, 1794," *South Carolina Historical Magazine* 69 (January 1968): 10–11; Linda Grant DePauw, ed., *The Documentary History of the First Federal Congress*, 17 vols. (Baltimore and London, 1972), 1: 153–154 (cited hereafter as *DHFFC*).

40 Bowling and Veit, eds., *Diary of Maclay*, published as vol. 9 in *DHFFC*, 243, 245, 255 (quotation on 255).

41 DePauw, ed., *DHFFC*, 1: 420, 438, 536; Gunn to Telfair, January 26, 1791, Keith Read Collection, Hargrett Rare Book and Manuscript Library, University of Georgia, Athens (hereafter cited as Hargrett Library).

42 Lamplugh, *Politics on the Periphery*, pp.64–65.

43 On reaction in Georgia to the Treaty of New York, see Dwight F. Henderson, ed., "Georgia Federal Grand Jury Presentments, 1791–1796," *GHQ* 55 (Summer 1971): 283–285; *Annals of Congress, 1st Cong., 3rd Sess.*, December 11, 1791; *American State Papers: Indian Affairs*, 2 vols. (Washington, 1832), 2: 791; Gunn to Hamilton, November 11, 1790, Syrett, ed., *Papers of Hamilton*, 7: 147–148.

44 The "Anas" of Thomas Jefferson, in A.A. Lipscomb and A.E. Bergh, eds., *The Writings of Thomas Jefferson*, 20 vols. (Washington, D.C., 1900–1904), 1: 285.

45 Jackson to Milledge, November 7, 1792, T.U.P. Charlton, *The Life of James Jackson* (Augusta, Ga., 1809; reprint, Atlanta, 1897), pp.138–140.

46 Gunn to Wayne, January 31, 1793, Anthony Wayne Papers, History Society of Pennsylvania, Philadelphia.

47 Jackson to Milledge, November 4, 1793, Harriet Milledge Salley, ed., *Correspondence of John Milledge, Governor of Georgia, 1802–1806* (Columbia, S.C., 1948), p.31.

48 Carnes to Seaborn Jones, George Walker, Peter Carnes, January 20, 1794, Seaborn Jones Papers, Rare Book, Manuscript, and Special Collections Library, Duke University.

49 For earlier efforts, both by the national government and by private companies, to procure Georgia's western territory, consult Lamplugh, *Politics on the Periphery*, pp.64–77.

50 *Ibid.*, pp.76–77. Judge Pendleton later stated that he had arrived in Augusta on or about November 17, 1794—*Columbian Museum and Savannah Advertiser*, April 12, 1796 (cited hereafter as *CMSA*).

[51] David Ross to John B. Scott, November 14, 1794, *American State Papers: Public Lands*, 8 vols. (Washington, D.C., 1832), 1: 199 (hereafter cited as *ASP: PL*).

[52] Thomas Carr to Samuel Hammond, October 31, 1794, Carr Collection, Hargrett Library, UGa; James Jackson to John Milledge, November 12, 1794, Salley, ed., *Correspondence of Milledge*, p.38.

[53] "Cassius," *Augusta Chronicle and Gazette of the State*, December 13, 1794. The first quotation, according to "Cassius," was from a handbill, written by "A Citizen," being circulated in Augusta in mid-December. "Cassius" was a favorite pseudonym of James Gunn. For example, when a writer signing himself "Cassius" publicly attacked the brigade orders of militia General James Jackson in the autumn of 1787, Jackson identified "Cassius" as Gunn and ordered his arrest and court martial on the charge of belittling the orders of a superior officer.

[54] Gunn to Wilson, November 28, 1794, Old Congress File, Case 1, Box 6, Gratz Collection, Historical Society of Pennsylvania, Philadelphia.

[55] The articles of agreement and the list of shareholders in the Georgia Company are in *ASP: PL* 1: 140–142. One of Gunn's partners in the Georgia Company, Zachariah Cox, followed a similar practice in connection with the Tennessee Company, of which he was co-organizer (*ibid.*, 143). The Georgia Mississippi Company, composed primarily of Augusta speculators, undoubtedly did likewise, but no list of shareholders in that company is extant because, according to a treasurer of that company, "the accounts were opened, not in the names of persons, but by numbers of certificates" (*ibid.*, 146). The fourth company involved in the purchase, the Upper Mississippi Company (formed by Thomas Scott after he had withdrawn the bid of the Virginia Yazoo Company), apparently restricted its largess to a few upcountry Georgians.

[56] *ASP: PL*, 1: 141–142; "Another Citizen," broadside, Savannah, *ca.* October 1795, mistakenly bound following page 2 of *Georgia Gazette*, July 23, 1793, in the microfilm edition of that paper. Although the name of Thomas Gibbons appears nowhere in the surviving documents dealing with the Yazoo sale, Thomas Young, an affluent Savannah merchant with whom "Another Citizen" claimed Gibbons joined to purchase ten million acres of the western territory, did buy at least four "money shares" in Gunn's Georgia Company. It seems likely that Gibbons, who was serving another term as mayor of Savannah at the time of the Yazoo sale, elected to contribute his money, but not his name, to the venture. (*ASP: PL*, 1: 141)

[57] Affidavits of Henry Mitchell, Peter Van Allen, Clement Lanier, and James Lucas, *ibid.*, 145–148.

[58] *Ibid.*, 141–143; *CMSA*, April 12, 1796. On the failure of the Yazoo sale of 1789, seen Lamplugh, *Politics on the Periphery*, pp.66–72.

59 *ASP: PL*, 1: 141, 143, 150, 201.

60 A comparison of the members of the convention with the lists of known shareholders in the purchasing companies reveals that eighteen delegates were interested in the purchase. Two others, Thomas Gibbons and Thomas King, were probably shareholders, and if the Georgia Mississippi Company's list were extant, the number would undoubtedly be found to be greater.

61 *ASP: PL*, 1: 145.

62 *Ibid.*, 146; Hawes, ed., "Papers of Jackson," pp.30–31. Raines' affidavit is in *ASP: PL*, 1: 149. It should be noted, however, that the Georgia House of Representatives adjourned on February 19, 1796, without acting against any of those charged with complicity in the Yazoo business. See *GG*, March 3, 1796.

63 *ASP: PL*, 1: 147–148.

64 James Jackson to General John Twiggs, March 5, 1795, Jackson Papers, Rare Book, Manuscript, and Special Collections Library, Duke; *Annals of Congress, 3rd Cong., 2nd Sess.*, 841; *Southern Centinel*, March 26, 1795. The foreman of the Richmond grand jury was General John Twiggs, James Jackson's correspondent in the letter of March 5.

65 Hamilton to King, June 20, 1795, Syrett, ed., *Papers of Hamilton,* 18: 383; *Annals of Congress, 3rd Cong., 3rd Sess.*, 862.

66 "Extract of a letter from a gentleman in Savannah, Charleston, July 29," *Federal Intelligencer & Baltimore Gazette,* August 14, 1795.

67 Gunn to King, August 10, 1795 (first quotation), August 22, 1795 (second quotation), both in Rufus King Papers, New York Historical Society, New York City; James Greenleaf to Chairman of House Committee on Georgia Land Claims, March 12, 1812, *ASP: PL*, 2: 882.

68 Everett Somerville Brown, ed., *William Plumer's Memorandum of Proceedings in the United States Senate, 1803–1807* (New York, 1923), p.627.

69 For Jackson's anti-Yazoo campaign in the summer and fall of 1795, see Lamplugh, *Politics on the Periphery,* pp.128–132. The work of Jackson's committee and the progress of the Rescinding Act through the lower house may be followed in House Journal, January 14–15, 18, 22, 25–29; February 1, 4, 9, 13, 1796, Ga Arch. The committee report and affidavits upon which it was based have published in *ASP: PL*, 1: 144–149, the Rescinding Act, *ibid.*, 156–158.

70 *GG*, March 3, 1796.

71 James Gunn to editor, *Gazette of the United States,* March 25, 1796, reprinted in *Federal Gazette & Baltimore Daily Advertiser,* April 6, 1796.

72 Baldwin's speech is in *Annals of Congress, 4th Cong., 1st Sess.*, 402–403; documents on Gunn's challenge and its sequel are *ibid.*, 786–798; James Jackson to John Milledge, April 11, 1796, Salley, ed., *Correspondence of Milledge,* pp.42–44.

Gunn's effort against Baldwin was very similar to his unsuccessful attempt earlier in his career to force General Nathanael Greene to a duel.

73 Thomas Gamble, *Savannah Duels and Duellists, 1733–1877* (Savannah, Ga., 1923), p.45; William Omer Foster, Sr., *James Jackson, Duelist and Militant Statesman, 1757–1806* (Athens, Ga., 1960), p.127; Jackson to Milledge, April 11, 1796, Salley, ed., *Correspondence of Milledge*, p.43 (quotation).

74 Robert Goodloe Harper to Seaborn Jones, January 4, 1797, Seaborn Jones Papers, Rare Book, Manuscript, and Special Collections Library, Duke (first quotation); Lachlan McIntosh to Elisha B. Hopkins, February 6, 1797, Lilla M. Hawes, ed., "The Papers of Lachlan McIntosh," *Collections of the Georgia Historical Society* (Savannah, Ga., 1957), pp.161–162 (second quotation).

75 Obituary of Mrs. Mary Jane Gunn, *CMSA*, May 16, 1797; James Jackson to John Milledge, June 11, 1797, Charlton, *Life of Jackson*, p.171.

76 James Seagrove to James Gunn, August 12, 1797, Letters of Application and Recommendation During the Administration of John Adams, 1797–1801, microfilm, reel 2, National Archives; William Mowbray to Gunn, August 12, 1797, and Gunn to Oliver Wolcott, January 5, 1798, *ibid.* On Mowbray's share of the Yazoo lands, see *ASP: PL*, 1: 141.

77 James Jackson to John Milledge, February 23, 1798," Salley, ed., *Correspondence of Milledge*, p.53; Albert B. Saye, ed., "The Journal of the Georgia Constitutional Convention of 1798," *GHQ* 36 (December, 1952): 350–393.

78 Copy of protest from the *Southern Centinel*, June 7, 1798, Georgia Miscellaneous Papers State, Rare Book, Manuscript, and Special Collections Library, Duke; letter from James M. Simmons, convention secretary, *Augusta Chronicle and Gazette of the State*, August 4, 1798.

79 *Southern Centinel*, June 28, 1798. On the ensuing loyalty oath controversy, see Lamplugh, *Politics on the Periphery*, pp.147–148.

80 Gunn to Adams, October 1, 1798, Adams Papers, 53:251, microfilm, reel 391, Massachusetts Historical Society, Boston; *CMSA*, October 9, 1798. The "XYZ Affair" refers to efforts by three officials of the French Directory to bribe three American diplomats sent to Paris by Adams to discuss strained relations between the two nations. On the split within the Federalists over the XYZ Affair and the outbreak of the so-called "Quasi-War" with France, see Stanley Elkins and Eric McKitrick, *The Age of Federalism: The Early American Republic, 1788–1800* (New York, 1993), pp.615–690.

81 Hamilton to Gunn, December 16, Syrett, ed., *Papers of Hamilton*, 22: 367; Gunn to Hamilton, December 19, *ibid.*, 374–375; Hamilton to Gunn, December 22, 1798, *ibid.*, 390.

[82] Sedgwick to King, January 20, 1799, Charles R. King, ed., *The Life and Correspondence of Rufus King*, 6 vols. (New York, 1894–1900), 2: 516.

[83] The "Anas" of Thomas Jefferson, January 19, 1799, Lipscomb and Bergh, eds., *Writings of Jefferson*, 1: 432.

[84] Alexander Hamilton to James Gunn, December 22, 1798, Syrett, ed., *Papers of Hamilton*, 22: 388–390; Hamilton to James McHenry, January 14, 1799, Bernard C. Steiner, *The Life and Correspondence of James McHenry* (Cleveland, Ohio, 1907), p.366; Gunn to Hamilton, January 23, 1799, John C. Hamilton, ed., *The Works of Alexander Hamilton*, 7 vols. (New York, 1850–1851), 5: 195. See also, *Annals of Congress, 5th Cong., 3rd Sess.*, 2204, 2206, 2209, 2213, 2217, 2221, 2222–2224, 2239; Elkins and McKitrick, *Age of Federalism*, p.616.

[85] Pinckney to Harper, June 13, 1799, Robert Goodloe Harper Papers, Library of Congress (microfilm, University of Chicago).

[86] Gunn to Jones, December 19, 1799, Seaborn Jones Papers, Rare Book, Manuscript, and Special Collections Library, Duke.

[87] Anonymous, *Louisville Gazette and Republican Trumpet*, August 5, and "D," *ibid.*, August 19 (hereafter cited as *LGRT*); "Otho" [William Stith], August 23, and letter from Judge David B. Mitchell, September 20, *Augusta Chronicle and Gazette of the State*; James Jackson to John Milledge, n.d., but *ca.* November 20; Jackson to Abraham Baldwin, November 26, Abraham Baldwin Papers, Yale; Jackson to Baldwin, December 10, 1800, Abraham Baldwin Papers, Hargrett Library, UGa.

[88] Gunn to Rutledge, May 12, 1800, Rutledge Papers, Southern Historical Collection, Louis Round Wilson Library, University of North Carolina, Chapel Hill (first quotation); Gunn to Rutledge, May 15, 1800, Broussard, *Southern Federalists*, p.27 (second quotation).

[89] Gunn to Hamilton, December 13, 1800, Syrett, ed., *Papers of Hamilton*, 25: 254.

[90] Gunn to Hamilton, December 18, *ibid.*, 25: 263; Hamilton to Theodore Sedgwick, December 22, 1800, quoted in Elkins and McKitrick, *Age of Federalism*, p.687.

[91] Gunn to President Adams, February 21, 1801, Adams Papers, 21: 257 (microfilm, reel 400); Sidney Aronson, *Status and Kinship in the Higher Civil Service: Standards of Selection in the Administrations of John Adams, Thomas Jefferson, and Andrew Jackson* (Cambridge, Mass., 1964), Appendix C. For Jackson's outraged reaction to Gibbons' appointment, see his letters to James Madison, May 15, June 4, 1801, Madison Papers, Library of Congress (microfilm, reel 6).

[92] Letter from Louisville, dated July 31, 1801, *GG*, August 6, 1801.

[93] *LGRT*, August 8 (first quotation); *CMSA*, August 14, 1801 (second quotation).

[94] "A & Z," *CMSA*, September 11, 1801.

95 For references to Gunn's stature, see James Jackson to John Milledge, November 7, 1792, Charlton, *Life of Jackson*, p.139; and letter from John Clark, *Southern Centinel*, January 15, 1795.

96 Edgar Erskine Hume, *General Washington's Correspondence Concerning the Society of the Cincinnati* (Baltimore, 1941), 370n; *GG*, July 12, 1792.

97 On the evolution of the ideology of Southern Federalists, see Rose, *Prologue to Democracy*, and Broussard, *The Southern Federalists.*

Notes—11

1 On these early, unsuccessful efforts to dispose of Georgia's public domain, see George R. Lamplugh, *Politics on the Periphery: Factions and Parties in Georgia, 1783–1806* (Newark, Del., 1986), pp. 31–37, 66–77.

2 On the passage of the Yazoo Act, see Thomas P. Abernethy, *The South in the New Nation, 1789–1819* (Baton Rouge, 1961), 136–147; Lisle A. Rose, *Prologue to Democracy: The Federalists in the South, 1789–1800* (Lexington, Ky., 1968), 85–92; and Lamplugh, *Politics on the Periphery*, 104–119.

3 Lilla M. Hawes, ed., "The Papers of James Jackson, 1781–1798," *Collections* of the Georgia Historical Society, 11 (1955): 101; House Journal, January 14–15, 18, 22, 25–29, February 12, 20, 1796, Georgia Archives, Morrow, Georgia (cited hereafter as Ga. Arch.); *American State Papers: Public Lands* (Washington, D.C., 1834), I: 124–129 [hereafter, *ASP:PL*]; "Pliny," [Savannah] *Georgia Gazette* (hereafter cited as *GG*), April 18, 1796; "Benedict," [Augusta] *Southern Centinel* [cited hereafter as *SC*], March 17, 1796.

4 For Jackson's successful effort to build the Jeffersonian Republican Party in Georgia between 1796 and 1806, see Lamplugh, *Politics on the Periphery*, chs. 7–8.

5 On Jackson's efforts to frustrate the state's Yazooists, see Lamplugh, *Politics on the Periphery*, pp.140–144, 185–186.

6 On the Georgia Mississippi Company, see *ASP: PL*, 1: 146; on distributions of Yazoo lands in the upcountry, see Lamplugh, *Politics on the Periphery*, pp.108–109. Walton's "Brutus" letters were published in *SC*, March 15, 27; April 5, 19; May 10, 17, 31; June 14; July 12; August 9, 1798. James Jackson identified Walton as "Brutus" in a letter to John Milledge, Harriet Milledge Salley, ed., *Correspondence of John Milledge* (Columbia, S.C., 1949), p.60 [hereafter cited as Salley, ed., *Milledge Correspondence*].

7 Jackson to Milledge, March 13, 1798, Salley, ed., *Milledge Correspondence*, pp.60–61; same to same, n.d. but *ca*. November 20, 1800, *ibid*., pp.110–111; Jackson to

Abraham Baldwin, November 26, 1800, Abraham Baldwin Papers, Yale; same to same, December 10, 1800, Abraham Baldwin Papers, UGa.

8 House Journal, November 28, December 1, 1800, Ga. Arch. Governor Jackson defended his conduct toward the Watkinses in his November 1800 address to the General Assembly, *Columbian Museum and Savannah Advertiser* (cited hereafter as *CMSA*), November 21, 1800; the Watkins brothers had their say in an "Address to the Public," pp. iii–iv of their *Digest of the Laws of the State of Georgia* (Philadelphia, 1800). The expurgated compilation by Marbury and Crawford was printed in Savannah in 1802.

9 "Expono," *SC*, January 15, 1795; House Journal, December 12, 1789, Ga. Arch.

10 *SC*, January 29, 1795; "Mentor," *Augusta Chronicle and Gazette of the State* (cited hereafter as *ACGS*), October 24, 31, November 7, 14, 28.

11 House Journal, January 14, 15, 18, 22, 25–29, 1796; February 1, 4, 9, 13, 1796, Ga. Arch.; Robert Goodloe Harper to Seaborn Jones, January 4, 1797, Seaborn Jones Papers, Duke University; House Journal, February 8, 10, 1797, Ga. Arch.

12 On Watkins, Gunn, and Glascock in the 1798 constitutional convention and the resulting "loyalty oath" controversy, see Lamplugh, *Politics on the Periphery*, pp.146–148.

13 A pro-Watkins version of this encounter is furnished in an "Extract of a letter from Augusta, (Georgia) [February 26, 1796]," *Federal Gazette & Baltimore Daily Advertiser*, March 19, 1796; Jackson offered his side in a letter to John Milledge, March 8, 1796, Salley, ed., *Milledge Correspondence*, pp.38–41.

14 A detailed, pro-Watkins version of the second Jackson-Watkins fracas and its sequel can be found in "Extract of a letter from Augusta, dated May 13," *Gazette of the United States*, June 6, 1796. Jackson described the encounter more concisely to John Milledge, May 14, 1796, Salley, ed., *Milledge Correspondence*, p.45.

15 Since mid-1794 Carnes had been preparing the House for some kind of independent effort by Georgia to resolve her Indian problems. He constantly attacked the federal government's policy toward the Southern tribes, especially the Creeks, and on a number of occasions came close to disavowing the Treaty of New York; *Annals of Congress*, 3rd Cong., 2nd Sess., 777–778, 992, 1156; *ibid.*, 851–852; James Jackson to John Twiggs, March 5, 1795, James Jackson Papers, Duke University.

16 *GG*, March 3, 1796.

17 Baldwin's speech on speculators is in *Annals of Congress*, 4th Cong., 1st Sess., 402–403; documents on Gunn's challenge and its sequel are *ibid.*, 786–798, *passim*; Jackson to John Milledge, April 11, 1796, Salley, ed., *Milledge Correspondence*, pp.42–44.

18 Jackson to Milledge, September 1, 1801, Salley, ed., *Milledge Correspondence*, p.75.

[19] Jackson to John Twiggs, March 5, 1795, James Jackson Papers, Duke University.

[20] On Jackson's refusal to pay M'Millan, see his message to the legislature, February 13, 1799, Governor's Letterbook, January 11–October 30, 1799, Ga. Arch. On December 5, 1801, the House finally appropriated, by the slim margin of 23–21, $1,090 to compensate M'Millan for printing the 1799 legislative journals—House Journal, Ga. Arch.

[21] "B," *Augusta Herald* (*AH*), June 11, 1800; editorial, *Louisville Gazette & Republican Trumpet* (*LGRT*), June 17, 1800; "An Up Countryman," *LGRT*, July 1, October 7, December 10, 1800; "B," *AH*, July 9, August 27, October 22, 1800.

[22] *CMSA*, February 12; *Washington Federalist*, February 27; *CMSA*, September 14, 1802; James Jackson to John Milledge, March 16, 1803, Salley, ed., *Milledge Correspondence*, pp.99–100.

[23] "A Back-Country Citizen," *ACGS*, November 3, 1798.

[24] For a more detailed treatment of the emergence of William Harris Crawford and John Clark, see Lamplugh, *Politics on the Periphery*, chapter 9.

[25] House Journal, November 26, 1801, Ga. Arch.; *LGRT*, June 9, 1802.

[26] Documents concerning this series of disputes were published in *ACGS*, May 29, June 12, July 3, 31, August 7, September 18, 1802. See also Garnett Andrews, *Reminiscences of an Old Georgia Lawyer* (Atlanta, 1870), p.61; E. Merton Coulter, "A Famous Duel That Was Never Fought," *Georgia Historical Quarterly* 43 (1959): 365–377.

[27] John Clark inaugurated the exchange in the Washington (Ga.) *Monitor* early in November 1804, and he and Crawford sniped at one another in the columns of *LGRT* during the meeting of the General Assembly. Most of this correspondence, as well as the decision of the court of honor, is reprinted in J.E.D. Shipp, *Giant Days or the Life of William H. Crawford* (Americus, Ga., 1909), pp.50–65.

[28] Shipp, *Giant Days*, chapter 7, discusses the events of 1806–1807; on Clark's public humiliation of Tait, see Andrews, *Reminiscences*, p.61.

[29] On this phase of the Yazoo controversy, see Thomas Perkins Abernethy, *The South in the New Nation, 1789–1819* (Baton Rouge, La., 1961), pp.162–168.

[30] On Troup, Adams, and the Creeks, see Charles S. Sydnor, *The Development of Southern Sectionalism, 1819–1848* (Baton Rouge, La., 1948), pp.151–152, 182–184; Ulrich B. Phillips, *Georgia and State Rights* (1902; reprint, Macon, Ga., 1984), pp.55–67; Michael D. Green, *The Politics of Indian Removal* (Lincoln, Neb., and London, 1982), chs. 4–6.

[31] Literature on Georgia, the Cherokees, and the "Trail of Tears" is vast. For a sampling, see Phillips, *Georgia and State Rights*, ch.3; Theda Perdue and Michael D. Green, *The Cherokee Nation and the Trail of Tears* (New York, 2007); Thurman Wilkins, *Cherokee Tragedy: The Ridge Family and the Decimation of a People* (2nd

ed., revised; Norman, Okla., 1986); and Brian Hicks, *Toward the Setting Sun: John Ross, the Cherokees, and the Trail of Tears* (New York, 2011).

32 "Enquirer," [Milledgeville] *Southern Recorder*, August 21, 1821; "History of the Yazoo Fraud," *ibid.*, November 6, 1821.

33 Editorial, [Milledgeville]*Federal Union*, August 8, 1835; "Constitution, No. III," [Milledgeville] *Georgia Journal*, August 25, 1835.

Notes—12

1 For the concept of "versatile Georgians," see George R. Lamplugh, *Politics on the Periphery: Factions and Parties in Georgia, 1783–1806* (Newark, Del., 1986), pp.22–26.

2 On Jackson and Gunn, see chapters 9 and 10, above.

3 Basic information on Mitchell's early career may conveniently be found in Kenneth Coleman and Steve Gurr, eds., *Dictionary of Georgia Biography* (2 vols; Athens, Ga., 1983), II: 722–723; the online *New Georgia Encyclopedia* (http://www.georgiaencyclopedia.org/nge/Article.jsp?path=/HistoryArchaeology/AntebellumEra/People1&id=h-2825); and chapter 1 in Thomas Henry Rentz, Sr., "The Public Life of David B. Mitchell" (M.A. thesis, UGa, 1955).

4 On the significance of the Yazoo fraud for the creation of a Jeffersonian Republican party in Georgia, see Lamplugh, *Politics on the Periphery,* chapters 6–7. For Mitchell's affidavit before a legislative committee investigating the land fraud, see Walter Lowrie and Matthew St. Clair Clarke, eds., *American State Papers: Public Lands* (Washington, 1832), I, 148 (hereafter *ASP: PL)*; on his election as the state's attorney-general, see Ms. House Journal, Feb. 20, 1796, p.145, Georgia Archives (hereafter Ga. Arch.).

5 "Extract of a Letter from a gentleman in Savannah, to a friend in [Washington]," *Washington Federalist*, April 30, 1802.

6 Jefferson to Jackson, May 1, 1802, Jefferson Papers, LC (for Jackson's explanation of the charge against Mitchell, see Jackson to Jefferson, May 1, 1802, *ibid*) ; *Columbian Museum and Savannah Advertiser* (hereafter *CMSA*), August 31, 1802.

7 On John Clark, see Kenneth Coleman and Steve Gurr, eds., *Dictionary of Georgia Biography* (2 vols; Athens, Ga., 1983), I, 192–193; *New Georgia Encyclopedia*, online, at http://www.georgiaencyclopedia.org/nge/Article.jsp?path=/HistoryArchaeology/AntebellumEra/People1&id=h-2485; and Lamplugh, *Politics on the Periphery,* pp.190–196. On the rivalry between John Clark and William Harris Crawford, see Lamplugh, *Politics on the Periphery*, pp. 193–196.

[8] For evidence that Mitchell was the acknowledged leader of the state's Republican interest, see Thomas Fitch to Daniel Mulford, 5 April 1810, Daniel Mulford Papers, Georgia Historical Society (GHS); and Joel Crawford to William Jones, October 17, 1811, William Jones Papers, GHS.

[9] According to one Georgia Republican, Mitchell was first elected governor because the incumbent, Jared Irwin, had remitted John Clark's $2000 fine for horsewhipping Judge Charles Tait—Bolling Hall to Mitchell, May 26, 1809, in Chester M. Destler, ed., "Correspondence of David Brydie Mitchell," *GHQ*, 21 (1937), 383–384.

[10] D. B. Mitchell, *An Exposition of the Case of the Africans, Taken to the Creek Agency, by Captain William Bowen, on or about the 1st Dec'r 1817* (Milledgeville, 1821), p.162 (hereafter Mitchell, *Exposition*).

[11] Kenneth S. Greenberg, *Honor & Slavery* (Princeton, N.J., 1996), p.55; George R. Gilmer, *Sketches of Some of the First Settlers of Upper Georgia* (reprint; Baltimore, 1965), p.159.

[12] A.S. Clayton to Milledge, October 20, 1813, in Harriet Milledge Salley, ed., *Correspondence of John Milledge, Governor of Georgia, 1802–1806* (Columbia, S.C., 1949), pp. 161–162 (hereafter Salley, *Milledge Correspondence*). See also Thomas W. Cobb to Charles Harris, October 21, 1813, Keith Read Collection, University of Georgia; William B. Bulloch to Mitchell, December 6, 1813, Bulloch Papers, Southern Historical Collection, University of North Carolina—Chapel Hill (cited hereafter as Bulloch Papers).

[13] Crawford to James Monroe, August 6, 1812, Monroe Papers, LC [Mic., reel 5]. On Mitchell's ill-starred efforts in East Florida, see James G. Cusick, *The Other War of 1812: The Patriot War and the American Invasion of Spanish East Florida* (Gainesville, Fla., 2003), chapters 10, 12.

[14] On the defeat of Early's reelection bid and the victory of Mitchell, see editorial, *Augusta Herald*, November 15, 1816; Coleman and Gurr, eds., *Dictionary of Georgia Biography*, I: 282–283; and the *New Georgia Encyclopedia*, *http://www.georgiaencyclopedia.org/articles/government-politics/peter-early-1773-1817*. A modern treatment of the Embargo and its consequences is in Gordon S. Wood, *Empire of Liberty: A History of the Early Republic, 1789–1815* (Oxford and New York, 2009), pp. 646–658.

[15] Crawford to Madison, June 19, August 8, 1816, Madison Papers, LC.

[16] Crawford to Madison, August 30, 1816, *ibid.*

[17] Crawford to Mitchell, October 2, 1816, Mitchell Papers, Ayer Collection, Newberry Library, Chicago (hereafter Mitchell Papers).

[18] Crawford to Mitchell, October 28, 1816, *ibid.*

[19] Crawford to Mitchell, November 22, 1816, Mitchell Papers.

20 Clark, *Considerations* ..., p.131. This was one charge that Mitchell apparently never refuted in his published responses to Clark's pamphlet.

21 William B. Bulloch to Mitchell, October 29, [1816], Bulloch Papers; James C. Bonner, "Tustunugee Hutkee and Creek Factionalism on the Georgia-Alabama Frontier," *Alabama Review*, 10 (1957), 117; Michael D. Green, *The Politics of Indian Removal: Creek Government and Society in Crisis* (Lincoln, Neb., 1982), p.54.

22 William Baldwin to William Darlington, Apr. 19, 1817, quoted in Michael D. Green, *The Politics of Indian Removal: Creek Government and Society in Crisis* [Lincoln, Neb., 1982], p. 52; *GaJ*, June 10, 1817.

23 Benjamin W. Griffith, Jr., *McIntosh and Weatherford, Creek Indian Leaders* (Tuscaloosa and London, 1988), p.201; Daniel Hughes to Thomas L. McKenney, March 23, 1818, in Clarence Edwin Carter, ed., *The Territorial Papers of the United States. Volume XVIII: The Territory of Alabama, 1817–1819* (Washington, D.C., 1952), 275; Mitchell to Calhoun, June 17, 1818, *ibid.*, 351–353; McKenney to Mitchell, October 9, 1818, *ibid.*, 432–433; McKenney to Hughes, October 7, 1818, *ibid.*, 433.

24 Mitchell to Secretary of War, Mar. 30, 1817, *ASP: IA, II:* 156; Mitchell to Acting Secretary of War George Graham, Dec. 14, 1817, *ibid.*, 161. For a modern treatment that essentially agrees with this interpretation, see David S. Heidler and Jeanne T. Heidler, *Old Hickory's War* (Mechanicsburg, Pa., 1996), especially pp.124–125. On Mitchell's charge that Gaines was responsible for the outbreak of the Seminole War, see Mitchell to Governor of Alabama Territory William Wyatt Bibb, Dec. 15, 1817, Carter, ed., *TPUS, XVIII*: 215–216; Mitchell to Secretary of War, Feb. 3, 1818, *ibid.*, 247; and Mitchell's testimony before U.S. Senate committee on the Seminole War, in *AC, 15th Congress, 2nd Session*, 2291–2296, and *ASP: MA, I*: 748–749.

25 This and the following four paragraphs are based on Dr. Antonio J. Waring, "The Case of the Africans," no pagination, Waring Papers, GHS; *ASP: Misc.*, II: 961; affidavit of Joseph Thorn, David B. Mitchell, *An Exposition*, pp. 14–15.

26 Wirt's discussion of the division of the Africans is in *ASP: Misc.*, II, 964–965; McIntosh's report, *ibid.*, 965.

27 Gaines to editor, January 23, 1818, *Georgia Journal*, January 27, 1818.

28 Mitchell's letter to Rabun was published in the *Georgia Journal*, February 17, and in the *Reflector* on February 24, 1818.

29 Charlotte Adams Ford, "The Public Career of Tomlinson Fort, M.D.," (M.A. thesis, Georgia Southern College, 1964), p.102. Later, in May 1820, Fort was a member of the grand jury for the state's sixth judicial circuit that investigated the "slave trade charges," condemned the smuggling of Africans as a "flagrant

violation" of American laws, and recommended that "the slave trade operations be brought to the attention of Congress and department heads." *Ibid.*, p.103, citing [Milledgeville] *Southern Recorder*, May 16, 1820.

30 *Ibid.*

31 Heidler and Heidler, *Old Hickory's War,* pp.124, 125, 132, 155. On Arbuthnot's view of Mitchell, see Arbuthnot to Mitchell, January 19, 1818, James Parton, *Life of Andrew Jackson* (3 vols., New York, 1860), II: 439.

32 Letter reprinted from the *Savannah Republican* in *Reflector*, April 7, 1818.

33 *Reflector*, April 28, 1818. The "Philanthropist" letters were published in *Georgia Journal*, August 18, 25; September 1, 8, 15; October 13, 27; November 10, 1818 (quote from issue of August 25).

34 On Castro, see *Georgia Journal*, August 4, 1818; on Crawford's presence and the sale of the Africans, see *Reflector*, August 11, 1818. In its August 18 editorial, the *Georgia Journal* informed its readers that the Africans were sold for a total of $41,710; the highest price paid was $892, while the lowest (except one) was $380; the average price paid for one of the blacks was $662.

35 Editorial, *Georgia Journal,* September 8, 1818.

36 *Reflector,* September 15, 1818.

37 "One of Thousands," *Reflector*, September 15, 1818; affidavits, *Georgia Journal*, September 29, 1818.

38 This paragraph is based on Heidler and Heidler, *Old Hickory's War,* pp.191–193. Though conceding Mitchell's "questionable business deals" while Creek agent, the Heidlers assert that what brought him down were his long affiliation with Crawford and his temporary opposition to Jackson's Florida scheme, concluding that "Mitchell fell not because he was a thief and a corruptionist. He had committed a far greater crime than that. He had gotten in Andrew Jackson's way." (193) Their interpretation is too neat, for they underestimate the tenacious campaign waged against both Mitchell and Crawford by John Clark. It was this effort, not the campaign by Jackson and Gaines, which ultimately led to Mitchell's dismissal in 1821.

39 Robert V. Remini, *Andrew Jackson* (3 vols.; New York, 1998), I: 370–374; James Parton, *Life of Andrew Jackson* (3 vols.; Boston, 1866), II: 551.

40 Mitchell to Crawford, December 30, 1818, Mitchell Papers, Ayer Collection, Newberry Library, Chicago; quote from Mitchell to Secretary of War Calhoun, January 22, 1819, Carter, ed., *TPUS*, 18: 543.

41 For Mitchell's testimony, see Walter Lowrie and Matthem St. Clair Clarke, eds., *American State Papers: Military Affairs* (7 vols.; Washington, 1832–1861), I: 748–749; for Gen. Gaines's complaints to Secretary of War Calhoun, see *ibid.*, II:125–132.

[42] Rabun's message to the legislature, November 11, 1818, in *Journal of the Georgia Senate* (Milledgeville, Ga., 1819), pp.8, 18; *Niles'*, 15 (Jan. 2, 1819): 357–359. Rabun's reference to "several hundred [more slaves illegally] held by individuals in different parts of the state" seemed calculated to lessen the impact of the smuggling charge against Mitchell. It might have been, in other words, part of what we would call a "cover up," a point made by John Quincy Adams in his diary.

[43] For Governor Rabun's posthumous message to the legislature (November 1819), see *Niles'*, 17 (Dec. 4, 1819): 222.

[44] The arrival of The Rev. Mr. Meade was reported in *Georgia Journal*, May 11, 1819, as was news of the formation of the "Auxiliary Society"; for the letter from "Aristides," see *ibid.*

[45] "Amadis," *Reflector*, August 25, 1818.

[46] "Limner," *Georgia Journal*, June 1819.

[47] *Ibid.*, August 31; September 7,14, 1819.

[48] Jackson to Clark, April 20, 1819, Bassett, ed., *Correspondence of Jackson,* 2: 416; Clark to Jackson, May 24, 1819, *ibid.,* 2: 416–418; Remini, *Jackson, Vol. I: The Course of American Empire,* p.378.

[49] Clark's pamphlet was *Considerations on the Purity of the Principles of William H. Crawford, Esq.* (Augusta, 1819). Despite the 1819 date, the pamphlet was much delayed, with part of it appearing in late May 1820 and a complete edition only in October 1820. See Crawford to Charles Tait, October 2, 1820, Tait Family Papers, Alabama Department of Archives and History, Montgomery (ADAH); Crawford to Bolling Hall, October 2, 1820, Hall Family Papers, *ibid*; and John Quincy Adams's diary entry for October 5, 1820, C.F. Adams, ed., *Memoirs of John Quincy Adams,* V: 185.

[50] John Quincy Adams's diary, Oct. 5, 14, 1820, in C.F. Adams, ed., *Memoirs of JQA* V: 185–186; Crawford to Mitchell, Apr. 3, 1818, excerpt in Mitchell, *An Exposition*, p. 62; Collector of Darien to Crawford, May 12, collector of Savannah to Crawford, May 23, 1818, both in *GaJ*, Feb. 8, 1820.

[51] See entries for February 2 and February 24, 1820, both in Adams Family Papers, Massachusetts Historical Society [microfilm, reel 34]; June 18, 1820, C.F. Adams, ed., *Memoirs of John Quincy Adams,* IV: 154–155; and October 18, 1820, *ibid.,* V: 185–186. On Mitchell's removal from office, see Calhoun to Mitchell, Feb. 16, 1821, published at the behest of Governor John Clark, in both the *Georgia Journal* and the *Southern Recorder* on Mar. 27, 1821.

[52] D. B. Mitchell, *An Exposition of the Case of the Africans ...* (Milledgeville,1821).

[53] Jackson to Calhoun, January 12, 1822, W. Edwin Hemphill, ed., *The Papers of John C. Calhoun, Volume 6* (Columbia, S.C., 1972): 618–619.

[54] Remini, *Jackson, Volume 2: The Course of American Freedom, 1822–1832,* 14.

[55] Griffith, *McIntosh and Weatherford*, p.219, citing Judge Cuyler to Crowell, July 14, 1825, in HR 98 19/2, 388.

[56] Crawford to Mitchell, March 14, 1822, Mitchell Papers, Ayer Collection, Newberry Library, Chicago; Crawford to William Rutherford, July17, 1821, Keith Read Collection, UGa.

[57] Joel Crawford to Bolling Hall, September 28, 1821, Hall Family Papers, ADAH.

[58] Crawford to Charles Tait, November 27, 1819, Tait Family Papers, ADAH; Crawford to Mitchell, November 27, 1819, Keith Read Collection, UGa.; Crawford to Tait, November 23, 1823, Tait Family Papers, ADAH.

[59] *Georgia Laws, 1820*, Dec. 19, 1820, p.117, available at http://metis.galib.uga.edu/ssp/cgi-bin/legis-idx.pl?sessionid=63be8857-e6b2274961-3110&type=law&byte=5024583&lawcnt=22&filt=doc; Gov. Clark's annual message, Nov. 6, 1821, *Journal of the Georgia House of Representatives, 1821* (Milledgeville, 1822), p. 9.

[60] *Journal of the Georgia House of Representatives, 1821*, Dec. 20, 1821, pp. 273–275.

[61] Clark's annual message, Nov. 6, 1822, *Journal of the Georgia House of Representatives, 1822* (Milledgeville, 1823), p. 15; *GaJ*, Nov. 19, 1822; extract of a letter from Milledgeville, *Sava Repub*, Nov. 11, 1822.

[62] *GaJ*, Oct. 14, 21, 28, 1823.

[63] *GaJ*, Feb. 24, 1824.

[64] Governor Troup to legislature, Nov. 3, 1824, *Journal of the Georgia House of Representatives, 1824* (Milledgeville, 1824), pp. 30–32.

[65] *Journal of the Georgia Senate, 1825* (Milledgeville, 1825), Dec.15, 1825, p. 180; *ibid.*, Dec. 16, 1825, pp.190–191.

[66] The debate may be followed in *Journal of the Georgia Senate, 1826* (Milledgeville, 1826), Nov. 15, 21, 22, Dec. 4, 1826; pp. 52–53, 77, 80–81, 144, 155. The resolution, passed on Dec. 4, 1826, may be found at http://metis.galib.uga.edu/ssp/cgi-bin/legis-idx.pl?sessionid=fa13db79-1b531e6348-9978&type=law&byte=8170626&lawcnt=5&filt=doc)

[67] "Holograph Notes of James Monroe on Fiscal and Foreign Affairs, 1817–1824," Monroe Papers, UVa ; C.F. Adams, ed., *Memoirs of John Quincy Adams*, 6: 335–336, 339 [entries for and May17, 18, 1824]; Monroe to Crawford, May 17, 1824, Hamilton, ed., *Writings of Monroe*, 7:21–22. For Crawford's response to allegations that he had "suppressed" several documents, including two letters from Mitchell, see *Niles*, 26 (July10, 1824): 303–305.

Notes—13

1 George R. Lamplugh, *Politics on the Periphery: Factions and Parties in Georgia, 1783–1806* (Newark, Del.), p.186.

2 Mary Herschberger, "Mobilizing Women, Anticipating Abolition: The Struggle against Indian Removal in the 1830s," *Journal of American History* 86 (June 1999): 16.

3 Michael D. Green, *The Politics of Indian Removal: Creek Government and Society in Crisis* (Lincoln, Neb., and London, 1982), pp. 81, 86–90, 92–93.

4 *Ibid.*, pp. 116–119, 122–125; and chapter 6.

5 Editorial, *Georgia Journal*, May 22, 1827. For an interesting, provocative overview of the Indian removal crisis, see Mary Young, "Racism in Red and Black: Indians and Other Free People of Color in Georgia Law, Politics, and Removal Policy," *Georgia Historical Quarterly* 73 (Fall 1989): 492–518.

6 On "civilizing" the Cherokees, see Henry Thompson Malone, *Cherokees of the Old South: A People in Transition* (Athens, Ga., 1956), chs. 6–10; Theda Perdue and Michael D. Green, *The Cherokee Nation and the Trail of Tears* (New York, 2007), ch. 2; John Ehle, *Trail of Tears: The Rise and Fall of the Cherokee Nation* (New York, 1988), chs. 8–11; Daniel Blake Smith, *An American Betrayal: Cherokee Patriots and the Trail of Tears* (New York, 2011), chs. 1–2, 4; Theda Perdue and Michael D. Greene, *The Cherokee Removal: A Brief History with Documents* (2nd ed.; Boston, 2005), pp.7–19.

7 Perdue and Green, *Cherokee Nation*, pp.53–59, 61–63, 66–67.

8 Kenneth Penn Davis, "Chaos in the Indian Country: The Cherokee Nation, 1828–1835," in Duane H. King, ed., *The Cherokee Indian Nation: A Troubled History* (Knoxville, 1979), p.129.

9 Herschberger, "Mobilizing Women," p. 21.

10 Thurman Wilkins, *Cherokee Tragedy: The Ridge Family and the Decimation of a People* (2nd ed., rev.; Norman, Okla., 1986), pp. 208–210.

11 *Ibid.*, pp. 150–153.

12 Elias Boudinot, "An Address to the Whites," in Theda Perdue, ed., *Cherokee Editor: The Writings of Elias Boudinot* (Athens, Ga., 1996), pp. 68–83 (quotes on p.76 and pp.78–79).

13 *Cherokee Phoenix* (cited hereafter as *CP*), Feb. 21, 1828.

14 Boudinot, "Address to the Whites," in Perdue, *Cherokee Editor*, p.72; *CP*, May 14, June 18, 1828.

15 *CP*, Jan. 28, May 27, 1829 (quote).

16 *Ibid.*, July 1, 1829; Perdue, *Cherokee Editor*, p. 149, note 46.

17 Perdue and Green, *The Cherokee Removal*, p.103.

[18] On the Cherokee legal strategy and Jackson's reaction to it, see Perdue and Green, *Cherokee Nation*, pp.77–89; key court cases have been conveniently reprinted in Jill Norgren, ed., *The Cherokee Cases: The Confrontation of Law and Politics* (New York, 1996), pp. 155–186.

[19] *CP*, June 26, 1830.

[20] Perdue and Green, *Cherokee Nation and the Trail of Tears*, pp.83–86, and the following items in *CP*: John Ridge to Elias Boudinot, June 1, 1831, published June 4; same to same, June 14, 1831, published July 9, 1831. Boudinot reported on excesses by the Georgia Guard and their commander, Colonel Nelson *ibid.*, Mar. 5, 26; May 7; July 2, 9, 16; Aug. 27; Sept. 3, 10, 17, 24, 1831.

[21] *CP*, July 17, 1830; Dec. 3, 1831; Feb. 18, Mar. 24, 1832.

[22] John Ridge to Elias Boudinot, May 17, 1831, published *ibid.*, May 21, 1831; Boudinot's commentary on Principal Chief John Ross's message to the Council, *ibid.*, Aug. 11, 1832.

[23] *Ibid.*, July 21, Aug. 17, Sept. 8, 1832.

[24] Editorials, *CP*, Sept. 8,22,29; Oct. 6, 1832.

[25] *CP*, Nov. 23, 1833.

[26] *Ibid.*, Feb. 22, Mar. 8, 1834; Davis, "Chaos in Indian Country," p.128.

[27] For accounts of the final days of the *Cherokee Phoenix*, see Brian Hicks, *Toward the Setting Sun: John Ross, the Cherokees, and the Trail of Tears* (New York, 2011), p.264; A.J. Langguth, *Driven West: Andrew Jacksokn and the Trail of Tears to the Civil War* (New York, 2010), p.224; Perdue, ed., *Cherokee Editor*, p. 227, note 13; Perdue and Green, *The Cherokee Removal*, p. 135; Smith, *An American Betrayal*, p. 166; Wilkins, *Cherokee Tragedy*, p. 281.

[28] On the Treaty of New Echota, see Hicks, *Towards the Setting Sun*, pp. 277–282; Langguth, *Driven West*, pp. 231–235; Perdue, ed., *Cherokee Editor*, pp. 26–30; Perdue and Green, *The Cherokee Removal*, pp. 145–153; Smith, *An American Betrayal*, pp. 173–184; Wilkins, *Cherokee Tragedy*, pp. 285–290.

[29] Boudinot's reply to Ross is reprinted in Perdue, *Cherokee Editor*, pp. 159–225.

[30] On the Ross faction's bloody settling of scores with the leaders of the Treaty Party, see Hicks, *Toward the Setting Sun*, pp. 315–335; Langguth, *Driven West*, pp. 315–321; Perdue, ed., *Cherokee Editor*, pp. 30–33; Smith, *An American Betrayal*, pp. 251–264; Wilkins, *Cherokee Tragedy*, pp. 329–339.

[31] Perdue, ed., *Cherokee Editor*, pp. 15–16, 28, 58, 80 (note 9).

[32] *Ibid., p.* 33.

Notes—Epilogue

1 Cobb to Mrs. Mary Ann Lamar Cobb, Sept. 8, 1850, Howell Cobb Papers, UGa. Other efforts to tell this story include: U.B. Phillips, *Georgia and State Rights* (reprint; Macon, Ga., 1984), Ch. 6; Richard Harrison Shryock, *Georgia and the Union in 1850* (Durham, N.C., 1926); Horace Montgomery, *Cracker Parties* (Baton Rouge, 1950); Robert Preston Brooks, "Howell Cobb and the Crisis of 1850," *MVHR* IV (1917–1918): 279–298; Horace Montgomery, "The Compromise of 1850 and Its Effects on Political Parties in Georgia," *GHQ* 34 (1950): 293–322; Anthony Gene Carey, *Politics, Slavery, and the Union in Antebellum Georgia* (Athens and London, 1997), Ch. 6.

2 See, for example, editorials in the Columbus *Southern Sentinel*, Sept. 12, and *Macon Telegraph*, Sept. 17, both cited in Brooks, "Cobb and the Crisis of 1850," 289.

3 F.N. Boney, "The Politics of Expansion and Secession," Ch. XI in Kenneth Coleman, gen.ed., *A History of Georgia, 2nd Ed.* (Athens and London, 1991), p.141.

4 On the Georgia Platform, see David M. Potter, *The Impending Crisis, 1848–1861* (New York, 1976), pp.128–129; Allan Nevins, *Ordeal of the Union, Vol. I: Fruits of Manifest Destiny, 1847–1852* (New York and London, 1947), 355–356; Phillips, *Georgia and State Rights*, p. 165; Carey, *Politics, Slavery, and the Union in Antebellum Georgia*, pp.168–169; and Michael F. Holt, *The Rise and Fall of the American Whig Party: Jacksonian Politics and the Onset of the Civil War* (New York and Oxford, 1999) pp.613–614.

5 Editorial, Columbus *Southern Sentinel*, Sept. 12, 1850.

6 Brooks, "Cobb and the Crisis of 1850," 291.

7 On Cobb's role in helping to secure the Compromise of 1850 while Speaker of the House, see Holman Hamilton, *Prologue to Conflict: The Crisis and Compromise of 1850* (New York, 1966), pp. 67, 155–160, 164–165.

8 J.W.H.Underwood to Cobb, Dec. 22, 1850, Cobb Papers, UGa.

9 See, for example, Robert Toombs to Absalom H. Chappell and Others, Feb. 15, 1851, Phillips, *Correspondence*, p.228.

10 Hull to Cobb, Feb. 3, 1851, Cobb Papers, UGa.

11 James F. Cooper to Cobb, May 5, 1851, Phillips, *Correspondence*, p.234.

12 Holt, *American Whig Party*, p.614; Dougherty to Berrien, Mar. 31, 1851, *ibid.*

13 For minutes of the Constitutional-Union Party convention, see Auga*Chron&Sent*, June 5, 1851; for the Southern Rights convention, see Albany *Patriot*, June 6, 1851.

14 Toombs to Cobb, June 9, 1851, Brooks, ed., "Cobb Papers," *GHQ* V (September, 1921): 45.

15 Cobb to Buchanan (Private), June 9, 1851, Cobb Papers, UGa.

16 Cobb to James A. Meriwether and Others, June 24, 1851, Phillips, *Correspondence*, pp.238–241.

17 This and the next two paragraphs are based on Cobb to John Rutherford and Others, Aug. 12, 1851, *ibid.*, pp. 249–259.

18 Boney, "Politics of Expansion and Secession," p.142; Nevins, *Ordeal*, p.374; Potter, *Impending Crisis*, p.129; Carey, *Parties, Slavery, and the Union*, p.173; Holt, *American Whig Party*, pp.614–615.

19 Minutes of the Milledgeville meeting, published in *Albany Patriot*, Dec. 5, 1851.

20 Cobb to Mrs. Cobb, Mar. 2, 1852, Brooks, ed., "Cobb Papers," *GHQ* V (Dec. 1921), 45–46.

21 Chastain to Cobb, Feb. 8, 29 1852, Cobb Papers, UGa; for Chastain's speech, see Appendix to *Congressional Globe, 1st Sess., 32nd Cong. Vol. XXV*: 256–258.

22 The text of Cobb's Tammany Hall address may be found in the Athens *Weekly SBan*, Mar. 25, 1852.

23 For Hillyer's speech, see Appendix to *Cong. Globe, 1st Sess., 32nd Cong., Vol. XXV*: 319–322. The invective-laden commentary on Cobb's presence during Hillyer's speech, as well as a more sweeping denunciation of his entire New York excursion, may be found in the Columbus *Weekly Southern Sentinel*, Mar. 26, 1852.

24 Toombs to Cobb (Private), June 24, 1852, Cobb Papers, UGa.

25 Stephens to James Jones, June 28, 1852, in *AugaChron&Sent*, July 15, 1852.

26 Henry R. Jackson, to John B. Lamar, June 26, Cobb Papers, UGa; John H. Lumpkin to Cobb, July 11, Phillips, ed., *Correspondence*, pp.309–310; Lamar to Cobb, July 1, 1852, *ibid.*, pp. 307–308.

27 Editorial, Augusta *Daily Constitutionalist*, Sept. 10, 1852.

28 Cobb to John B. Lamar, Sept. 18, 1852, Phillips, ed., *Correspondence*, pp. 320–321.

29 Milledgeville *SRec*, Sept. 28, 1852, cited in Greene, "Politics in Georgia, 1830–1854," pp.324–325.

30 Editorial, Marietta *Union*, reprinted in *AugaChron&Sent*, Sept. 25, 1852.

31 Notice of this meeting, under the headline "Strange Bedfellows," appeared in the Oct. 17, 1852 issue of the *AugaChron&Sent*.

32 Cobb to Thomas D. Harris (Private), Jan. 12, 17 1853, Miscellaneous File, Georgia Archives, Morrow, Ga.

33 See, for example, John W. Forney to Cobb, July 29, Phillips, ed., *Correspondence*, p.330; editorial, Augusta *Daily Constitutionalist*, Oct. 26, 1853.

34 Cobb to Mrs. Cobb, Nov. 8, 1853, Cobb Papers, UGa.

35 A.H. Stephens to Linton Stephens, Dec. 4, 1853, Stephens Papers, Manhattanville College (Microfilm), Emory University.

36 Thomas C. Howard and H.K. Green to Cobb, Dec. 3, Phillips, ed., *Correspondence*, pp.337–338; for Cobb's speech, see Albany *Patriot*, Dec. 30, 1853.

[37] John H. Lumpkin to Cobb, Dec. 28, 1853, Phillips, ed. *Correspondence,* pp.338–339.

[38] Herschel V. Johnson to Cobb, Jan. 10, 1854, and John H. Lumpkin to Cobb, Jan. 18, 1854, Brooks, ed., "Cobb Papers," *GHQ* VI (June, 1922): 148–149.

Index

C

D

E

F

G

H

I

J

K

L

M

N

O

P

Q

R

S

T

U

V

W

X

Y

Z

Printed in the United States
By Bookmasters